Better Homes and Gardens®
BIGGEST BOOK OF
LOW-CARB
RECIPES

I0565766

Meredith® Books
Des Moines, Iowa

BIGGEST BOOK OF LOW-CARB RECIPES

Editor: Stephanie Karpinske, R.D.
Contributing Editors: Janet Figg, Mary Williams
Design Director: Matt Strelecki
Contributing Designer: Joyce DeWitt
Cover Designer: Daniel Pelavin
Copy Chief: Terri Fredrickson
Publishing Operations Manager: Karen Schirm
Edit and Design Production Coordinator: Mary Lee Gavin
Managers, Book Production: Pam Kvitne, Marjorie J. Schenkelberg,
   Rick von Holdt, Mark Weaver
Contributing Copy Editor: Karen Fraley
Contributing Proofreaders: Judy Friedman, Jeanne LeDoux, Jody Speer
Indexer: Spectrum Communication Services, Inc.
Editorial Assistant: Cheryl Eckert
Test Kitchen Director: Lynn Blanchard
Test Kitchen Product Supervisor: Jennifer Kalinowski
Test Kitchen Home Economists: Juliana Hale; Laura Harms;
   Maryellyn Krantz; Jill Moberly; Colleen Weeden; Lori Wilson

Meredith® Books
Editor in Chief: Linda Raglan Cunningham
Design Director: Matt Strelecki
Managing Editor: Gregory H. Kayko
Executive Editor: Jennifer Dorland Darling

Publisher: James D. Blume
Executive Director, Marketing: Jeffrey Meyers
Executive Director, New Business Development: Todd M. Davis
Executive Director, Sales: Ken Zagor
Director, Operations: George A. Susral
Director, Production: Douglas M. Johnston
Business Director: Jim Leonard

Vice President and General Manager: Douglas J. Guendel

Better Homes and Gardens® Magazine
Editor in Chief: Karol DeWulf Nickell
Deputy Editor, Food and Entertaining: Nancy Hopkins

Meredith Publishing Group
President, Publishing Group: Stephen M. Lacy
Vice President-Publishing Director: Bob Mate

Meredith Corporation
Chairman and Chief Executive Officer: William T. Kerr

In Memoriam: E. T. Meredith III (1933-2003)

All of us at Meredith Books are dedicated to providing you with the information and ideas you need to create delicious foods. We welcome your comments and suggestions. Write to us at: Meredith Books, Cookbook Editorial Department, 1716 Locust St., Des Moines, IA 50309-3023.

If you would like to purchase any of our cooking, crafts, gardening, home improvement, or home decorating and design books, check wherever quality books are sold.
Or visit us at: **bhgbooks.com**

Our Better Homes and Gardens® Test Kitchen seal on the back cover of this book assures you that every recipe in *Biggest Book of Low-Carb Recipes* has been tested in the Better Homes and Gardens® Test Kitchen. This means that each recipe is practical and reliable and meets our high standards of taste appeal. We guarantee your satisfaction with this book for as long as you own it.

LOW-CARB BASICS

Good food relates to good health. But what foods are best for weight loss? Instead of focusing exclusively on eliminating fats, researchers are now looking into how carbohydrates affect health. Whether you're cutting back on carbs or almost eliminating them, this book gives you the recipes you need for a low-carb lifestyle. The recipes include common ingredients and accessible specialty foods to make low-carb cooking easy and enjoyable.

WHAT'S A CARBOHYDRATE?

Carbohydrates are one of three basic macronutrients (along with protein and fat) required for life. They're found in many foods, such as fruits, vegetables, baked goods, dairy products, and beverages.

Refined carbohydrates, sometimes called simple sugars, go through extensive processing, which often removes valuable nutrients, leaving mostly calories. Unrefined, or complex, carbohydrates go through minimal processing, leaving fiber, essential vitamins, and minerals intact.

Fiber is a type of carbohydrate that is not digested and, therefore, provides no calories. Because of this, many food manufacturers list net carbohydrates on food labels. Net carbohydrates, as used in this book, are calculated by subtracting the grams of fiber in a food from its total grams of carbohydrates.

IMPORTANT NOTE ABOUT THE BIGGEST BOOK OF LOW-CARB RECIPES

This book includes recipes for a variety of low-carb diet plans. It is not intended to address the needs of a specific diet but instead offers a wide array of recipes so you can and choose what works best for you and your meal plan.

You'll also notice that throughout this book we have called for the use of a no-calorie, able granular sugar substitute (Splenda) in place of sugar. This type of heat-stable er is necessary in baked products. In foods that are not cooked or heated, any ve sweetener can be used.

TABLE OF CONTENTS

THE RISE AND FALL OF SUGAR LEVELS

When you eat foods containing any carbohydrates (except fiber), your body converts them into glucose, a simple sugar. Glucose raises blood sugar levels and stimulates the pancreas to release a hormone called insulin. Insulin allows your body to absorb glucose and use it for energy or store it. If your body has all the glucose it needs, any extra glucose will be stored as fat.

Foods high in refined carbohydrates, such as sweet rolls, candy bars, and white bread, cause blood glucose levels to rise rapidly. This spike signals your body to release large amounts of insulin. In some people, repeated large blood sugar/insulin spikes may cause insulin resistance. The American Diabetes Association calls this pre-diabetes, a condition where normal amounts of insulin are not able to remove the glucose from your blood. This may also contribute to heart disease by causing high blood pressure, increasing triglyceride levels, and lowering HDL (good) cholesterol.

Consuming minimally processed foods or foods that contain a mix of protein or fat with carbohydrates allows blood sugar and insulin levels to increase gradually. So, less total glucose is absorbed and less insulin is released, avoiding peaks and valleys in blood sugar levels.

WHY LOW-CARB DIETS WORK

Many low-carb diets claim that insulin creates hunger. That's because after a high-carbohydrate meal, insulin levels rise to high levels to remove the excess glucose from the bloodstream and deliver it to the cells. When blood sugar levels drop, people feel hungry and want to eat again. If they choose candy, regular soda, or another food high in refined carbohydrates, insulin levels spike again and they end up in a vicious eating cycle that never cures their hunger pangs.

This may explain why some people say low-carb diets increase satiety, the feeling of fullness that comes from eating. Carbohydrates also are digested faster than proteins or fats, making people feel hungry sooner on a high-carb diet. When more fat and protein is included in your meal, you'll feel full, eat less, and lose weight.

KETOSIS: GOOD OR BAD?

Very strict low-carbohydrate diets limit carb consumption so much that there's not even enough glucose to meet energy needs. The body responds by burning fat for energy. When fat is broken down, the body releases ketones, which are sent to the heart and brain to be used for energy or are excreted—a state called ketosis. Although still controversial, some researchers feel this is an advantage, making it easier to lose weight. Other researchers believe a low-carb diet could lead to a buildup of ketones in the blood, which over time increases the risk for gout (a painful joint swelling), bone loss, and kidney disease.

TIPS FOR SUCCESS

No matter what type of low-carb diet you follow, it's important to realize that a healthy lifestyle is more than purchasing specialty low-carb foods or taking the bun off your burger. You still need to make good food choices, watch portions, and exercise. Following are some guidelines to keep in mind while on a low-carb diet.

Consider foods with low glycemic index or glycemic load

Foods with low glycemic indexes or loads are less likely to cause spikes in blood sugar levels. Fruits and vegetables with low glycemic indexes include apples, asparagus, broccoli, Brussels sprouts, cauliflower, celery, cherries, cucumbers, grapefruits, green beans, lettuce, mushrooms, onions, peaches, pears, plums, spinach, strawberries, tomatoes, and zucchini.

Eating protein, fat, or fiber at the same time as you eat a food with a higher glycemic index or load slows the rate of absorption of the entire meal. So if you top a bowl of high-glycemic oatmeal with a few high-fiber, low-glycemic toasted walnuts, you'll reduce the impact of the oatmeal on your blood sugar.

Count starchy vegetables as starches

Some vegetables are very similar to grains because of their high starch content. These include corn, potatoes, sweet potatoes, lima beans, black-eyed peas, lentils, plantains, winter squash, and some canned or dried beans. They contain lots of carbohydrates but also provide fiber and nutrients needed for good health.

Skip soft drinks

Regular soda, soft drinks sweetened with sugar, sports drinks, and sweetened juices are loaded with carbohydrates. Worse yet, minimal nutrients are associated with these products. Instead shop for diet sodas, sugar-free drink mixes, or mineral water—they don't provide many nutrients, but they don't add carbs to your diet either.

Choose lean meats and poultry

Switching to a low-carb diet is not permission to pile high-fat meats on your plate. Instead choose lean cuts. For beef, select tenderloin, top loin, sirloin, top round, eye of round, or flank cuts. For lamb, choose leg or sirloin cuts. The leanest cuts of pork include tenderloin, sirloin, rib chops, lean ham, or Canadian bacon. Venison, ostrich, and bison tend to be very lean as well.

Make wise poultry purchases

Skinless chicken and turkey are naturally low in fat and make good choices. But carefully read labels when purchasing ground turkey. Both ground turkey breast (which has the least fat) and low-fat ground turkey make good choices. Packages of ground turkey that do not specify fat content may contain ground skin and have far more fat.

Eat plenty of fish

Fish is a lean protein that makes a great low-carb diet choice. Even fatty fish are good selections because they contain healthy omega-3 fatty acids, which protect against heart disease and contribute to healthy nerve function.

Make good fat choices

When carbohydrate is limited in a diet, researchers suggest adding moderate amounts of fat back into the diet. The key is making good fat choices such as monounsaturated fats found in olive oil, peanut oil, and canola oil or polyunsaturated fats found in fish, corn oil, sunflower oil, and soybean oil. They help protect against heart disease.

GLYCEMIC INDEX VERSUS GLYCEMIC LOAD

Not all carbohydrates are equal, especially when considering how quickly they raise your blood sugar levels. You might think that all refined carbohydrates increase blood sugar levels quickly and all unrefined carbohydrates raise it more slowly. However, researchers have found this is not the case. So they developed the glycemic index that indicates how rapidly a particular food turns into sugar. Unfortunately, it doesn't take into consideration how many carbohydrates are in a serving of that food.

Glycemic load provides a better explanation of how a food affects blood sugar levels. It multiplies the grams of carbohydrates in a food by the food's glycemic index. This provides information on both how fast the carbohydrate turns into sugar and how many carbohydrates are in a food—two important factors that influence blood sugar levels. In the future, food labels may boast about low glycemic load!

Cut portion sizes

Starting a low-carb diet isn't a license to eat unlimited amounts of any low-carbohydrate food. Overindulging on low-carb cheesecake will only hinder your weight loss. Eating more protein or fat than your body needs also can lead to weight gain, even on a low-carb diet.

Plan ahead for meals out

Look for restaurants that offer several good low-carb choices, such as broiled, baked, or roasted seafood, steaks, or poultry. Then substitute a nutrient-packed salad or vegetable in place of potato and bread.

Check low-fat labels

Many low-fat foods have added carbohydrates to make up for the missing fat. Scan the nutrition labels of low-fat foods. Often the grams of sugar on low-fat versions are higher than they are on the standard foods.

Scan condiment labels

Carbohydrates regularly hide in popular condiments. Catsup and relish both contain about 4 carbohydrate grams per tablespoon, while barbecue sauce packs a walloping 8 grams per tablespoon. Mustard and cider vinegar have about 1 carbohydrate gram per tablespoon, but an equal amount of balsamic vinegar contains twice as much.

QUESTIONS AND ANSWERS

Many people have questions about low-carb diets, especially since there is so much conflicting information in the media. Here are a few commonly asked questions.

How can I tell if a food has added sugars?

Watch for any ingredient ending in "–ose." That indicates sugar. Also scrutinize labels for brown sugar, cane sugar, corn sweeteners, corn syrup, crystallized cane sugar, dextrin, maltodextrin, evaporated cane juice, fruit juice concentrate, fruit juice, high-fructose corn syrup (HFCS), honey, invert sugar, malt, malt extract, syrup, molasses, raw sugar, mannitol, sorbitol, xylitol, lactitol, isomalt, and maltitol. They're all sweeteners and add at least a few carbohydrates to your diet.

Do I have to purchase special low-carb foods to follow a low-carb diet?

Special low-carb foods abound in both grocery and health food stores, but they're not needed to follow a low-carb diet. Some low-carb foods are high in calories and may cause weight gain. The low-carb recipes in this book contain common ingredients. You won't have to go to a health food store to purchase the ingredients.

Will a high-protein and low-carbohydrate diet cause me to lose bone density or damage my kidneys?

Some researchers are concerned that ketosis, which results from burning fat while on a very low-carb diet, may cause kidney damage and bone loss. Scientific research is not yet complete, so there is no consensus about how long people can safely stay in a state of ketosis.

If you're on a low-carb diet, take steps to minimize risks to your bones and kidneys. Eat plenty of low-carb, calcium-rich foods, such as cheese, dark green leafy vegetables, almonds, salmon, and sardines. Participate in weight-bearing exercises to strengthen your bones. Most important, ask your doctor or dietitian for advice before changing your diet, especially if you already have kidney disease or osteoporosis.

Will eating a low-carb diet cause fatigue?

Low-carb diets are not likely to make you feel tired. Some people report fatigue during the first day or two of the diet change, but usually the symptoms disappear after a couple of days. To minimize potential for exhaustion, include a variety of foods in your new low-carb eating plan and maintain a regular exercise schedule.

What's the best kind of fat to include in a low-carb diet?

Some fats are more harmful than others. The "good" fats are the unsaturated ones. Several fats fall into this category. Mono-unsaturated fats come from olive oil, canola oil, peanut oil, olives, cashews, almonds, and avocados. They lower LDL (bad) cholesterol and improve HDL (good) cholesterol. Poly-unsaturated fats include both the omega-3 and omega-6 fats. Omega-3 fats are found in fish, flaxseed oil, walnuts, and canola oil. Although they have little effect on cholesterol levels, they lower triglycerides (blood fats). Omega-6 fats come from corn, soybeans, and sunflowers. They lower LDL (bad) cholesterol and raise HDL (good) cholesterol.

What are the sugar alcohols listed in the ingredients of some low-carb products? Are they safe? Do they have any side effects?

The term sugar alcohols is the consumer-friendly name given to sweeteners whose chemical structures resemble both sugar and alcohol. These sweeteners—mannitol, sorbitol, xylitol, lactitol, isomalt, and maltitol—are often used in sugar-free foods. They're called alcohols because of their chemical structure. They don't contain the type of alcohol (ethanol) found in alcoholic beverages.

Low-carb foods often use a lot of sugar alcohols since they convert to glucose more slowly than sugar and require less insulin during metabolism. Some food manufacturers choose to subtract them from the total carbohydrate number when calculating net carbs.

Sugar alcohols are safe to eat, but there are potential side effects. Bloating, abdominal cramping, and diarrhea are the most common problems associated with eating too many sugar alcohols.

How do you include fiber in a low-carb diet?

Fiber is harder to work into low-carb diets than into low-fat diets. However, by carefully selecting carbs, you'll be able to keep some fiber in your diet. Choose unrefined carbohydrates that are high in fiber and have a low glycemic index such as strawberries, spinach, asparagus, broccoli, cauliflower, oranges, plums, grapefruit, cherries, green beans, and Brussels sprouts. Other slightly higher glycemic index foods that provide both nutrients and fiber are 100% whole wheat bread and pumpernickel bread.

After losing weight, what's the best way to keep it off?

The key to keeping off weight is to remember that a diet is how you eat every day, instead of a plan you follow just until you reach your goal weight. As every dieter knows, if you go back to old eating and exercise habits after reaching your goal weight, the numbers on the scale will creep back up. It's important to continue monitoring portion sizes, making good food choices, and exercising.

THE SECRET INGREDIENT TO ANY DIET

The key to successful diets is exercise. The National Weight Control Registry looked at nearly 800 people who lost at least 30 pounds and kept the weight off for an average of 5½ years. They found that 89% of these people combined both dietary changes and physical activity to lose the weight.

Official guidelines from the American College of Sports Medicine suggest expending about 1,000 calories per week through physical activity. Successful dieters in the National Weight Control Registry burned almost 3,000 calories per week through exercise.

Don't panic—you don't have to spend hours sweating in a gym to reach that level. Daily activities like walking, climbing stairs, raking leaves, and dancing all burn calories. The following list gives you an idea of how many calories are expended when a 180-pound person actively participates in 30 minutes of various pastimes. If you weigh less than 180 pounds, you use slightly fewer calories, and if you weigh more than 180 pounds, you burn slightly more calories.

Activity	Calories Burned
Ballroom dancing	180 calories
Baseball	205 calories
Dusting the house	95 calories
Golf *(without cart)*	155 calories
Grocery shopping	140 calories
Jogging	400 calories
Mowing the lawn *(without riding mower)*	190 calories
Raking leaves	205 calories
Shoveling snow	240 calories
Swimming	360 calories
Volleyball *(casual game)*	120 calories
Walking the dog	175 calories
Walking *(brisk)*	235 calories
Yoga	215 calories

*Based on 180 pound person and 30 minutes of activity.

CARB COUNT CHARTS

When you're planning meals for a low-carb lifestyle, check out this chart of calorie, carb, and net carb values. Use it to compare the regular versions of your favorite foods with the low-carb versions you may be using. Or these charts can help you decide which fruit you want to purchase at the grocery store or which vegetable is the best choice for dinner tonight. This list is for reference only. It is not meant to be part of a specific low-carb diet. Many low-carb meal plans vary on total carbs allowed per day and what foods are okay to eat.

CARB COUNTS OF DAIRY, FISH, MEATS, AND POULTRY

	serving size	calories	carb (g)	net carb (g)
DAIRY				
Cheese				
Cheddar	1 oz.	114	0	0
Cottage (2% fat)	1 cup	203	8	8
Cottage (4% fat)	1 cup	233	6	6
Cream (regular)	1 tbsp.	51	0	0
Cream (fat-free)	1 tbsp.	15	1	1
Feta	1 oz.	75	1	1
Mozzarella (part skim)	1 oz.	79	1	1
Muenster	1 oz.	104	0	0
Parmesan, grated	1 tbsp.	23	0	0
Provolone	1 oz.	100	1	1
Swiss	1 oz.	107	1	1
Processed American	1 oz.	106	0	0
Milk and Cream				
Light cream	1 tbsp.	29	1	1
Whipping cream	1 tbsp.	52	0	0
Whole milk	1 cup	150	11	11
Reduced fat milk (2% fat)	1 cup	121	12	12
Nonfat skim milk	1 cup	86	12	12
Pressurized whipped topping	1 tbsp.	8	0	0
Yogurt				
Fruit-flavored	8 oz.	231	43	43
Plain	8 oz.	144	16	16
Fruit-flavored with low-cal sweetener	8 oz.	98	17	17

* NOTE: *Nutrient information on carb count charts taken from the USDA National Nutrient Database for Standard Reference*

	serving size	calories	carb (g)	net carb (g)
FISH AND SEAFOOD				
Flounder, cooked	3 oz.	99	0	0
Orange roughy, cooked	3 oz.	76	0	0
Lobster, cooked	3 oz.	83	0	0
Salmon, cooked	3 oz.	184	0	0
Shrimp, unbreaded, cooked	3 oz.	84	0	0
Sardines, canned	3 oz.	177	0	0
Swordfish, cooked	3 oz.	132	0	0
Tuna, cooked	3 oz.	118	0	0
BEEF				
83% lean ground beef, cooked	3 oz.	218	0	0
73% lean ground beef, cooked	3 oz.	246	0	0
Bottom round, cooked	3 oz.	178	0	0
Chuck blade, cooked	3 oz.	213	0	0
Eye of round, cooked	3 oz.	143	0	0
Loin, top, cooked	3 oz.	176	0	0
Ribs, cooked	3 oz.	195	0	0
Sirloin, cooked	3 oz.	166	0	0
Tenderloin, cooked	3 oz.	189	0	0
LAMB				
Arm chop, cooked	3 oz.	237	0	0
Loin, cooked	3 oz.	184	0	0
Leg, cooked	3 oz.	162	0	0
Rib, cooked	3 oz.	197	0	0
PORK				
Bacon, cooked	3 slices	109	0	0
Canadian-style bacon, cooked	2 oz.	86	1	1
Lean ham	3 oz.	133	0	0
Loin chop, cooked	3 oz.	172	0	0
Rib chop, cooked	3 oz.	190	0	0
Baby back ribs, cooked	3 oz.	315	0	0
Country-style ribs, cooked	3 oz.	252	0	0
Spareribs, cooked	3 oz.	337	0	0
Shoulder cut, cooked	3 oz.	211	0	0
Tenderloin, cooked	3 oz.	159	0	0
SAUSAGES				
Bologna	2 oz.	180	2	2
Brown-and-serve links, cooked	2 links	103	1	1
Frankfurters, cooked	1 medium	144	1	1
Pork sausage, cooked	1 patty	100	0	0
Salami	2 oz.	143	1	1
VEAL				
Cutlet, cooked	3 oz.	179	0	0
Rib, cooked	3 oz.	194	0	0
POULTRY				
Chicken				
Batter-dipped fried breast	½ breast	364	13	13
Batter-dipped fried drumstick	1 drumstick	193	6	6
Breast, cooked	½ breast	142	0	0
Drumstick, cooked	1 drumstick	76	0	0
Turkey				
Dark meat, cooked	3 oz.	159	0	0
Light meat, cooked	3 oz.	133	0	0

CARB COUNTS OF BREADS AND CEREALS

	serving size	calories	carb (g)	net carb (g)
BREADS				
Bagels				
Cinnamon-raisin	One 3½ inch bagel	195	39	37
Egg	One 3½ inch bagel	197	38	36
Oat-bran	One 3½ inch bagel	181	38	35
Plain	One 3½ inch bagel	195	38	36
Banana bread	1 slice	196	33	32
Biscuits				
Baking powder from recipe	1 medium	212	27	26
Low-fat from refrigerated dough	1 medium	63	12	12
Regular from refrigerated dough	1 medium	93	13	13
Bread crumbs, plain	1 cup	427	78	75
Bread crumbs, seasoned	1 cup	440	84	79
Bun, frankfurter	1 medium	123	22	21
Bun, hamburger	1 medium	123	22	21
Cinnamon roll with raisins	1 medium	223	31	30
Cornbread	One 2½ inch square	173	28	26
Cracked wheat bread	1 slice	65	12	11
Croissant	1 croissant	231	26	24
Croutons, seasoned	1 cup	186	25	23
Dinner roll	1 medium	84	14	13
Egg bread	1 slice	115	19	18
French bread	1 slice	69	13	12
French toast	1 slice	149	16	15
Hard rolls	1 medium	167	30	29
Italian bread	1 slice	54	10	10
Matzo, plain	1 medium	112	24	23
Mixed grain bread	1 slice	65	12	10
Muffins				
Blueberry	1 medium	158	27	26
Bran-raisin	1 medium	106	19	16
Corn	1 medium	174	29	27
English	1 medium	134	26	24
Oat-bran	1 medium	154	28	25
Oatmeal bread	1 slice	73	13	12
Pancakes, plain	One 4-inch	82	16	15
Pita bread	1 large	165	33	32
Pumpernickel bread	1 slice	80	15	13
Raisin bread, unfrosted	1 slice	71	14	13
Rye bread, reduced-calorie	1 slice	47	9	6
Rye bread, regular	1 slice	83	15	13
Stuffing, made from mix	½ cup	178	22	19
Taco shell	1 medium	62	8	7
Tortilla, corn	1 medium	58	12	11
Tortilla, flour	1 medium	104	18	17
Waffle, low-fat	One 4-inch	83	15	15
Waffle, plain	One 4-inch	87	13	12
White bread, reduced-calorie	1 slice	48	10	8
White bread, regular	1 slice	67	12	11
Whole wheat bread	1 slice	69	13	11

	serving size	calories	carb (g)	net carb (g)
CEREALS				
Bite-size square corn cereal	1 cup	113	26	26
Bite-size square rice cereal	1¼ cups	117	27	27
Bite-size square wheat cereal	1 cup	104	24	21
Corn flakes	1 cup	102	24	23
Crisp rice cereal	1¼ cups	124	29	29
Crisp rice cereal, chocolate-flavored	¾ cup	120	27	27
Farina, cooked	1 cup	112	24	23
Granola with raisins, low-fat	½ cup	195	40	37
Granola, plain	¾ cup	248	36	32
Hominy grits, cooked	1 cup	145	31	30
Honey-graham cereal	¾ cup	116	26	25
Oat bran, cooked	1 cup	88	25	19
Oat square cereal, sweetened	¾ cup	121	25	23
Oatmeal				
Apple and cinnamon, instant	1 pkt.	125	26	24
Maple and brown sugar, instant	1 pkt.	153	31	28
Old-fashioned, cooked	1 cup	145	25	21
Peanut butter cereal	¾ cup	112	22	21
Puffed corn cereal	1 cup	118	28	28
Puffed rice cereal	1 cup	56	13	13
Puffed wheat cereal	1 cup	44	10	10
Raisin bran cereal	1 cup	178	43	38
Rice and wheat flakes	1 cup	115	22	21
Shredded wheat biscuits	2 biscuits	156	38	33
Toasted oat cereal	1 cup	110	23	20
Wheat cereal, cooked	1 cup	133	28	26
Wheat flakes cereal	¾ cup	95	23	18
Pasta				
Couscous, cooked	1 cup	176	36	34
Macaroni, elbow, cooked	1 cup	197	40	38
Noodles, egg, cooked	1 cup	213	40	38
Noodles, rice, cooked	1 cup	192	44	42
Noodles, spinach, cooked	1 cup	211	39	35
Spaghetti, cooked	1 cup	197	40	38
Spaghetti, whole wheat, cooked	1 cup	174	37	31
Rice and Grains				
Barley, cooked	1 cup	193	44	38
Buckwheat groats, cooked	1 cup	155	33	28
Bulgar, cooked	1 cup	151	34	26
Millet, cooked	1 cup	207	41	39
Rice, instant, cooked	1 cup	162	35	34
Rice, long-grain brown, cooked	1 cup	216	45	42
Rice, long-grain white, cooked	1 cup	205	45	44
Rice, wild, cooked	1 cup	166	35	32
Wheat germ, toasted	1 tbsp.	27	3	2

CARB COUNTS OF FRUITS AND VEGETABLES

	serving size	calories	carb (g)	net carb (g)
FRUITS				
Apple juice	1 cup	117	29	29
Apples, dried	5 rings	78	21	18
Apples, unpeeled	1 small	81	21	17
Applesauce, unsweetened	1 cup	105	28	25
Apricot nectar	1 cup	141	36	34
Apricots, dried	10 halves	83	22	19
Apricots, unpeeled	1 medium	17	4	3
Bananas	1 medium	109	28	25
Blackberries	1 cup	75	18	10
Blueberries	1 cup	81	20	16
Cantaloupe, cubed	1 cup	56	13	12
Cherries, sour, canned	1 cup	88	22	19
Cherries, sweet	1 cup	91	23	20
Cranberries, dried	¼ cup	92	24	22
Dates, whole	5 dates	116	31	28
Figs, dried	2 figs	97	25	20
Grape juice	1 cup	154	38	38
Grapefruit	½ grapefruit	37	9	8
Grapefruit juice	1 cup	96	23	23
Grapes, seedless	10 grapes	36	9	8
Honeydew melon, cubed	1 cup	60	16	15
Kiwi fruit	1 medium	46	11	8
Mangoes, sliced	1 cup	107	28	25
Nectarines	1 medium	67	16	14
Orange juice	1 cup	112	26	26
Oranges	1 small	62	15	12
Papayas, cubed	1 cup	55	14	12
Peaches	1 medium	42	11	9
Peaches, canned (juice pack)	1 cup	109	29	26
Peaches, dried	3 halves	93	24	21
Pear juice	1 cup	124	32	28
Pears	1 medium	98	25	21
Pineapple chunks, canned (juice pack)	1 cup	149	39	37
Pineapple juice, unsweetened	1 cup	140	34	34
Pineapple, cubed	1 cup	76	19	17
Plums	1 medium	36	9	8
Plums, canned (juice pack)	1 cup	146	38	36
Raisins, seedless	1 cup	435	115	109
Raspberries	1 cup	60	14	6
Strawberries	1 cup	50	12	8
Tangerines	1 medium	37	9	7
Watermelon, cubed	1 cup	49	11	10
VEGETABLES				
Artichokes, cooked	1 cup	84	19	10
Asparagus, cooked	1 cup	43	8	5
Bamboo shoots, canned	1 cup	25	4	2
Bean sprouts, cooked	1 cup	26	5	4
Beans				
Baked with pork and tomato sauce	1 cup	248	49	37
Baked, vegetarian	1 cup	236	52	39
Black, cooked	1 cup	227	41	26
Garbanzo, cooked	1 cup	269	45	32
Great Northern, cooked	1 cup	209	37	25
Green, cooked	1 cup	44	10	6
Pinto, cooked	1 cup	234	44	29
Red kidney, cooked	1 cup	225	40	27
Beets, cooked	1 cup	75	17	14
Black-eyed peas, cooked	1 cup	200	36	25
Broccoli, cooked	1 cup	44	8	4

	serving size	calories	carb (g)	net carb (g)
Broccoli, raw	1 cup	25	5	2
Brussels sprouts, cooked	1 cup	61	14	10
Cabbage, cooked	1 cup	33	7	4
Cabbage, raw	1 cup	18	4	2
Carrots, cooked	1 cup	70	16	11
Carrots, raw	1 medium	31	7	5
Cauliflower, cooked	1 cup	29	5	2
Cauliflower, raw	1 cup	25	5	2
Celery, cooked	1 cup	27	6	4
Celery, raw	1 stalk	6	1	0
Corn, cooked	1 cup	131	32	28
Corn, cream style, cooked	1 cup	184	46	43
Cucumber, unpeeled	1 cup	14	3	2
Eggplant, cooked	1 cup	28	7	4
Green onion, raw	1 medium	5	1	1
Green or red sweet peppers, cooked	1 cup	38	9	7
Green or red sweet peppers, raw	1 cup	40	10	7
Green soybeans, cooked	1 cup	254	20	12
Greens				
Beet, cooked	1 cup	39	8	4
Collard, cooked	1 cup	49	9	4
Dandelion, cooked	1 cup	35	7	4
Mustard, cooked	1 cup	21	3	0
Kale, cooked	1 cup	36	7	4
Kohlrabi, cooked	1 cup	48	11	9
Leeks, cooked	1 cup	32	8	7
Lentils, cooked	1 cup	230	40	24
Lettuce				
Butterhead	1 cup	7	1	0
Iceberg	1 cup	6	1	0
Leaf	1 cup	10	2	1
Romaine	1 cup	8	1	0
Mushrooms, cooked	1 cup	42	8	5
Mushrooms, raw	1 cup	18	3	2
Okra, cooked	1 cup	51	12	8
Onions, cooked	1 cup	92	21	18
Onions, raw	1 cup	61	14	11
Parsnips, cooked	1 cup	126	30	24
Peas, cooked	1 cup	67	11	6
Potatoes				
Baked with skin	1 medium	220	51	46
Boiled	1 cup	134	31	28
Sweet, baked with skin	1 medium	150	35	31
Pumpkin, canned	1 cup	83	20	13
Radishes	1 medium	1	0	0
Rutabagas, cooked	1 cup	66	15	12
Sauerkraut, canned	1 cup	45	10	4
Spinach, cooked	1 cup	41	7	3
Spinach, raw	1 cup	7	1	0
Split peas, cooked	1 cup	231	41	25
Summer squash, cooked	1 cup	36	8	6
Summer squash, raw	1 cup	23	5	3
Tomatillos, raw	1 medium	11	2	1
Tomato juice	1 cup	41	10	9
Tomato paste	1 cup	215	51	40
Tomato sauce	1 cup	74	18	15
Tomatoes, canned	1 cup	46	10	8
Tomatoes, dried	1 piece	5	1	1
Tomatoes, raw	1 cup	38	8	6
Turnips, cooked	1 cup	33	8	5
Vegetable juice cocktail	1 cup	46	11	9
Water chestnuts, canned	1 cup	70	17	14
Winter squash, cooked and cubed	1 cup	80	18	12

CARB COUNTS OF SNACK FOODS

	serving size	calories	carb (g)	net carb (g)
Almonds, whole	1 oz.	164	6	3
Brown rice cake, plain	1 medium	35	7	7
Candy-coated chocolate pieces	10 pieces	34	5	5
Candy-coated chocolate pieces with peanuts	10 pieces	103	12	11
Caramel	1 piece	39	8	8
Caramel corn with peanuts	1 cup	168	34	32
Caramel corn without peanuts	1 cup	152	28	26
Cashews, dry-roasted	1 oz.	163	9	8
Cereal mix	1 oz.	120	18	16
Cheese crackers	10 crackers	50	6	6
Cheese puffs	1 oz.	157	15	15
Cheese-flavored popcorn	1 cup	58	6	5
Chocolate fudge, plain	1 piece	65	14	14
Chocolate fudge, with nuts	1 piece	81	14	14
Chocolate-covered peanut butter cups	1 miniature	38	4	4
Corn chips, barbecue flavor	1 oz.	148	16	14
Corn chips, plain	1 oz.	153	16	15
Fruit and juice bar	1 medium	63	16	16
Fruit leather pieces	1 oz.	97	22	21
Granola bar, chocolate chip	1 medium	119	20	19
Granola bar, plain	1 medium	134	18	16
Gumdrops	1 medium	16	4	4
Gummy bears	10 pieces	85	22	22
Hard candy	1 piece	24	6	6
Hummus	1 tbsp.	23	2	1
Jelly beans	10 large	104	26	26
Macadamia nuts, dry-roasted	1 oz.	203	4	2
Melba toast	4 pieces	78	15	14
Milk chocolate bar	1.55 oz.	226	26	24
Milk chocolate bar with crisp rice cereal	1.55 oz.	230	29	28
Milk chocolate bar with almonds	1.45 oz.	216	22	20
Oyster crackers	1 cup	195	32	31
Peanut butter, chunky	1 tbsp.	94	3	2
Peanut butter, reduced-fat	1 tbsp.	94	6	5
Peanut butter, smooth	1 tbsp.	95	3	2
Peanuts, dry-roasted	1 oz.	166	6	4
Popcorn, air-popped	1 cup	31	6	5
Popcorn, oil-popped	1 cup	55	6	5
Potato chips, barbecue flavor	1 oz.	139	15	14
Potato chips, fat-free	1 oz.	75	17	16
Potato chips, plain	1 oz.	152	15	14
Potato chips, reduced-fat	1 oz.	134	19	17
Potato chips, sour cream and onion flavor	1 oz.	151	15	14
Pretzel sticks (2¼ inches long)	10 pretzels	11	2	2
Pretzels, twisted	10 pretzels	229	48	46
Pumpkin seeds, dry-roasted	1 oz.	148	4	3
Saltine crackers	4 crackers	52	9	9
Sunflower seeds, dry-roasted	1 oz.	165	7	4
Thin square wheat crackers	4 crackers	38	5	5
Tortilla chips, nacho cheese flavor	1 oz.	141	18	16
Tortilla chips, plain	1 oz.	142	18	16
Trail mix, regular	1 cup	707	66	57
Trail mix, tropical	1 cup	570	92	81
Whole wheat crackers	4 crackers	71	11	9

CARB COUNTS OF DESSERTS

	serving size	calories	carb (g)	net carb (g)
Brownies, unfrosted	One 2¾ inch square	227	36	35
Cakes				
Angel food	One 1-oz. slice	72	16	16
Chocolate, frosted	⅛ of 18-oz. cake	235	35	33
Pineapple upside-down	One 2½ inch square	367	58	57
Pound, fat-free	One 1-oz. slice	80	17	17
Pound, regular	One 1-oz. slice	109	14	14
Cheesecake	⅙ of 17-oz. cake	257	20	20
Cheese-filled Danish	1 medium	266	26	25
Cookies				
Butter	1 medium	23	3	3
Chocolate chip, reduced fat	1 medium	45	7	7
Chocolate chip, regular	1 medium	48	7	7
Chocolate chip, sugar free	1 medium	108	16	16
Chocolate, fat-free	1 medium	49	12	12
Chocolate-filled sandwich	1 medium	47	7	7
Fig bar	1 medium	56	11	10
Molasses	1 medium	65	11	11
Oatmeal, soft, regular	1 medium	61	10	10
Oatmeal, sugar-free	1 medium	106	16	16
Peanut butter	1 medium	72	9	9
Shortbread, plain	1 medium	40	5	5
Shortbread, pecan	1 medium	76	8	8
Sugar	1 medium	72	10	10
Vanilla wafer	1 medium	18	3	3
Vanilla-filled sandwich	1 medium	48	7	7
Éclair, filled	1 medium	262	24	23
Gingerbread	One 2½ inch square	263	36	35
Glazed doughnut	1 medium	242	27	26
Pies				
Apple	⅛ pie	277	40	38
Blueberry	⅛ pie	271	41	40
Boston cream	⅛ pie	232	39	38
Cherry	⅛ pie	304	47	46
Chocolate cream	⅛ pie	344	38	36
Coconut custard	⅛ pie	270	31	29
Lemon meringue	⅛ pie	303	53	52
Pecan	⅛ pie	452	65	61
Pumpkin	⅛ pie	229	30	27
Shortcake, biscuit type	1 medium	225	32	31
Shortcake, sponge type	1 medium	87	18	18
Frozen				
Ice cream, chocolate	½ cup	143	19	18
Ice cream, strawberry	½ cup	127	18	17
Ice cream, vanilla	½ cup	133	16	16
Ice cream, vanilla, no-sugar-added	½ cup	99	12	11
Italian ices	½ cup	61	16	16
Sherbet, orange	½ cup	102	22	22
Others				
Gelatin dessert, reduced-calorie	½ cup	8	1	1
Gelatin dessert, regular	½ cup	80	19	19
Pudding, chocolate, instant	½ cup	150	28	27
Pudding, tapioca	½ cup	134	22	22
Pudding, vanilla, instant	½ cup	148	28	28

MENU PLANS - WEEK 1

Make low-carb eating even easier with these helpful menu plans. There are two full weeks' worth of meals! The carb count levels in these menus are very low but are meant to fit with the first week of many popular low-carb diets. Add carbs as needed to fit your specific low-carb eating plan.

DAY 2 — Net Carbs

Breakfast
Spinach & Cheese Omelet (p. 55)	1 g
3 ounces broiled ham	1 g
1/2 cup fresh strawberries	4 g
Hot coffee	

Lunch
Alpine Cheese Soup (p. 101)	7 g
Celery sticks	0 g
1 cup broccoli flowerets	2 g
Sugar-free lemon-flavored iced tea	0 g

Dinner
Peppercorn Beef (p. 148)	1 g
1/2 cup cooked mushrooms	1 g
Melted Tomato Salad (p. 132)	2 g
Sparkling water with lime wedge	0 g

Snack
Hot & Spicy Walnuts (p. 49)	2 g

Total grams net carbs	21 g

DAY 1 — Net Carbs

Breakfast
2 fried eggs	0 g
Apple Breakfast Patties (p. 52)	3 g
Hot herbed tea	0 g

Lunch
Ham and Swiss cheese wrapped in romaine lettuce (2 ounces ham and 1 ounce Swiss cheese wrapped in 1 romaine lettuce leaf)	2 g
Scallion Mayonnaise (p. 378)	1 g
Iced Yellow Tomato Soup (p. 102)	6 g
Sparkling water with lime wedge	0 g

Dinner
Grilled Mustard-Glazed Pork (p. 184)	1 g
1 cup steamed broccoli	4 g
Sugar-free strawberry gelatin	0 g
Sugar-free iced coffee	0 g

Snack
Garlic-Feta Cheese Spread (p. 26)	1 g
Celery sticks	0 g

Total grams net carbs	18 g

DAY 3 — Net Carbs

Breakfast
2 fried eggs	0 g
1/2 cup vegetable juice cocktail	4 g
Hot hazelnut coffee	0 g

Lunch
Tossed salad (2 cups torn romaine lettuce, 3 ounces roasted turkey breast, 1 ounce cheddar cheese, 1/4 cup chopped tomato, 1 sliced green onion, and 1 sliced radish)	2 g
Oil-Free Herb Dressing (p. 394)	2 g
Sugar-free raspberry-flavored iced tea	0 g

Dinner
Peachy Pork Tenderloin (p. 183)	6 g
1 cup steamed asparagus	5 g
Tossed salad (2 cups torn Bibb lettuce, 1/2 cup sliced cucumber, 1 sliced green onion, and 1 sliced radish)	1 g
Jalapeño Dressing (p. 395)	2 g
Sparkling water with lime wedge	0 g

Snack
Mediterranean Walnut Spread (p. 311)	1 g
Celery sticks	0 g

Total grams net carbs	23 g

DAY 4

	Net Carbs
Breakfast	
Spinach-Feta Frittata (p. 62)	4 g
3 slices bacon	0 g
Hot herbed tea	0 g
Lunch	
Coconut Chicken Salad (p. 108)	6 g
Sparkling water with lime wedge	0 g
Dinner	
Java Swiss Steak (p. 144)	5 g
Asparagus Finger Salad (p. 129)	3 g
Sugar-free orange gelatin	0 g
Hot coffee	0 g
Snack	
½ cup fresh raspberries	3 g
Total grams net carbs	**21 g**

DAY 5

	Net Carbs
Breakfast	
Baked Eggs (p. 56)	1 g
3 ounces broiled ham	1 g
1 medium apricot	3 g
Sugar-free hot spiced tea	0 g
Lunch	
Garden Chicken Soup (p. 81)	9 g
Celery sticks	0 g
Sugar-free strawberry-kiwi gelatin	0 g
Sparkling water with lime wedge	0 g
Dinner	
Sesame-Ginger Grilled Salmon (p. 250)	1 g
Tossed salad (2 cups torn Boston lettuce, 1 sliced green onion, 2 cherry tomatoes, and 1 tablespoon toasted slivered almonds)	2 g
Lime Vinaigrette (p. 398)	1 g
Margarita Whip (p. 336)	1 g
Hot herbed tea	0 g
Snack	
Spiced Chili Nuts & Seeds (p. 316)	4 g
Total grams net carbs	**23 g**

DAY 6

	Net Carbs
Breakfast	
1 scrambled egg	1 g
3 ounces Canadian-style bacon	1 g
Hot coffee	0 g
Lunch	
Tossed Salad with Shrimp & Oranges (p. 120)	7 g
Sugar-free lemonade	0 g
Dinner	
Dijon-Crusted Lamb Rib Roast (p. 167)	2 g
Zucchini à la Romano (p. 283)	2 g
Creamy Lemon Blueberry Dessert (p. 343)	4 g
Hot herbed tea	0 g
Snack	
Savory Nuts (p. 48)	2 g
Total grams net carbs	**19 g**

DAY 7

	Net Carbs
Breakfast	
1 poached egg	0 g
Maple-Mustard Sausages (p. 58)	2 g
½ cup fresh blackberries	5 g
Hot espresso	0 g
Lunch	
Peanut-Pumpkin Soup (p. 97)	6 g
½ cup cucumber sticks	1 g
Sugar-free lemonade	0 g
Dinner	
Teriyaki Fish Steaks (p. 237)	2 g
1 cup steamed spinach	3 g
½ fresh peach, sliced	5 g
Sugar-free lemon gelatin	0 g
Hot herbed tea	0 g
Snack	
Hot Reuben Dip (p. 30)	1 g
Celery sticks	0 g
Total grams net carbs	**25 g**

MENU PLANS - WEEK 2

DAY 1

	Net Carbs
Breakfast	
Zucchini-Pepperoni Frittata (p. 63)	7 g
Hot tea with lemon wedge	0 g
Lunch	
Tossed salad (2 cups torn romaine lettuce, 3 ounces roasted chicken breast, ½ ounce dry-roasted sunflower seeds, 1 sliced green onion, and 1 sliced radish)	2 g
Roquefort Salad Dressing (p. 391)	1 g
Sugar-free lemon-flavored iced tea	0 g
Dinner	
Filet Mignon with Cognac Sauce (p. 147)	4 g
Italian Vegetable Salad (p. 133)	5 g
Sugar-free raspberry-strawberry gelatin with 1 tablespoon frozen whipped dessert topping, thawed	1 g
Hot herbed tea	0 g
Snack	
1 tablespoon chunky peanut butter in celery sticks	2 g
Total grams net carbs	**22 g**

DAY 2

	Net Carbs
Breakfast	
1 hard-cooked egg	0 g
1 ounce cheddar cheese	0 g
½ cup fresh raspberries	3 g
Hot tea with lemon wedge	0 g
Lunch	
Hot Italian Beef Salad (p. 117)	5 g
Sparkling water	0 g
Dinner	
Grilled Jerk Chicken (p. 217)	4 g
Marinated Cucumbers (p. 278)	4 g
Mocha Pots de Crème (p. 332)	6 g
Hot hazelnut coffee	0 g
Snack	
Herbed Soy Snacks (p. 317)	1 g
Total grams net carbs	**23 g**

DAY 3

	Net Carbs
Breakfast	
Cheesy Ham & Egg Bake (p. 58)	9 g
Hot coffee	0 g
Lunch	
Turkey and mozzarella cheese wrapped in romaine lettuce (2 ounces roasted turkey breast and 1 ounce mozzarella cheese wrapped in 1 romaine lettuce leaf)	1 g
Roasted Garlic Mayonnaise (p. 379)	1 g
Three-Mushroom Soup (p. 100)	3 g
Sugar-free iced tea	0 g
Dinner	
Marinated Prime Rib (p. 145)	0 g
Mustard Greens Salad (p. 127)	2 g
Herbed-Yogurt Baked Tomatoes (p. 274)	6 g
Hot espresso	0 g
Snack	
Creamy Cheese Spread (p. 310)	1 g
Celery sticks	0 g
Total grams net carbs	**23 g**

DAY 4

	Net Carbs
Breakfast	
Chile-Cheese Squares (p. 57)	5 g
3 ounces Canadian-style bacon	1 g
Hot coffee	
Lunch	
Cabbage & Chicken with Sesame Dressing (p. 109)	6 g
Sugar-free lemonade	0 g
Dinner	
Pork with Nutty Pear Stuffing (p. 177)	8 g
½ cup steamed broccoli	2 g
Sugar-free wild berry gelatin	0 g
Sugar-free iced coffee	0 g
Snack	
Wrap-&-Roll Basil Pinwheels (p. 301)	2 g
Total grams net carbs	**24 g**

DAY 5

	Net Carbs
Breakfast	
1 scrambled egg	1 g
3 slices bacon	0 g
½ cup cubed cantaloupe	6 g
Hot coffee	0 g
Lunch	
Chicken and Nectarine Salad (p. 110)	9 g
Tropical Berry Squares (p. 341)	3 g
Sugar-free lemon-flavored iced tea	0 g
Dinner	
Halibut in Hazelnut Butter (p. 241)	1 g
Summer Squash with Peppers (p. 268)	4 g
Raspberry & Chocolate Tulips (p. 326)	3 g
Hot coffee	0 g
Snack	
Icy Shrimp Cocktail (p. 43)	6 g
Total grams net carbs	**33 g**

DAY 6

	Net Carbs
Breakfast	
Baked Spinach-Ham Frittata (p. 65)	4 g
Hot herbed tea	0 g
Lunch	
Beef & Blue Cheese Salad (p. 116)	7 g
Sugar-free raspberry-flavored iced tea	0 g
Dinner	
Coriander Pork Chops (p. 195)	4 g
Tangy Green Beans (p. 273)	4 g
Tossed salad (2 cups mesclun lettuce, ½ cup cauliflower flowerets, 2 cherry tomatoes, and 1 sliced radish)	2 g
with Apricot Nectar Dressing (p. 399)	2 g
Sparkling water with lemon wedge	0 g
Snack	
Salmon-Artichoke Dip (p. 29)	0 g
Celery sticks	0 g
Total grams net carbs	**23 g**

DAY 7

	Net Carbs
Breakfast	
Weekend Scramble (p. 67)	2 g
½ cup fresh raspberries	3 g
2 links turkey breakfast sausage	1 g
Hot tea with lemon wedge	0 g
Lunch	
Oriental Chicken & Shrimp Soup (p. 78)	5 g
1 cup mixed cucumber sticks and cauliflower flowerets	2 g
Sparkling water with lime wedge	0 g
Dinner	
Kansas City Strip Steak (p. 143)	8 g
Soy-Sauced Broccoli & Peppers (p. 272)	3 g
Sugar-free cranberry gelatin	0 g
Hot hazelnut coffee	0g
Snack	
Crab & Vegetable Roll-Ups (p. 304)	0 g
Total grams net carbs	**24 g**

NOTE: *For this book, net carbs are calculated by subtracting fiber from the number of total carbohydrates.*

APPETIZERS

When best friends or coworkers come for appetizers, there's no need to stray from your low-carb lifestyle. Whether you're sharing laughs, celebrating memories of past adventures, or planning your next work project, the savory bites in this chapter will tease everyone's taste buds. Offer several appetizers for a party or pick a special one to serve before dinner.

1

For a pretty presentation, serve the creamy dip in an artichoke half. Be sure to brush the cut artichoke with lemon juice to preserve its summer green color.

DILLY CRAB DIP

PREP:

15 minutes

CHILL:

2 hours

MAKES:

12 (2-tablespoon) servings

1	cup flaked, cooked crabmeat (cartilage removed)
½	cup mayonnaise or salad dressing
½	cup dairy sour cream
1	teaspoon dried dillweed
2	teaspoons finely chopped onion or green onion
½	teaspoon finely shredded lime peel
1	teaspoon lime juice
2	dashes bottled hot pepper sauce
	Dash cayenne pepper (optional)
3	sprigs fresh dillweed (optional)
	Celery, zucchini, or cucumber sticks (optional)

1 Reserve a few flakes of crabmeat for garnish; chill until ready to serve.

2 In a bowl stir together mayonnaise, sour cream, the remaining flaked crabmeat, dillweed, onion, lime peel, lime juice, hot pepper sauce, and, if desired, cayenne pepper; mix well. Transfer to a serving bowl; chill for 2 hours or overnight.

3 Just before serving, sprinkle dip with reserved crabmeat and, if desired, garnish with fresh dill sprigs. If desired, serve with vegetable sticks.

Nutrition Facts per serving: 93 cal., 10 g total fat (2 g sat. fat), 24 mg chol., 105 mg sodium, 1 g carbo., 1 g fiber, 3 g pro.

This easy stir-together dip delivers big flavor and takes just minutes to prepare.

1 g net carb

THAI SPINACH DIP

1	cup chopped fresh spinach
1	8-ounce carton dairy sour cream
1	8-ounce carton plain yogurt
¼	cup snipped fresh mint
¼	cup finely chopped peanuts
¼	cup natural peanut butter
1	tablespoon soy sauce
1	to 2 teaspoons crushed red pepper
	Low-carb tortilla chips (optional)

1 In a medium bowl stir together spinach, sour cream, and yogurt. Stir in mint, peanuts, peanut butter, soy sauce, and crushed red pepper. Cover and chill for 2 to 24 hours. If desired, serve with low-carb tortilla chips.

Nutrition Facts per serving: 31 cal., 3 g total fat (1 g sat. fat), 3 mg chol., 41 mg sodium, 1 g carbo., 0 g fiber, 1 g pro.

PREP:
15 minutes

CHILL:
2 hours

MAKES:
40 (1-tablespoon) servings

Feta, a brine-cured sheep's milk cheese, provides a tangy backdrop for garlic and herbs. Its naturally salty flavor pairs nicely with raw vegetable sticks.

GARLIC-FETA CHEESE SPREAD

START TO FINISH:

15 minutes

MAKES:

12 (3-slice) servings

4	ounces feta cheese, crumbled
½	of an 8-ounce package cream cheese, softened
⅓	cup mayonnaise or salad dressing
1	clove garlic, minced
¼	teaspoon dried basil, crushed
¼	teaspoon dried oregano, crushed
⅛	teaspoon dried dillweed
⅛	teaspoon dried thyme, crushed
36	¼-inch cucumber or zucchini slices
	Fresh dill sprigs

1 In a food processor bowl or mixing bowl combine feta cheese, cream cheese, mayonnaise, garlic, and dried herbs. Cover and process or beat with an electric mixer on medium speed until combined. Immediately spoon about 2 teaspoons spread onto each vegetable slice. Garnish each with a small sprig of fresh dill.

Nutrition Facts per serving: 106 cal., 10 g total fat (4 g sat. fat), 21 mg chol., 166 mg sodium, 1 g carbo., 0 g fiber, 2 g pro.

The exotic artichoke dip makes the list of all-time favorites. Mayonnaise and Parmesan cheese make it extra creamy.

CLASSIC ARTICHOKE DIP

2   14-ounce cans artichoke hearts, drained and chopped

1   cup mayonnaise or salad dressing

1   cup grated Parmesan cheese

    Low-carb tortilla chips or vegetable dippers (optional)

1 In a medium bowl stir together artichokes, mayonnaise, and cheese. Transfer to a 1-quart casserole. Bake, uncovered, in a 350° oven about 25 minutes or until heated through. Serve warm. If desired, serve with low-carb tortilla chips.

Nutrition Facts per serving: 86 cal., 8 g total fat (2 g sat. fat), 8 mg chol., 217 mg sodium, 2 g carbo., 1 g fiber, 2 g pro.

PREP:

5 minutes

BAKE:

25 minutes

OVEN:

350°F

MAKES:

26 (2-tablespoon) servings

To keep this rich dip warm during your party, place it on a warming tray or in an electric fondue pot.

2 g net carb

ARTICHOKE CHILE DIP

PREP:

10 minutes

BAKE:

20 minutes

OVEN:

350°F

MAKES:

about 20 (2-tablespoon) servings

1   14-ounce can artichoke hearts, drained and chopped

1   4½-ounce can chopped green chile peppers, drained

1   cup mayonnaise or salad dressing

½   cup grated Parmesan cheese

   Low-carb tortilla chips (optional)

1 In a medium bowl stir together artichoke hearts, chile peppers, mayonnaise, and Parmesan cheese. Spread mixture in a 9-inch pie plate. Bake in a 350° oven about 20 minutes or until heated through. Serve warm. If desired, serve with low-carb tortilla chips.

Nutrition Facts per serving: 28 cal., 2 g total fat (1 g sat. fat), 3 mg chol., 94 mg sodium, 2 g carbo., 0 g fiber, 1 g pro.

Impress your guests with a party-time classic that sports a salmon twist.

0 g net carb

SALMON-ARTICHOKE DIP

2   14-ounce cans artichoke hearts, drained and chopped

1   cup mayonnaise or salad dressing

1   cup grated Parmesan cheese

1   7½-ounce can red salmon, drained, flaked, and skin and bones removed

2   ounces cream cheese, softened

Celery, cucumber, and/or zucchini sticks (optional)

1 In a medium bowl stir together artichoke hearts, mayonnaise, and Parmesan cheese. Stir in salmon and cream cheese. Transfer mixture to a 1-quart casserole. Bake, uncovered, in a 350° oven about 25 minutes or until heated through. Serve warm. If desired, serve with vegetable sticks.

Nutrition Facts per serving: 88 cal., 8 g total fat (2 g sat. fat), 13 mg chol., 210 mg sodium, 1 g carbo., 1 g fiber, 3 g pro.

PREP:
10 minutes
BAKE:
25 minutes
OVEN:
350°F
MAKES:
32 (2-tablespoon) servings

It's everything you find in a Reuben sandwich minus the bread. The melted cheddar cheese deepens the flavor and makes the savory mixture a better dipping consistency.

HOT REUBEN DIP

PREP:

10 minutes

BAKE:

25 minutes

OVEN:

350°F

MAKES:

20 (¹/₄-cup) servings

1   14- or 16-ounce can sauerkraut, rinsed and well drained

1¹/₂   cups shredded cheddar cheese (6 ounces)

1¹/₂   cups shredded Swiss cheese (6 ounces)

6   ounces corned beef, chopped (about 1 cup)

1   cup mayonnaise or salad dressing
   Low-carb tortilla chips (optional)

① Pat rinsed and drained sauerkraut dry with paper towels. In a large bowl stir together the sauerkraut, cheddar cheese, Swiss cheese, corned beef, and mayonnaise. Spread in a 9-inch quiche dish or 1¹/₂-quart casserole. Bake, uncovered, in a 350° oven for 25 minutes or until hot and bubbly. Serve warm. If desired, serve with low-carb tortilla chips.

Nutrition Facts per serving: 223 cal., 21 g total fat (7 g sat. fat), 39 mg chol., 943 mg sodium, 1 g carbo., 1 g fiber, 8 g pro.

Deviled ham blends in smoothly and adds smoky zip to this rich, cheesy spread.

1 g net carb

DEVILED HAM & CHEESE BALL

2   4¼-ounce cans deviled ham
1   8-ounce package cream cheese, softened
2   cups shredded cheddar cheese (8 ounces)
½   cup finely chopped green sweet pepper
1   teaspoon dry ranch salad dressing mix
¾   cup unsalted, dry-roasted sunflower seeds
    Low-carb tortilla chips (optional)

PREP:
10 minutes
CHILL:
2 hours
MAKES:
24 (2-tablespoon) servings

1 In a medium bowl stir together deviled ham, cream cheese, cheddar cheese, sweet pepper, and salad dressing mix. Divide mixture in half. Cover and chill for 1 to 1½ hours or until firm enough to handle.

2 Form each portion into a ball. Roll the balls in sunflower seeds to coat. Cover and chill at least 1 hour before serving. If desired, serve with low-carb tortilla chips.

Nutrition Facts per serving: 129 cal., 11 g total fat (5 g sat. fat), 26 mg chol., 231 mg sodium, 2 g carbo., 1 g fiber, 5 g pro.

You'll be amazed that so few ingredients generate so much flavor.

SPANISH OLIVE SPREAD

PREP:

15 minutes

CHILL:

4 hours

MAKES:

about 20 (2-tablespoon) servings

1½ cups finely shredded Swiss cheese (6 ounces)

1 3-ounce jar pimiento-stuffed green olives, drained and chopped

½ cup mayonnaise or salad dressing

Low-carb tortilla chips (optional)

1 In a medium bowl stir together Swiss cheese and green olives. Stir in mayonnaise until combined. Cover and chill for 4 to 24 hours. Before serving, gently stir mixture. If desired, serve with low-carb tortilla chips.

Nutrition Facts per serving: 76 cal., 7 g total fat (2 g sat. fat), 10 mg chol., 140 mg sodium, 0 g carbo., 0 g fiber, 2 g pro.

If smoked whitefish is unavailable where you live, substitute smoked trout or haddock.

SMOKED FISH SPREAD

6 ounces smoked skinless, boneless whitefish

2 tablespoons mayonnaise or salad dressing

½ of an 8-ounce package cream cheese, softened

2 tablespoons Dijon-style mustard

¼ teaspoon ground white pepper

Low-carb tortilla chips (optional)

1 Using a fork, finely flake the fish. (Or place fish in a food processor bowl. Cover and process with several on-off turns until fish is finely chopped.) Set aside.

2 In a medium bowl gradually stir mayonnaise into the softened cream cheese. Stir in mustard and white pepper. Gently stir in the fish. Cover and chill for 4 to 24 hours. If desired, serve with low-carb tortilla chips.

Nutrition Facts per serving: 104 cal., 8 g total fat (4 g sat. fat), 34 mg chol., 320 mg sodium, 0 g carbo., 0 g fiber, 6 g pro.

PREP:

10 minutes

CHILL:

4 hours

MAKES:

8 (2-tablespoon) servings

As the garlic bakes, it becomes sweet and tender, melding delectably with the creamy Brie.

BAKED BRIE WITH ROASTED GARLIC

PREP:

35 minutes

BAKE:

10 minutes

OVEN:

400°F

MAKES:

4 servings

1   head garlic

2   tablespoons olive or cooking oil

1   8-ounce round Brie, well chilled

2   tablespoons Greek black olives, pitted and quartered

1   teaspoon finely snipped parsley

1 To roast garlic, place an unpeeled head of garlic in a heavy saucepan with oil. Cook and stir over medium heat for 5 minutes. Cover and reduce heat to medium-low. Cook about 15 minutes more or until garlic is soft. Remove garlic from oil. Drain on paper towels and cool.

2 Slice the thin rind off one of the flat sides of the Brie. Place cut side up on a baking sheet. Divide head of garlic into cloves; peel cloves. Slice each garlic clove with repeated diagonal cuts, being careful not to completely sever the cloves. Gently press sliced garlic cloves into a fan. Arrange garlic fans and olives on top of Brie.

3 Bake, uncovered, in a 400° oven for 10 to 12 minutes or until Brie is warm and slightly softened. To serve, sprinkle with parsley.

Nutrition Facts per serving: 231 cal., 20 g total fat (10 g sat. fat), 56 mg chol., 376 mg sodium, 2 g carbo., 0 g fiber, 12 g pro.

This chunky Mediterranean-style appetizer tastes garden-fresh even in the middle of winter.

MARINATED ARTICHOKE HEARTS

2	9-ounce packages frozen artichoke hearts
¾	cup oil-and-vinegar salad dressing
1	cup halved cherry tomatoes
¼	cup chopped cucumber
¼	cup chopped green sweet pepper
¼	cup snipped fresh basil leaves

1 Cook artichokes according to package directions. Drain and cool. Place in a medium bowl. Pour salad dressing over artichokes and stir to coat. Cover and marinate in the refrigerator for 4 hours or overnight.

2 About 1 hour before serving, stir in tomatoes, cucumber, green pepper, and basil. Transfer to a serving bowl. Serve with a slotted spoon.

Nutrition Facts per serving: 114 cal., 10 g total fat (2 g sat. fat), 0 mg chol., 35 mg sodium, 6 g carbo., 3 g fiber, 1 g pro.

PREP:
15 minutes

CHILL:
4 hours

MAKES:
10 servings

The crushed red pepper takes the kalamata and green olives from mellow to memorable.
If you like foods spicy hot, use the 1 teaspoon crushed red pepper.

1 g net carb

LEMONY-HERBED OLIVES

PREP:

15 minutes

STAND:

30 minutes

MARINATE:

4 hours

MAKES:

56 servings

1   pound pitted kalamata olives and/or green olives (3½ cups)

1   tablespoon olive oil

½   teaspoon finely shredded lemon peel

1   tablespoon lemon juice

2   teaspoons snipped fresh oregano or ½ teaspoon dried oregano, crushed

½   to 1 teaspoon crushed red pepper

    Lemon peel curls (optional)

1 Place olives in a self-sealing plastic bag set in a bowl. For marinade, in a bowl stir together olive oil, lemon peel, lemon juice, oregano, and crushed red pepper. Pour over olives; seal bag. Marinate in the refrigerator for 4 to 24 hours, turning bag occasionally.

2 To serve, let olives stand at room temperature for 30 minutes. Drain and serve. If desired, garnish olives with curled strips of lemon peel.

Nutrition Facts per serving: 15 cal., 1 g total fat (0 g sat. fat), 0 mg chol., 94 mg sodium, 1 g carbo., 0 g fiber, 0 g pro.

Look for Easter egg and French breakfast radishes, as well as the more common red or icicle varieties. Scrub the radishes and leave the roots and a quarter-inch or so of the tops.

SWEET & SOUR RADISHES

2	cups small whole or halved radishes
⅓	cup vinegar
3	tablespoons water
4	teaspoons no-calorie, heat-stable granular sugar substitute (Splenda)
1	tablespoon snipped fresh dillweed
1	small fresh red serrano or Thai chile pepper, seeded and sliced* (optional)
1½	teaspoons bottled minced garlic (3 cloves)
¼	teaspoon salt

PREP:

10 minutes

MARINATE:

6 hours

MAKES:

6 servings

1 Place radishes in a self-sealing plastic bag. In a small bowl stir together vinegar, water, sugar substitute, dill, chile pepper (if desired), garlic, and salt. Pour over radishes; seal bag.

2 Marinate in the refrigerator for 6 to 8 hours, turning bag occasionally. Drain radishes before serving.

*NOTE: Hot peppers contain oils that can burn eyes, lips, and skin. Wear plastic gloves while preparing them and be sure to wash your hands and nails thoroughly afterward.

Nutrition Facts per serving: 12 cal., 0 g total fat (0 g sat. fat), 0 mg chol., 107 mg sodium, 3 g carbo., 1 g fiber, 0 g pro.

For easy drizzling, pour the flavored oil into a plastic squeeze bottle.

3 g net carb

GRILLED ENDIVE WITH PROSCIUTTO

PREP:

15 minutes

GRILL:

25 minutes

MAKES:

4 servings

1	tablespoon olive oil
1	tablespoon Dijon-style mustard
¼	teaspoon black pepper
2	heads Belgian endive, trimmed and halved lengthwise
4	thin slices prosciutto (1½ to 2 ounces)
½	of a medium red sweet pepper, cut into thin strips
½	of a medium yellow sweet pepper, cut into thin strips
1	green onion, bias-sliced
1	recipe Herbed Oil (see below)

1 In a small bowl stir together olive oil, mustard, and black pepper; brush over endive halves. Wrap each endive half in a thin slice of prosciutto; secure with wooden toothpicks.

2 For a charcoal grill, in a covered grill arrange medium-hot coals around a drip pan. Test for medium heat above the pan. Place endive on grill rack over drip pan. Cover and grill about 25 minutes or until endive is tender and prosciutto is golden brown, turning once halfway through grilling. (For a gas grill, preheat grill. Reduce heat to medium. Adjust grill for indirect cooking. Grill as above.)

3 Meanwhile, in a small bowl combine sweet peppers and green onion; divide among 4 salad plates. Top with grilled endive. Drizzle each serving with Herbed Oil. Discard any remaining oil. Serve immediately.

HERBED OIL: In a blender container combine ¼ cup olive oil, ⅓ cup coarsely chopped fresh flat-leaf parsley, 3 tablespoons snipped fresh chives, 4 teaspoons snipped fresh lemon thyme or thyme, and ¼ teaspoon salt. Cover and blend until smooth. Strain herb mixture through a fine-mesh sieve, pressing on solids to extract all oil; discard herb mixture. Place oil in a squeeze bottle. Refrigerate for up to 2 days. (For food safety reasons, do not store oil any longer than 2 days.) To serve, bring to room temperature; shake well.

Nutrition Facts per serving: 206 cal., 20 g total fat (2 g sat. fat), 0 mg chol., 361 mg sodium, 4 g carbo., 1 g fiber, 4 g pro.

Herbes de Provence, a classic French combination of basil, fennel seed, lavender, marjoram, rosemary, sage, summer savory, and thyme, seasons these tasty appetizers.

4 g net carb

HERBED LEEK TORTILLA WEDGES

4	8- to 9-inch low-carbohydrate multigrain or whole wheat flour tortillas
4	medium leeks, thinly sliced (1⅓ cups)
3	cloves garlic, minced
2	tablespoons olive oil
1	teaspoon dried herbes de Provence or dried basil, crushed
2	tablespoons Dijon-style mustard
1	cup shredded Gruyère or Swiss cheese (4 ounces)
¼	cup pine nuts or chopped almonds, toasted

PREP:
20 minutes

BAKE:
8 minutes per batch

OVEN:
425°F

MAKES:
24 wedges

1 Put 2 tortillas on a baking sheet. Bake in a 425° oven for 5 minutes. Repeat with remaining 2 tortillas.

2 Meanwhile, in a large skillet cook leeks and garlic in olive oil over medium heat for 5 to 8 minutes or until tender, stirring frequently. Remove from heat. Stir in herbes de Provence. Spread mustard over tortillas. Top with leek mixture, cheese, and nuts.

3 Bake tortillas, 2 at a time, for 3 to 5 minutes or until cheese is melted. Cut each tortilla into 6 wedges.

Nutrition Facts per square: 114 cal., 8 g total fat (2 g sat. fat), 10 mg chol., 174 mg sodium, 7 g carbo., 3 g fiber, 5 g pro.

The 12 garlic cloves mellow as they cook, blending with apricot and ginger undertones.

5 g net carb

ZESTY TURKEY MEATBALLS

PREP:

15 minutes

BAKE:

20 minutes

OVEN:

375°F

MAKES:

18 (2-meatball) servings

12   large cloves garlic, halved

3   tablespoons grated fresh ginger

     Several dashes bottled hot pepper sauce

¾   cup sugar-free apricot preserves

2   teaspoons finely shredded lemon peel

½   teaspoon toasted sesame oil

¼   cup rice vinegar

1   beaten egg white

⅓   cup finely chopped green or red sweet pepper

⅓   cup quick-cooking rolled oats

½   teaspoon salt

1   pound lean ground turkey

1 For sauce, in a blender container combine garlic, ginger, hot pepper sauce, preserves, lemon peel, sesame oil, and vinegar. Cover and blend until smooth. Set aside.

2 In a medium bowl stir together egg white, sweet pepper, oats, salt, and ⅓ cup of the sauce. Add turkey; mix well. Shape into 1½-inch balls. Arrange meatballs in a 15×10×1-inch baking pan.

3 Bake, uncovered, in a 375° oven for 15 minutes or until thoroughly cooked. Brush with some of the remaining sauce and bake about 5 minutes more or until golden and glazed. Remove from oven and drain on paper towels. Cook remaining sauce in a saucepan over medium heat until heated through and slightly thickened. Spoon sauce over meatballs.

Nutrition Facts per serving: 58 cal., 2 g total fat (1 g sat. fat), 20 mg chol., 86 mg sodium, 5 g carbo., 0 g fiber, 53 g pro.

Four ingredients combine for a cheesy meatball dish that's like pizza without the crust.

4 g net carb

EASY TWICE-BAKED MEATBALLS

1   32-ounce jar spaghetti sauce

2   16-ounce packages frozen cooked meatballs

¼   teaspoon crushed red pepper

12   ounces shredded mozzarella cheese (3 cups)

1 Spoon about ⅓ of the jar of spaghetti sauce into a 13×9×2-inch baking dish. Arrange the meatballs in the sauce. Pour the remaining sauce over the meatballs. Sprinkle with pepper; top with mozzarella.

2 Bake, uncovered, in a 350° oven for 30 to 40 minutes or until meatballs are hot and cheese is bubbly.

Nutrition Facts per serving: 116 cal., 8 g total fat (4 g sat. fat), 15 mg chol., 371 mg sodium, 5 g carbo., 1 g fiber, 6 g pro.

PREP:

5 minutes

BAKE:

30 minutes

OVEN:

350°F

MAKES:

35 servings

These party snacks are so easy and delicious everyone will want the recipe. Four ingredients and four hours—that's all you need.

ITALIAN COCKTAIL MEATBALLS

PREP:

15 minutes

COOK:

4 hours

MAKES:

16 (2-meatball) servings

1   16-ounce package frozen cooked meatballs (32), thawed

½   cup bottled roasted red and/or yellow sweet peppers, cut into 1-inch pieces

⅛   teaspoon crushed red pepper

1½ cups bottled onion-garlic pasta sauce

1 Place meatballs and peppers in a 1½-quart slow cooker.* Sprinkle with crushed red pepper. Pour sauce over mixture in cooker.

2 Cover and cook for 4 to 5 hours. Skim fat from sauce. Stir gently before serving.

*NOTE: The 1½-quart slow cooker does not have a low or high setting. It cooks on one heat setting only.

Nutrition Facts per serving: 99 cal., 8 g total fat (3 g sat. fat), 10 mg chol., 322 mg sodium, 4 g carbo., 1 g fiber, 4 g pro.

Chilled shrimp appetizers shine with very little encouragement. Here chopped orange and snipped cilantro give them an island flavor.

ICY SHRIMP COCKTAIL

1	orange, peeled, sectioned, and coarsely chopped
20	cooked, peeled, and deveined large shrimp
¼	cup snipped fresh cilantro
	Dash salt
	Dash black pepper

1 In a bowl gently toss together the chopped orange, shrimp, cilantro, salt, and pepper. Cover and chill for 2 hours.

Nutrition Facts per serving: 123 cal., 3 g total fat (0 g sat. fat), 129 mg chol., 402 mg sodium, 7 g carbo., 1 g fiber, 18 g pro.

PREP:
15 minutes
CHILL:
2 hours
MAKES:
4 servings

If fresh mozzarella is not available, substitute another fresh soft cheese, such as queso fresco or feta.
For even more flavor, use an olive oil infused with herbs or roasted garlic instead of plain olive oil.

MARINATED MOZZARELLA WITH BASIL

PREP:

15 minutes

CHILL:

1 hour

MAKES:

14 to 16 servings

¼ cup fresh basil leaves, chopped

¼ cup extra virgin olive oil

1 tablespoon coarsely ground black pepper

1 to 2 teaspoons balsamic vinegar

16 ounces fresh mozzarella cheese, cut into 1-inch cubes

1 In a medium bowl stir together basil, oil, pepper, and vinegar. Add cheese cubes; toss gently to coat. Cover and chill for 1 hour or up to 5 days.

Nutrition Facts per serving: 126 cal., 11 g total fat (5 g sat. fat), 25 mg chol., 120 mg sodium, 1 g carbo., 0 g fiber, 6 g pro.

Reserve the marinade from the artichoke hearts to infuse the zucchini, tomato, and green onion with tangy flavor.

ENDIVE LEAVES WITH ARTICHOKE CAVIAR

1	6-ounce jar marinated artichoke hearts
½	cup finely chopped zucchini
1	medium tomato, peeled, seeded, and finely chopped
1	green onion, chopped
2	tablespoons snipped fresh basil or 1 teaspoon dried basil, crushed
1	teaspoon lemon juice
2	cloves garlic, minced
3	heads Belgian endive (36 leaves)
	Fresh basil sprigs (optional)

PREP:

15 minutes

MARINATE:

2 hours

MAKES:

36 servings

1 Drain artichoke hearts, reserving marinade (about ⅓ cup). Set aside. Finely chop artichoke hearts.

2 In a medium bowl combine the chopped artichoke hearts, zucchini, tomato, and green onion. In a small bowl stir together the reserved artichoke marinade, basil, lemon juice, and garlic. Whisk to mix well. Pour over artichoke mixture. Cover and marinate in the refrigerator for 2 to 6 hours, stirring occasionally.

3 To serve, drain mixture. Cut away the bitter core from Belgian endive heads. Separate endive leaves. Spoon about 2 teaspoons mixture into each leaf. If desired, garnish with fresh basil sprigs.

Nutrition Facts per serving: 6 cal., 0 g total fat (0 g sat. fat), 0 mg chol., 15 mg sodium, 1 g carbo., 0 g fiber, 0 g pro.

The lime-and-cilantro marinade has just the right amount of zing to kick off conversation.

1 g net carb

MARINATED LIME SHRIMP APPETIZER

PREP:

15 minutes

MARINATE:

2 hours

MAKES:

6 servings

12	ounces fresh or frozen peeled, deveined, cooked shrimp
1	teaspoon finely shredded lime peel
1/3	cup lime juice
1/4	cup cooking oil
2	tablespoons snipped fresh cilantro or parsley
1	fresh jalapeño pepper, seeded and finely chopped, or 1 tablespoon canned chopped jalapeño pepper
1	clove garlic, minced
	Lettuce (optional)

1 Thaw shrimp, if frozen. Rinse shrimp; pat dry. In a medium bowl stir together lime peel, lime juice, oil, cilantro, jalapeño pepper, and garlic. Add shrimp and toss to coat.

2 Cover and marinate in the refrigerator for 2 to 3 hours, stirring the mixture twice.

3 To serve, drain shrimp and discard marinade. If desired, arrange on lettuce-lined plate. Serve with toothpicks.

Nutrition Facts per serving: 101 cal., 6 g total fat (1 g sat. fat), 86 mg chol., 84 mg sodium, 1 g carbo., 0 g fiber, 12 g pro.

Easy and quick, these bite-size salmon morsels feature Asian flavor.

0 g net carb

PISTACHIO-SALMON NUGGETS

- 1 pound fresh or frozen skinless salmon fillets, cut 1 inch thick
- 2 tablespoons water
- 2 tablespoons soy sauce
- 1 tablespoon grated fresh ginger
- 2 teaspoons toasted sesame oil or cooking oil
- 1 tablespoon cooking oil
- 1 tablespoon finely chopped pistachio nuts

PREP:
15 minutes
COOK:
6 minutes
MARINATE:
30 minutes
MAKES:
10 to 12 servings

1 Thaw fish, if frozen. Rinse fish; pat dry with paper towels. Cut fish into 1-inch chunks. Place fish in a self-sealing plastic bag set in a shallow dish.

2 For marinade, in a small bowl stir together the water, soy sauce, ginger, and sesame oil. Pour marinade over salmon chunks; seal bag. Marinate at room temperature for 30 minutes, turning bag occasionally.

3 Drain salmon, discarding marinade. In a large nonstick skillet heat the cooking oil over medium-high heat.

4 In the skillet cook and gently stir half of the salmon chunks for 3 to 5 minutes or until fish flakes easily with a fork; remove from skillet and place on paper towels. Cook and stir remaining fish; remove and place on paper towels. Transfer to a serving dish; sprinkle with pistachio nuts.

Nutrition Facts per serving: 64 cal., 4 g total fat (1 g sat. fat), 8 mg chol., 130 mg sodium, 0 g carbo., 0 g fiber, 7 g pro.

Set out a bowl of nuts at your next party and they'll disappear in no time—even faster if they're these herb-accented macadamias.

SAVORY NUTS

2 g net carb

PREP:

5 minutes

BAKE:

12 minutes

OVEN:

350°F

MAKES:

16 (2-tablespoon) servings

2 cups macadamia nuts, broken walnuts, and/or unblanched almonds

2 tablespoons white wine Worcestershire sauce

1 tablespoon olive oil

½ teaspoon dried thyme, crushed

¼ teaspoon salt

¼ teaspoon dried rosemary, crushed

⅛ teaspoon cayenne pepper

1 Spread nuts in a 13×9×2-inch baking pan. In a small bowl stir together Worcestershire sauce, olive oil, thyme, salt, rosemary, and cayenne pepper; drizzle over nuts. Toss to coat.

2 Bake in a 350° oven for 12 to 15 minutes or until nuts are toasted, stirring occasionally. Spread on foil; cool. Store in an airtight container for up to 2 weeks.

Nutrition Facts per serving: 258 cal., 27 g total fat (4 g sat. fat), 0 mg chol., 193 mg sodium, 5 g carbo., 3 g fiber, 3 g pro.

This is a zesty twist on an already popular snack food.

HOT & SPICY WALNUTS

1	teaspoon ground coriander
1	teaspoon ground cumin
½	teaspoon salt
¼	teaspoon freshly ground black pepper
⅛	teaspoon cayenne pepper
2	cups walnut halves
1	tablespoon cooking oil

1 In a small bowl stir together coriander, cumin, salt, black pepper, and cayenne pepper; set aside. Place nuts in a 13×9×2-inch baking pan. Drizzle with oil, stirring to coat. Sprinkle with spice mixture; toss lightly.

2 Bake in a 300° oven for 20 minutes or until nuts are lightly toasted, stirring once or twice. Cool in pan for 15 minutes. Turn out onto paper towels; cool completely. Store in an airtight container for up to 2 weeks.

Nutrition Facts per serving: 214 cal., 21 g total fat (2 g sat. fat), 0 mg chol., 147 mg sodium, 4 g carbo., 2 g fiber, 5 g pro.

PREP:
10 minutes
BAKE:
20 minutes
COOL:
15 minutes
OVEN:
300°F
MAKES:
8 (¹/₄-cup) servings

BREAKFAST & BRUNCH

As kids we're taught that a healthful breakfast is the most important meal of the day. That folksy truth asserts itself repeatedly in nutrition research, especially for dieters. Give your metabolism a jump-start by launching the day with one of these taste-tempting recipes.

Chopped apple lends a touch of sweetness to these patties. Make them on a weekend morning when you have a few extra minutes to cook.

3 g net carb

APPLE BREAKFAST PATTIES

PREP:

15 minutes

COOK:

8 minutes

MAKES:

8 patties

1	slightly beaten egg white
½	cup finely chopped fresh apple
¼	cup finely chopped onion
3	tablespoons quick-cooking oats
2	tablespoons snipped fresh parsley
½	teaspoon salt
½	teaspoon ground sage
¼	teaspoon ground nutmeg
¼	teaspoon black pepper
	Dash cayenne pepper
8	ounces lean ground pork or uncooked ground turkey
	Nonstick cooking spray

1 In a medium bowl stir together egg white, apple, onion, oats, parsley, salt, sage, nutmeg, black pepper, and cayenne pepper. Add ground pork. Mix well. Shape the mixture into eight 2-inch-diameter patties.

2 Lightly coat a 10-inch skillet with cooking spray. Heat over medium-low heat. Cook patties in skillet for 8 to 10 minutes or until done (160°F for pork, 165°F for turkey), turning once. Drain off fat.

Nutrition Facts per patty: 51 cal., 2 g total fat (0 g sat. fat), 13 mg chol., 151 mg sodium, 3 g carbo., 0 g fiber, 4 g pro.

Syrup and sausages have kept company on breakfast plates for generations. This time, glaze the sausages with a sweet-sharp syrup and mustard combination.

2 g net carb

MAPLE-MUSTARD SAUSAGES

- 1   12-ounce package frozen link pork sausage, thawed
- 2   tablespoons sugar-free maple-flavored syrup with no-calorie, heat-stable sugar substitute
- 2   teaspoons brown mustard

① In a large skillet cook sausages according to package directions. Drain fat from skillet. Meanwhile, in a small bowl stir together syrup and mustard; add mixture to sausages in skillet. Cook, uncovered, over medium-low heat for 3 to 4 minutes or until sausages are glazed, stirring frequently. Serve immediately.

Nutrition Facts per serving: 199 cal., 16 g total fat (7 g sat. fat), 32 mg chol., 318 mg sodium, 2 g carbo., 0 g fiber, 7 g pro.

PREP:
10 minutes
COOK:
about 15 minutes
MAKES:
6 servings

Be sure to use a skillet that can withstand the heat of the oven. A cast-iron skillet does the job nicely.

3 g net carb

SPICY CHICKEN OMELET

START TO FINISH:

25 minutes

OVEN:

350°F

MAKES:

2 servings

4 eggs, separated

¼ teaspoon salt

⅛ teaspoon black pepper

2 tablespoons water

1 tablespoon butter

⅔ cup shredded Monterey Jack cheese with jalapeño peppers or cheddar cheese

1 6-ounce package refrigerated cooked Southwestern-style chicken breast strips, chopped

2 tablespoons salsa or picante sauce

Salsa or picante sauce (optional)

1 In a medium mixing bowl beat egg whites, salt, and pepper with an electric mixer on medium to high speed until frothy. Add water; continue beating about 1½ minutes or until stiff peaks form (tips stand straight). Fold in yolks.

2 In a large ovenproof skillet heat butter over medium-high heat until a drop of water sizzles. Spread egg mixture in skillet. Cook about 3 minutes or until bottom is just golden. Bake in a 350° oven for 3 to 4 minutes or until dry on top and edges are light brown.

3 Loosen the omelet from the sides of the skillet. Make a shallow cut slightly off center across the omelet. Sprinkle cheese over the larger side. Top with chicken and the 2 tablespoons salsa. Fold smaller side of omelet over larger side. Cut omelet in half. If desired, serve with additional salsa.

Nutrition Facts per serving: 464 cal., 31 g total fat (16 g sat. fat), 537 mg chol., 1,540 mg sodium, 3 g carbo., 0 g fiber, 41 g pro.

A tangy red pepper relish adorns these cheese-and-spinach-filled omelets. This breakfast classic makes a quick, easy weeknight supper, too.

1 g net carb

SPINACH & CHEESE OMELET

Nonstick cooking spray

4 eggs

Dash salt

Dash cayenne pepper

¼ cup shredded sharp cheddar cheese (1 ounce)

1 tablespoon snipped fresh chives, flat-leaf parsley, or chervil

1 cup spinach leaves

1 recipe Red Pepper Relish (see below)

START TO FINISH:
20 minutes
MAKES:
2 servings

1 Lightly coat an 8-inch nonstick skillet with flared sides or a crepe pan with cooking spray. Heat skillet over medium-high heat.

2 In a medium bowl beat together eggs, salt, and cayenne. Pour egg mixture into skillet. Cook over medium heat without stirring until mixture begins to set on bottom and around edge. Using a large spatula, lift and fold the partially cooked mixture so that the uncooked portion flows underneath.

3 Continue cooking until egg mixture is set but is still glossy and moist. Sprinkle with cheese and chives. Top with ¾ cup of the spinach and 2 tablespoons of the Red Pepper Relish. Using the spatula, lift and fold an edge of the omelet partially over filling. Top with the remaining ¼ cup spinach and 1 tablespoon of the relish. (Reserve the remaining relish for another use.) Cut the omelet in half.

RED PEPPER RELISH: In a small bowl combine ⅔ cup chopped red sweet pepper, 2 tablespoons finely chopped onion, 1 tablespoon cider vinegar, and ¼ teaspoon black pepper. Makes about ⅔ cup.

Nutrition Facts per serving: 214 cal., 15 g total fat (6 g sat. fat), 440 mg chol., 303 mg sodium, 3 g carbo., 2 g fiber, 17 g pro.

Baked eggs sometimes are referred to as shirred (SHERD) eggs. This is an old-fashioned but deliciously easy way to prepare eggs.

1 g net carb

BAKED EGGS

PREP:
10 minutes

BAKE:
25 minutes

OVEN:
325°F

MAKES:
3 servings

Butter or margarine

6 eggs

Snipped fresh chives or desired herb

Salt

Black pepper

6 tablespoons shredded cheddar, Swiss,
or Monterey Jack cheese

1 Generously grease three 10-ounce casseroles with butter. Carefully break 2 eggs into each casserole; sprinkle with chives, salt, and pepper. Set casseroles in a 13×9×2-inch baking pan; place on an oven rack. Pour hot water around casseroles in pan to a depth of 1 inch.

2 Bake in a 325° oven for 20 minutes. Sprinkle cheese on top of eggs. Bake for 5 to 10 minutes more or until eggs are cooked and cheese melts.

Nutrition Facts per serving: 167 cal., 12 g total fat (4 g sat. fat), 430 mg chol., 147 mg sodium, 1 g carbo., 0 g fiber, 13 g pro.

For a low-carb breakfast everyone will applaud, pair these Tex-Mex cheese-and-egg squares with some crisp bacon and a fresh fruit medley.

5 g net carb

CHILE-CHEESE SQUARES

10	eggs
¼	cup butter or margarine, melted
½	cup unbleached all-purpose flour
1	tablespoon baking powder
2	cups shredded cheddar or Monterey Jack cheese (8 ounces)
2	cups small-curd cottage cheese
2	4-ounce cans diced green chile peppers, undrained

1 In a large bowl beat eggs slightly with a wire whisk. Whisk in melted butter. In a small bowl stir together flour and baking powder; whisk into egg mixture until combined. Stir in cheddar cheese, cottage cheese, and undrained chile peppers.

2 Grease a 3-quart rectangular baking dish; pour cheese mixture into prepared baking dish. Bake, uncovered, in a 350° oven about 40 minutes or until a knife inserted near the center comes out clean and top is golden. Let stand for 10 minutes before serving. Cut into squares to serve.

Nutrition Facts per serving: 185 cal., 13 g total fat (7 g sat. fat), 170 mg chol., 404 mg sodium, 5 g carbo., 0 g fiber, 12 g pro.

PREP:
15 minutes

BAKE:
40 minutes

STAND:
10 minutes

OVEN:
350°F

MAKES:
15 servings

Because it can be made ahead, this breakfast entrée is perfect for those mornings when you are short on time.

9 g net carb

CHEESY HAM & EGG BAKE

PREP:

20 minutes

BAKE:

15 minutes

OVEN:

350°F

MAKES:

2 servings

1	tablespoon butter or margarine
2	teaspoons unbleached all-purpose flour
	Dash black pepper
½	cup milk
¼	cup shredded American cheese (1 ounce)
4	eggs
1	tablespoon grated Parmesan or Romano cheese
	Dash black pepper
1	tablespoon butter or margarine
⅓	cup diced fully cooked ham or fully cooked smoked turkey
½	of a 2½-ounce jar (¼ cup) sliced mushrooms, drained
1	green onion, thinly sliced

1 For sauce, in a small saucepan melt 1 tablespoon butter. Stir in flour and dash of pepper. Add the milk all at once. Cook and stir over medium heat until thickened and bubbly. Cook and stir for 1 minute more. Stir in American cheese until melted. Remove from heat. Set aside.

2 In a small bowl beat together eggs, Parmesan cheese, and dash of pepper.

3 In a medium skillet melt 1 tablespoon butter. Pour egg mixture into the skillet. Cook over medium heat, without stirring, until mixture begins to set on the bottom and around edge. Using a large spatula, lift and fold the partially cooked egg mixture so that the uncooked portion flows underneath. Continue cooking for 2 to 3 minutes more or until egg mixture is cooked through but is still glossy and moist.

4 Spoon the eggs into two small casseroles. Sprinkle with ham and mushrooms. Pour sauce over ham and mushrooms.

5 Bake, covered, in a 350° oven for 15 to 20 minutes or until heated through. Sprinkle with green onion.

Nutrition Facts per serving: 409 cal., 31 g total fat (15 g sat. fat), 491 mg chol., 907 mg sodium, 9 g carbo., 0 g fiber, 24 g pro.

This versatile pie makes an enticing brunch or supper. Or for an appetizer, cut it into 16 wedges.

CHEESY EGG WEDGES

4	beaten eggs
⅓	cup milk
¼	cup unbleached all-purpose flour
½	teaspoon baking powder
⅛	teaspoon garlic powder
2	cups shredded cheddar or mozzarella cheese (8 ounces)
1	cup cream-style cottage cheese with chives
1	cup bottled meatless spaghetti sauce or salsa
	Fresh basil sprigs (optional)

PREP:
10 minutes

BAKE:
25 minutes

OVEN:
375°F

MAKES:
6 servings

1 In a medium bowl beat together eggs, milk, flour, baking powder, and garlic powder until combined. Stir in cheddar cheese and cottage cheese.

2 Lightly grease a 9-inch pie plate. Pour egg mixture into pie plate. Bake, uncovered, in a 375° oven for 25 to 30 minutes or until golden brown and a knife inserted near the center comes out clean.

3 Meanwhile, in a small saucepan heat the spaghetti sauce over medium-low heat about 5 minutes or until warm, stirring occasionally.

4 To serve, cut egg mixture into wedges. Top with spaghetti sauce. If desired, garnish with basil.

Nutrition Facts per serving: 273 cal., 18 g total fat (10 g sat. fat), 186 mg chol., 614 mg sodium, 9 g carbo., 0 g fiber, 20 g pro.

Bored with the same old egg dishes? Try this dynamite combination of spinach, poached eggs, and a vibrant mustard vinaigrette.

9 g net carb

EGGS WITH MUSTARD VINAIGRETTE

START TO FINISH:

20 minutes

MAKES:

4 servings

1   tablespoon coarse-grain brown mustard

2   tablespoons vinegar

2   tablespoons olive oil

      Cooking oil

4   eggs

2   cups spinach

1   tablespoon butter or margarine

      Salt

      Black pepper

1 For grainy mustard vinaigrette, in a small saucepan stir together mustard, vinegar, and olive oil. Bring to boiling, stirring to combine. Reduce heat; keep warm until serving.

2 Grease 4 cups of an egg poaching pan* with cooking oil. Place poacher cups over pan of boiling water (water should not touch bottoms of cups). Reduce heat to simmering. Break one of the eggs into a measuring cup. Carefully slide egg into a poacher cup. Repeat with remaining eggs. Cook, covered, for 6 to 9 minutes or until the whites are completely set and yolks begin to thicken but are not hard.

3 To serve, place spinach on 4 plates. Loosen poached eggs by running a knife around edge of each poacher cup; invert poacher cups and slip eggs onto spinach. Stir vinaigrette and pour over eggs. Season with salt and pepper.

*NOTE: If you don't have an egg poaching pan, lightly grease a medium skillet. Add water to half-fill the skillet. Bring water to boiling; reduce heat to simmering (bubbles should begin to break the surface of the water). Break one of the eggs into a measuring cup. Carefully slide egg into simmering water, holding the lip of the cup as close to the water as possible. Repeat with remaining eggs, allowing each egg an equal amount of space. Simmer eggs, uncovered, for 3 to 5 minutes or until the whites are completely set and yolks begin to thicken but are not hard. Remove poached eggs with a slotted spoon. Serve as directed in step 3.

Nutrition Facts per serving: 183 cal., 13 g total fat (3 g sat. fat), 213 mg chol., 257 mg sodium, 10 g carbo., 1 g fiber, 8 g pro.

Omelets and frittatas begin with similar egg mixtures. The extra ingredients are used as a filling for an omelet and are stirred into the egg mixture for a frittata.

9 g net carb

GREENS & BROWN RICE FRITTATA

6	egg whites
3	eggs
¼	teaspoon salt
⅛	teaspoon black pepper
½	cup cooked brown rice
¼	cup chopped onion
1	clove garlic, minced
1	tablespoon olive oil
2	cups packed mustard greens, stems trimmed and torn into 1-inch pieces
1	medium tomato, seeded and chopped (optional)
⅓	cup shredded fontina, provolone, or Gruyère cheese

PREP:
15 minutes
COOK:
8 minutes
BROIL:
1 minute
MAKES:
4 servings

1 In a medium bowl beat together egg whites, eggs, salt, and pepper. Stir in brown rice; set aside. In a large broiler-proof skillet cook onion and garlic in hot oil until tender. Stir in mustard greens; cook and stir about 2 minutes or until wilted. If desired, stir in tomato and cook 1 minute more.

2 Pour egg mixture over vegetables in skillet. Cook over medium-low heat without stirring until mixture begins to set on bottom and around edge. Using a large spatula, lift and fold the partially cooked mixture so the uncooked portion flows underneath. Continue cooking until egg mixture is almost set but is still glossy and moist. Sprinkle with cheese.

3 Place under broiler 4 to 5 inches from heat. Broil for 1 to 2 minutes or until top is just set and cheese melts.

Nutrition Facts per serving: 197 cal., 11 g total fat (4 g sat. fat), 172 mg chol., 370 mg sodium, 11 g carbo., 2 g fiber, 14 g pro.

If your favorite skillet isn't broilerproof, just remove it from the heat after adding the feta. Cover it and let stand for 3 to 4 minutes or just until the top of the frittata is set.

4 g net carb

SPINACH-FETA FRITTATA

START TO FINISH:

25 minutes

MAKES:

4 servings

6	eggs
¼	cup milk
1	teaspoon dried dill
¼	teaspoon salt
¼	teaspoon black pepper
½	cup chopped onion
1	clove garlic, minced
1	tablespoon butter or margarine
½	of a 10-ounce package frozen chopped spinach, thawed and well drained
¼	teaspoon lemon-pepper seasoning
¼	cup crumbled feta cheese (1 ounce)

1 In a medium bowl beat together eggs, milk, dill, salt, and pepper until combined. Set aside.

2 In a 10-inch broilerproof or regular skillet cook onion and garlic in hot butter until tender. Stir in spinach and lemon-pepper seasoning.

3 Pour egg mixture over spinach mixture in skillet. Cook over medium heat without stirring until egg mixture begins to set on the bottom and around edge. Using a large spatula, lift and fold the partially cooked egg mixture so that the uncooked portion flows underneath. Continue cooking until egg mixture is almost set but is still glossy and moist. Sprinkle with feta cheese.

4 Place broilerproof skillet under the broiler 4 to 5 inches from the heat. Broil for 1 to 2 minutes or just until top is set. (Or if using a regular skillet, remove skillet from heat; cover and let stand for 3 to 4 minutes or just until top is set.)

Nutrition Facts per serving: 183 cal., 12 g total fat (5 g sat. fat), 334 mg chol., 475 mg sodium, 5 g carbo., 1 g fiber, 12 g pro.

This quick-to-fix frittata sports an inviting pizza flavor.

7 g net carb

ZUCCHINI-PEPPERONI FRITTATA

3   cups thinly sliced zucchini

4   slightly beaten eggs

2   tablespoons unbleached all-purpose flour

¼   teaspoon salt

¼   teaspoon black pepper

2   teaspoons snipped fresh oregano or ½ teaspoon
    dried oregano, crushed

2   teaspoons snipped fresh thyme or ½ teaspoon
    dried thyme, crushed

2   teaspoons snipped fresh marjoram or ½ teaspoon
    dried marjoram, crushed

2   teaspoons snipped fresh basil or ½ teaspoon
    dried basil, crushed

2   tablespoons olive oil or cooking oil

2   ounces thinly sliced pepperoni

1   medium tomato, sliced (optional)

4   ounces thinly sliced mozzarella cheese

PREP:
20 minutes
COOK:
15 minutes
BROIL:
1 minute
MAKES:
4 servings

1 In a covered saucepan cook zucchini in a small amount of boiling water for 3 minutes; drain.

2 In a large bowl beat together eggs, flour, salt, and pepper. Stir in oregano, thyme, marjoram, basil, and zucchini; set aside.

3 Heat oil in an 8-inch broilerproof skillet over medium heat. Pour egg mixture into skillet. Cook without stirring over medium heat about 15 minutes or until egg mixture is almost set but is still glossy and moist.

4 Top with pepperoni, tomato (if desired), and mozzarella cheese. Place under broiler 4 to 5 inches from the heat. Broil for 1 to 2 minutes or until top is set, cheese has melted, and pepperoni is sizzling.

Nutrition Facts per serving: 303 cal., 23 g total fat (8 g sat. fat), 240 mg chol., 631 mg sodium, 8 g carbo., 1 g fiber, 17 g pro.

For breakfast, brunch, or supper, ham and eggs are a welcome pair on any plate. With a mix of pepper, tomato, and cheddar cheese, this recipe is especially colorful.

HAM & CHEESE FRITTATA

START TO FINISH:

25 minutes

MAKES:

6 servings

Nonstick cooking spray

1   cup chopped cooked ham (about 5 ounces)

½   cup chopped onion

½   cup chopped green or red sweet pepper

6   slightly beaten eggs

¾   cup cottage cheese

⅛   teaspoon black pepper

2   Roma tomatoes, thinly sliced (optional)

⅓   cup shredded cheddar cheese

1 Lightly coat a 10-inch ovenproof skillet with cooking spray. Heat skillet over medium heat. Cook ham, onion, and sweet pepper in hot skillet about 4 minutes or until vegetables are tender and ham is lightly browned.

2 Meanwhile, in a medium bowl stir together eggs, cottage cheese, and black pepper. Pour egg mixture over ham mixture in skillet. Cook over medium-low heat without stirring until mixture begins to set on bottom and around edge. Using a large spatula, lift and fold the partially cooked egg mixture so that the uncooked mixture flows underneath. Continue cooking and lifting edges until egg mixture is almost set but is still glossy and moist.

3 Place skillet under broiler 5 inches from heat. Broil for 1 to 2 minutes or until top is set. If desired, arrange tomato slices on top of frittata. Sprinkle with cheddar cheese. Broil 1 minute more.

Nutrition Facts per serving: 195 cal., 12 g total fat (5 g sat. fat), 239 mg chol., 528 mg sodium, 5 g carbo., 1 g fiber, 16 g pro.

Start your breakfast eggs on top of the stove and finish them in the oven while you make toast and coffee. It's no-fuss cooking at its best.

4 g net carb

BAKED SPINACH-HAM FRITTATA

8	eggs
1/3	cup milk
1/4	teaspoon dried basil, crushed
1/8	teaspoon black pepper
1/4	cup chopped onion
1	tablespoon butter or margarine
1	10-ounce package frozen chopped spinach, thawed and well drained
4	ounces thinly sliced cooked ham, chopped
2	tablespoons grated Parmesan cheese

1 In a medium bowl beat together eggs, milk, basil, and pepper. Set aside.

2 In a 10-inch ovenproof skillet cook onion in hot butter until tender. Remove from heat. Stir in spinach and ham. Pour egg mixture over spinach mixture in skillet. Bake, uncovered, in a 350° oven for 15 to 18 minutes or until a knife inserted near the center comes out clean.

3 Sprinkle with Parmesan cheese. Cover and let stand for 5 minutes before serving.

Nutrition Facts per serving: 270 cal., 18 g total fat (7 g sat. fat), 453 mg chol., 686 mg sodium, 6 g carbo., 2 g fiber, 21 g pro.

PREP:
10 minutes
BAKE:
15 minutes
STAND:
5 minutes
OVEN:
350°F
MAKES:
4 servings

Baking eggs in cups lined with ham rather than bread is a delicious low-carb innovation.

2 g net carb

WAKE-UP HAM-&-EGG BASKETS

PREP:
10 minutes

BAKE:
20 minutes

OVEN:
350°F

MAKES:
4 servings

4   pieces thinly sliced deli-style cooked ham (about 4 ounces)

4   eggs

     Salt

     Black pepper

4   teaspoons half-and-half or light cream

1 Lightly butter four 6-ounce custard cups. Place cups on a baking sheet. Line each custard cup with a piece of ham, pleating ham as needed to fit. Carefully break 1 egg into the center of each custard cup. Sprinkle with salt and pepper. Pour 1 teaspoon half-and-half over each egg; cover cups with foil.

2 Bake in a 350° oven for 20 to 25 minutes or until eggs are firm and whites are opaque.

Nutrition Facts per serving: 137 cal., 9 g total fat (4 g sat. fat), 235 mg chol., 476 mg sodium, 2 g carbo., 0 g fiber, 11 g pro.

Your family will gather around the table eagerly for this morning dish. It's so easy, you can prepare it while you're in your pj's and slippers.

2g net carb

WEEKEND SCRAMBLE

½ of a 4½- to 5-ounce round Brie or Camembert cheese

8 eggs

2 tablespoons milk

1 tablespoon snipped fresh chives or thinly sliced green onion tops

¼ teaspoon salt

⅛ teaspoon black pepper

3 slices bacon

1½ cups fresh mushrooms (such as morel, chanterelle, and/or button), sliced

1 If desired, remove rind from cheese. Cut cheese into bite-size pieces. In a medium bowl beat together eggs, milk, chives, salt, and pepper. Set aside.

2 In a large skillet cook bacon over medium heat until crisp. Drain on paper towels, reserving 2 tablespoons drippings in skillet. Crumble bacon; set aside.

3 Add mushrooms to reserved drippings in skillet. Cook over medium-high heat for 4 to 5 minutes or until tender. Reduce heat to medium. Return bacon to skillet.

4 Pour egg mixture over mushroom mixture in skillet. Cook over medium heat without stirring, until egg mixture begins to set on the bottom and around edge. Using a large spatula, lift and fold the partially cooked egg mixture so that the uncooked portion flows underneath.

5 Continue cooking over medium heat for 2 to 3 minutes or until egg mixture is cooked through but is still glossy and moist. Sprinkle with cheese. Remove from heat. Cover and let stand for 1 to 2 minutes or until cheese is softened.

Nutrition Facts per serving: 200 cal., 16 g total fat (6 g sat. fat), 301 mg chol., 301 mg sodium, 2 g carbo., 0 g fiber, 12 g pro.

START TO FINISH:
30 minutes
MAKES:
6 servings

One skillet is all you'll need to prepare this spicy egg combo. If you top your eggs with sliced avocado, add 3 grams of carbohydrate.

8 g net carb

SOUTHWESTERN SKILLET

START TO FINISH:

25 minutes

MAKES:

4 servings

2	tablespoons sliced almonds
1	yellow sweet pepper, cut into thin bite-size strips
1	fresh jalapeño pepper, seeded and chopped*
1	tablespoon olive oil or cooking oil
4	medium tomatoes, peeled and chopped
1	to 1½ teaspoons chili powder
½	teaspoon ground cumin
¼	teaspoon salt
4	eggs
	Salt
	Black pepper

1 In a large skillet cook almonds over medium heat for 4 to 5 minutes or until lightly browned, stirring occasionally. Remove from skillet; set aside.

2 In the same skillet cook sweet pepper and jalapeño pepper in hot oil about 2 minutes or until tender. Stir in tomatoes, chili powder, cumin, and the ¼ teaspoon salt. Bring to boiling; reduce heat. Simmer, covered, for 5 minutes.

3 Break one of the eggs into a measuring cup. Carefully slide the egg into simmering tomato mixture. Repeat with remaining eggs. Sprinkle eggs lightly with salt and black pepper.

4 Cook, covered, over medium-low heat for 3 to 5 minutes or until whites are completely set and yolks begin to thicken but are not firm.

5 To serve, with a slotted spoon transfer eggs to serving plates. Stir tomato mixture; spoon around eggs on plates. Sprinkle with toasted almonds.

*NOTE: Hot peppers contain oils that can burn your eyes, lips, and skin. Wear plastic or rubber gloves while preparing hot peppers and be sure to thoroughly wash your hands and nails in hot, soapy water afterward.

Nutrition Facts per serving: 172 cal., 11 g total fat (2 g sat. fat), 213 mg chol., 228 mg sodium, 11 g carbo., 3 g fiber, 9 g pro.

Skipping the crust cuts carbs but not flavor, thanks to a hearty three-cheese filling.

7 g net carb

CRUSTLESS FETA & CHEDDAR QUICHE

Nonstick cooking spray

4 beaten eggs

⅓ cup unbleached all-purpose flour

¼ teaspoon black pepper

⅛ teaspoon salt

1½ cups cottage cheese (12 ounces), drained

1 10-ounce package frozen chopped broccoli, cooked and drained

1 cup crumbled feta cheese (4 ounces)

1 cup shredded shredded cheddar cheese (4 ounces)

1 Lightly coat a 9-inch pie plate with cooking spray; set aside.

2 In a medium bowl stir together eggs, flour, pepper, and salt. Stir in cottage cheese, cooked broccoli, feta cheese, and cheddar cheese. Spoon into the prepared pie plate.

3 Bake in a 350° oven for 40 to 45 minutes or until a knife inserted near the center comes out clean. Cool on a wire rack for 5 to 10 minutes before serving.

Nutrition Facts per serving: 212 cal., 13 g total fat (8 g sat. fat), 144 mg chol., 530 mg sodium, 8 g carbo., 1 g fiber, 16 g pro.

PREP:

20 minutes

BAKE:

40 minutes

COOL:

5 minutes

OVEN:

350°F

MAKES:

8 servings

Try these buckwheat pancakes wrapped around sausage links for breakfast, brunch, or even a late evening snack.

9 g net carb

WHEAT CAKE WRAP-UPS

PREP:

20 minutes

COOK:

2 minutes per batch

OVEN:

300°F

MAKES:

10 wrap-ups

1 8-ounce package cooked heat-and-serve turkey sausage links (10 links)

1 cup buttermilk

1 egg yolk

2 tablespoons butter or margarine, melted

1 cup Buckwheat Pancake Mix (see recipe, page 71)

1 egg white

  Milk (optional)

  Sugar-free maple-flavored syrup

1 Heat sausage links according to package directions; keep warm. Meanwhile, in a medium bowl combine buttermilk, egg yolk, and butter. Add to Buckwheat Pancake Mix. Stir just until combined but still slightly lumpy.

2 In a small mixing bowl beat egg white with an electric mixer on medium to high speed until stiff peaks form (tips stand straight). Gently fold beaten egg white into batter, leaving a few puffs of egg white. Do not overbeat.

3 Heat a lightly greased griddle or heavy skillet over medium heat until a few drops of water sprinkled on griddle dance across the surface. For each pancake, pour about ¼ cup batter onto the hot griddle. Spread batter into a circle about 4 inches in diameter. (Pancakes need to be thin enough to roll easily. If batter is too thick to spread out properly, add milk, 1 tablespoon at a time, until desired consistency is reached.)

4 Cook over medium heat until pancakes are golden brown, turning to cook second sides when pancake surfaces are bubbly and edges are slightly dry (1 to 2 minutes per side). As soon as pancakes are removed from the griddle, roll each one around a cooked sausage link. Keep warm in a loosely covered ovenproof dish in a 300° oven. Serve with maple-flavored syrup.

Nutrition Facts per wrap-up: 136 cal., 8 g total fat (3 g sat. fat), 47 mg chol., 377 mg sodium, 10 g carbo., 1 g fiber, 7 g pro.

Chopped pears and vanilla add texture and taste to these hearty pancakes. A pat of butter melting on top adds a crowning touch.

BUCKWHEAT & PEAR PANCAKES

2	cups Buckwheat Pancake Mix (see below)
1¾	cups milk
2	slightly beaten eggs
2	tablespoons cooking oil
1	teaspoon vanilla
1	cup chopped, peeled pear or one 8-ounce can pear halves in light syrup, drained and chopped

PREP:
15 minutes
COOK:
2 minutes per batch
MAKES:
24 pancakes

1 In a bowl stir together Buckwheat Pancake Mix, milk, eggs, oil, and vanilla. Stir just until combined but still slightly lumpy. Stir in pear.

2 Heat a lightly greased griddle or heavy skillet over medium heat until a few drops of water sprinkled on griddle dance across the surface. For each pancake, pour a scant ¼ cup batter onto the hot griddle. Spread batter into a circle about 4 inches in diameter.

3 Cook over medium heat until pancakes are golden brown, turning to cook second sides when pancake surfaces are bubbly and edges are slightly dry (1 to 2 minutes per side). Serve immediately or keep warm in a loosely covered ovenproof dish in a 300°F oven.

Nutrition Facts per pancake: 63 cal., 2 g total fat (1 g sat. fat), 19 mg chol., 161 mg sodium, 9 g carbo., 1 g fiber, 2 g pro.

BUCKWHEAT PANCAKE MIX: In a large bowl stir together 2½ cups stone-ground buckwheat flour, 2½ cups whole wheat flour, 4 teaspoons baking powder, 4 teaspoons no-calorie, heat-stable sugar substitute, 2 teaspoons baking soda, and 2 teaspoons salt. Store in an airtight container for up to 6 weeks. To use, spoon into a measuring cup; level off with a straight-edged spatula. Makes 5 cups.

Top a stack of these tender pancakes with the berry-studded syrup.

8 g net carb

BLUEBERRY-RICOTTA PANCAKES

PREP:

20 minutes

COOK:

2 minutes per batch

MAKES:

16 pancakes

½   cup unbleached all-purpose flour

2   teaspoons baking powder

½   teaspoon salt

1   cup ricotta cheese

4   egg yolks

3   tablespoons no-calorie, heat-stable granular sugar substitute

¼   cup milk

1½   cups fresh or frozen blueberries

4   egg whites

1   recipe Blueberry Syrup (optional, see below)

1 In a bowl stir together flour, baking powder, and salt. In another bowl beat together ricotta cheese, egg yolks, and sugar substitute until well combined. Add cheese mixture to flour mixture; stir until smooth. Stir in milk. Fold in blueberries.

2 In a small mixing bowl beat the egg whites with an electric mixer on high speed until stiff peaks form (tips stand straight). Gently fold the beaten egg whites into batter, leaving a few puffs of egg white. Do not overbeat.

3 Heat a lightly greased griddle or heavy skillet over medium heat until a few drops of water sprinkled on griddle dance across the surface. For each pancake, pour about ¼ cup batter onto the hot griddle. Spread batter into a circle about 4 inches in diameter.

4 Cook over medium heat until pancakes are golden brown, turning to cook the second sides when pancake surfaces are bubbly and edges are slightly dry (1 to 2 minutes per side). Serve immediately or keep warm in a loosely covered ovenproof dish in a 300°F oven. If desired, serve with Blueberry Syrup.

BLUEBERRY SYRUP: In a medium saucepan combine 1 cup fresh or frozen blueberries; ½ cup water; ⅓ cup no-calorie, heat-stable granular sugar substitute; and 2 teaspoons lemon juice. Cook and stir over medium heat for 2 to 3 minutes or until well combined. Bring to boiling; reduce heat. Simmer, uncovered, for 15 to 20 minutes or until slightly thickened, stirring occasionally. Stir in 1 cup fresh or frozen blueberries and cook, stirring occasionally, for 2 to 3 minutes more or until blueberries become soft. Serve warm. Cover and chill remaining syrup for up to 1 week. Makes 1 cup.

Nutrition Facts per pancake: 72 cal., 3 g total fat (1 g sat. fat), 58 mg chol., 150 mg sodium, 8 g carbo., 0 g fiber, 4 g pro.

Tea does a good job of chasing the midafternoon slow-down. This version features ginger, which not only infuses its wonderful flavor but is said to calm a nervous stomach.

1 g net carb

GINGER-LEMON TEA

6   cups water

1   2-inch piece fresh ginger, thinly sliced

8   lemon peel strips (2½ x 1 inch each)*

6   green tea bags
     Sugar substitute (optional)
     Lemon slices (optional)

1 In a large saucepan stir together the water, ginger, and lemon peel strips. Bring to boiling; reduce heat. Simmer, uncovered, for 10 minutes. Remove ginger and lemon strips with a slotted spoon and discard.

2 Place tea bags in a teapot; immediately add simmering water mixture. Cover and let steep according to tea package directions (1 to 3 minutes). Remove tea bags, squeezing gently, and discard. Serve immediately in heatproof glass mugs or cups. If desired, sweeten to taste with sugar substitute and garnish with lemon slices.

***NOTE:** Remove lemon peel using a vegetable peeler. If necessary, use a sharp knife to scrape off any white pith that remains on the peel, as this can cause bitterness.

Nutrition Facts per serving: 4 cal., 0 g total fat (0 g sat. fat), 0 mg chol., 0 mg sodium, 1 g carbo., 0 g fiber, 0 g pro.

START TO FINISH:

25 minutes

MAKES:

5 to 6 servings

Has your local coffee shop made you a latte aficionado? Here's an easy but tempting alternative to make at home.

2 g net carb

ICED LATTE

START TO FINISH:

10 minutes

MAKES:

2 servings

1	cup cold water
1/3	cup ground French roast or espresso roast coffee
1/3	cup half-and-half or light cream
2	to 4 teaspoons sugar-free hazelnut-flavored syrup or 1 teaspoon vanilla (optional)
	Ice cubes
	Sugar substitute (optional)

1 Using a drip coffeemaker, add water and ground coffee. Brew according to manufacturer's directions. Pour coffee into a glass measuring cup. Stir in half-and-half and, if desired, hazelnut-flavored syrup.

2 Fill 2 tall glasses with ice. Pour coffee mixture into glasses. If desired, sweeten to taste with sugar substitute.

Nutrition Facts per serving: 54 cal., 5 g total fat (3 g sat. fat), 15 mg chol., 19 mg sodium, 2 g carbo., 0 g fiber, 1 g pro.

A little bit of red pepper, cinnamon, and cardamom in this iced coffee brew is enough to wake up your taste buds.

REALLY HOT ICED COFFEE

¹⁄₃   cup ground coffee

2   inches stick cinnamon

¹⁄₄   to ¹⁄₂ teaspoon crushed red pepper

6   pods cardamom, crushed, or ¹⁄₄ teaspoon ground cardamom
       Ice cubes
       Sugar substitute (optional)

¹⁄₂   cup whipped cream (optional)

¹⁄₂   teaspoon ground nutmeg (optional)

1 Measure coffee into a filter-lined coffeemaker basket. Add cinnamon, pepper, and cardamom. Prepare 10 to 12 cups coffee according to manufacturer's directions. Chill for at least 1 hour. Pour into an ice-filled pitcher. To serve, pour into tall, ice-filled glasses and, if desired, sweeten to taste with sugar substitute, top with whipped cream, and sprinkle with nutmeg.

Nutrition Facts per serving: 5 cal., 0 g total fat (0 g sat. fat), 0 mg chol., 5 mg sodium, 1 g carbo., 0 g fiber, 0 g pro.

PREP:
15 minutes
CHILL:
1 hour
MAKES:
10 servings

SOUPS

There's nothing quite like soup for a quick yet versatile meal or side dish. The delectable aromas and rich flavors of the soups in this chapter will encourage family and friends to linger around the dinner table. Try soups loaded with meat, fish, or poultry for a protein punch, or make a simple vegetable-based soup to complement a main dish.

3

3

This colorful and light soup combines crunchy vegetables with chicken and shrimp.

5 g net carb

ORIENTAL CHICKEN & SHRIMP SOUP

START TO FINISH:

45 minutes

MAKES:

6 to 8 servings

2 small chicken breast halves (12 ounces total)

2 cups water

4 cups chicken broth

1 tablespoon soy sauce

8 ounces small shrimp, peeled and deveined

8 ounces fresh bean sprouts

1 cup broccoli florets

½ of a 15-ounce jar straw mushrooms or one 8-ounce can mushrooms, drained

½ cup chopped red and/or green sweet pepper

4 green onions, diagonally sliced into 1-inch pieces

Freshly ground black pepper

① In a 4-quart Dutch oven combine chicken and water; bring to boiling. Reduce heat. Simmer, covered, for 20 to 25 minutes or until chicken is no longer pink. Remove chicken; cool slightly. Chop chicken, discarding skin and bones. Strain the cooking liquid. Wipe out Dutch oven and add strained liquid. Add chicken broth.

② Bring mixture to boiling; add soy sauce, chicken, shrimp, bean sprouts, broccoli, mushrooms, sweet pepper, and green onions. Return to boiling; cook, uncovered, 5 minutes. Season to taste with pepper.

Nutrition Facts per serving: 152 cal., 3 g total fat (1 g sat. fat), 76 mg chol., 849 mg sodium, 7 g carbo., 2 g fiber, 26 g pro.

The bright flavors of the Yucatan dance in your mouth as you sip this highly spiced soup. Lime juice provides a tangy surprise.

YUCATAN SOUP WITH LIME

12	ounces skinless, boneless chicken breasts, cut into bite-size pieces
3	cloves garlic, minced
1	tablespoon olive oil or cooking oil
1	tablespoon hot chili powder
½	teaspoon cumin seed, crushed, or ¼ teaspoon ground cumin
¼	to ½ teaspoon crushed red pepper (optional)
2	14-ounce cans chicken broth
½	cup chopped green onions
1	large tomato, chopped
3	tablespoons lime juice

START TO FINISH:

30 minutes

MAKES:

4 servings

1 In a Dutch oven cook chicken and garlic in hot oil over medium-high heat until chicken is no longer pink. Stir in chili powder, cumin, and, if desired, crushed red pepper. Cook and stir for 30 seconds. Stir in chicken broth and green onions. Bring to boiling; reduce heat. Simmer, uncovered, for 10 minutes. Remove from heat. Stir in tomato and lime juice.

Nutrition Facts per serving: 178 cal., 8 g total fat (1 g sat. fat), 45 mg chol., 719 mg sodium, 6 g carbo., 1 g fiber, 21 g pro.

Thin, lacy shreds of egg float to the top, making an attractive self-garnish for this simple soup.

CORN & CHICKEN SOUP

PREP:

15 minutes

STAND:

20 minutes

MAKES:

6 servings

2	small skinless, boneless chicken breast halves (6 ounces total)
¼	cup water
1	tablespoon rice wine or dry white wine
2	teaspoons soy sauce
1	teaspoon grated fresh ginger
1	teaspoon sesame oil
2½	cups chicken broth
1	cup loose-pack frozen corn
1	beaten egg

1 Finely chop chicken. In a bowl stir together the chicken, water, wine, soy sauce, ginger, and sesame oil. Cover and let stand at room temperature for 20 minutes.

2 In a wok or 3-quart saucepan combine chicken broth and corn; bring to boiling. Add chicken mixture, stirring constantly to separate chicken pieces. Return to boiling. Reduce heat and simmer, uncovered, about 2 minutes or until chicken is no longer pink, stirring often.

3 Pour beaten egg into the hot chicken mixture in a steady stream while stirring 2 or 3 times to create shreds. Remove from heat. Cover and let stand for 1 minute. Ladle into soup bowls.

Nutrition Facts per serving: 98 cal., 3 g total fat (1 g sat. fat), 54 mg chol., 466 mg sodium, 7 g carbo., 1 g fiber, 11 g pro.

For a real treat, search your local farmer's market for slender baby carrots. The packaged mini carrots commonly found in supermarkets are often trimmed mature carrots and may take a few extra minutes to cook.

9 g net carb

GARDEN CHICKEN SOUP

12	ounces packaged skinless, boneless chicken breast strips for stir-frying
1	tablespoon cooking oil
3	cups reduced-sodium chicken broth
12	baby carrots (about 6 ounces with ½-inch tops)
2	medium onions, cut into thin wedges
2	cloves garlic, minced
1	large yellow summer squash, halved lengthwise and sliced (about 2 cups)
2	cups shredded Swiss chard
1	tablespoon snipped fresh lemon thyme or thyme

START TO FINISH:

35 minutes

MAKES:

4 servings

1 In a very large skillet cook chicken in hot oil over medium-high heat about 3 minutes or until no longer pink.

2 Carefully add broth, carrots, onions, and garlic to skillet. Bring mixture to boiling; reduce heat. Simmer, covered, for 5 minutes. Add squash and chard. Simmer, covered, about 3 minutes more or until vegetables are just tender. Stir in thyme.

Nutrition Facts per serving: 217 cal., 8 g total fat (3 g sat. fat), 57 mg chol., 643 mg sodium, 12 g carbo., 3 g fiber, 26 g pro.

Cooking the cumin seeds toasts them, releasing their mellow flavor for an authentic south-of-the-border taste.

8 g net carb

MEXICAN CHICKEN & SHRIMP SOUP

START TO FINISH:

30 minutes

MAKES:

6 servings

6	ounces peeled and deveined fresh or frozen medium shrimp
1	large onion, chopped (1 cup)
1	teaspoon cumin seeds
1	tablespoon cooking oil
4½	cups reduced-sodium chicken broth
1	14½-ounce can Mexican-style stewed tomatoes, undrained
3	tablespoons snipped fresh cilantro
2	tablespoons lime juice
1⅔	cups shredded cooked chicken breast (about 8 ounces)

1 Thaw shrimp, if frozen. Rinse shrimp; pat dry with paper towels. Set aside.

2 In a large saucepan cook onion and cumin seeds in hot oil about 5 minutes or until onion is tender. Carefully add chicken broth, undrained tomatoes, cilantro, and lime juice.

3 Bring to boiling; reduce heat. Simmer, covered, for 8 minutes. Stir in shrimp and chicken. Cook about 3 minutes more or until shrimp turn opaque, stirring occasionally.

Nutrition Facts per serving: 159 cal., 4 g total fat (1 g sat. fat), 76 mg chol., 773 mg sodium, 9 g carbo., 1 g fiber, 21 g pro.

A sliced chicken breast half graces each serving of this flavorful soup.

6 g net carb

CHIPOTLE CHICKEN SOUP

3   14-ounce cans reduced-sodium chicken broth

1   canned chipotle pepper in adobo sauce, cut into 4 pieces

4   small skinless, boneless chicken breast halves (about 12 ounces total)

½   teaspoon ground cumin

2   teaspoons olive oil

1   small avocado, halved, seeded, peeled, and sliced

½   of a 14½-ounce can white or yellow hominy, drained and rinsed (about ¾ cup)

     Cilantro sprigs (optional)

1 In a 2-quart saucepan combine broth and chipotle pepper. Bring to boiling; reduce heat. Simmer, uncovered, for 20 minutes. Discard the pepper.

2 Rub both sides of chicken breasts with the ground cumin. In a large skillet cook chicken breasts in hot oil over medium-high heat for 10 to 12 minutes or until chicken is no longer pink, turning once.

3 To serve, bias-cut each breast half into ¼-inch slices and assemble in the bottom of a soup bowl. Add avocado and hominy to each bowl. Pour simmering broth into each bowl. If desired, garnish with cilantro sprigs.

Nutrition Facts per serving: 231 cal., 11 g total fat (2 g sat. fat), 49 mg chol., 902 mg sodium, 8 g carbo., 2 g fiber, 25 g pro.

START TO FINISH:
45 minutes
MAKES:
4 servings

Marsala is a fortified wine, which means that brandy is added to it, raising the alcohol content.

7 g net carb

TURKEY MARSALA SOUP

START TO FINISH:

40 minutes

MAKES:

8 servings

2 turkey thighs (about 2¾ pounds total), skinned, boned, and cut into 1-inch pieces

1 medium onion, chopped (½ cup)

2 cloves garlic, minced

1 tablespoon olive oil

3 cups water

1½ cups sliced carrots

1½ cups sliced celery

1 cup Marsala or dry white wine

1 tablespoon instant chicken bouillon granules

¼ teaspoon black pepper

2 cups sliced fresh mushrooms

¼ cup unbleached all-purpose flour

¼ cup cold water

1 In a large saucepan or Dutch oven cook turkey, onion, and garlic in hot oil about 8 minutes or until turkey is lightly browned. Carefully stir in the 3 cups water, carrots, celery, Marsala, bouillon granules, and pepper. Bring to boiling; reduce heat. Simmer, covered, for 20 minutes. Stir in mushrooms. Simmer, covered, about 10 minutes more or until mushrooms are tender.

2 Stir together flour and the ¼ cup cold water; gradually stir into turkey mixture. Cook and stir over medium heat until thickened and bubbly. Cook and stir for 1 minute more.

Nutrition Facts per serving: 200 cal., 7 g total fat (2 g sat. fat), 69 mg chol., 446 mg sodium, 8 g carbo., 1 g fiber, 22 g pro.

Fish sauce adds the distinctive Thai taste. Look for this salty condiment in Asian markets or specialty sections at most supermarkets. Once opened, it will keep indefinitely in the refrigerator.

THAI CHICKEN-COCONUT SOUP

1	pound skinless, boneless chicken breast halves or thighs
4	cups chicken broth
2	tablespoons fish sauce (optional)
2	tablespoons lemon juice or lime juice
1	tablespoon grated fresh ginger
1	teaspoon ground cumin
1½	cups broccoli florets
1	large red, yellow, or green sweet pepper cut into thin strips (1 cup)
1	jalapeño pepper, seeded and chopped*
3	green onions, sliced into ½-inch pieces
2	tablespoons snipped fresh cilantro
1	14-ounce can unsweetened coconut milk

PREP:
20 minutes
COOK:
25 minutes
MAKES:
4 servings

1 Cut chicken into bite-size strips. In a Dutch oven combine chicken, broth, fish sauce (if desired), lemon juice, ginger, and cumin. Bring to boiling; reduce heat. Simmer, covered, for 10 minutes.

2 Stir in broccoli, sweet pepper, jalapeño pepper, green onions, and cilantro. Return to boiling; reduce heat. Simmer, covered, about 10 minutes more or until vegetables are tender. Add coconut milk; heat through but do not boil.

*NOTE: Hot peppers contain oils that can burn your eyes, lips, and skin. Wear plastic or rubber gloves while preparing hot peppers and be sure to thoroughly wash your hands and nails in hot, soapy water afterward.

Nutrition Facts per serving: 461 cal., 33 g total fat (22 g sat. fat), 60 mg chol., 857 mg sodium, 9 g carbo., 2 g fiber, 31 g pro.

Exotic Asian flavors enhance this hearty pork soup.

GINGERED PORK & CABBAGE SOUP

START TO FINISH:

40 minutes

MAKES:

8 servings

6   cups reduced-sodium chicken broth

8   ounces boneless pork sirloin, cut ½ inch thick

1   cup chopped onion

2   teaspoons grated fresh ginger

4   cloves garlic, minced

1   tablespoon cooking oil

3   small tomatoes, chopped

2   medium carrots, finely chopped

4   cups thinly sliced Chinese cabbage (napa cabbage)

¼   cup snipped fresh mint

1 In a medium saucepan bring broth to boiling. Meanwhile, trim fat from pork. Cut pork into ½-inch cubes.

2 In a large saucepan cook pork, onion, ginger, and garlic in hot oil until pork is brown. Add hot broth; bring to boiling. Stir in tomatoes and carrots. Return to boiling; reduce heat. Simmer, covered, for 15 minutes. Stir in Chinese cabbage and mint.

Nutrition Facts per serving: 97 cal., 4 g total fat (1 g sat. fat), 18 mg chol., 492 mg sodium, 7 g carbo., 2 g fiber, 10 g pro.

Dress up onion soup mix with fresh mushrooms and onion for a treat that tastes like it came from the kitchen of a French bistro.

BEEFY MUSHROOM SOUP

1 small onion, thinly sliced

1 8-ounce package sliced fresh mushrooms

2 tablespoons butter or margarine

1 14-ounce can beef broth

1½ cups water

1 envelope (½ of a 1.8- to 2.2-ounce package) onion-mushroom or beefy onion soup mix

1 to 2 tablespoons dry sherry (optional)

1 In a 2-quart saucepan cook onion and mushrooms in hot butter for 5 minutes. Stir in beef broth, the water, and dry soup mix. Cook and stir over medium-high heat until bubbly. Reduce heat. Simmer, uncovered, for 5 minutes. If desired, stir in sherry.

Nutrition Facts per serving: 104 cal., 8 g total fat (4 g sat. fat), 16 mg chol., 861 mg sodium, 7 g carbo., 1 g fiber, 3 g pro.

START TO FINISH:

15 minutes

MAKES:

4 servings

This rich and satisfying chili-flavored dish is filled with chunks of beef and garden-fresh vegetables.

7 g net carb VEGETABLE-BEEF SOUP

PREP:

35 minutes

COOK:

2¹/₂ hours

MAKES:

8 servings

3   pounds meaty beef shank crosscuts

2   tablespoons cooking oil

6   cups water

2   cups tomato juice

4   teaspoons instant beef bouillon granules

1   tablespoon Worcestershire sauce

1   teaspoon chili powder

2   bay leaves

2   medium carrots, diagonally sliced (1 cup)

2   medium stalks celery, sliced (1 cup)

1   large potato, peeled and cubed (1 cup)

1   cup coarsely chopped cabbage

1   small onion, coarsely chopped (¹/₃ cup)

1 In a 4-quart Dutch oven brown meat, half at a time, in the hot oil; drain off fat. Return all meat to pan. Stir in the water, tomato juice, bouillon granules, Worcestershire sauce, chili powder, and bay leaves. Bring to boiling; reduce heat. Simmer, covered, for 2 hours. Remove beef. Skim fat from broth.

2 When cool enough to handle, remove meat from bones; discard bones. Coarsely chop meat.

3 Stir chopped meat, carrots, celery, potato, cabbage, and onion into broth. Bring to boiling; reduce heat. Simmer, covered, for 30 to 45 minutes or until vegetables and beef are tender. Discard bay leaves.

Nutrition Facts per serving: 185 cal., 5 g total fat (2 g sat. fat), 55 mg chol., 743 mg sodium, 9 g carbo., 2 g fiber, 26 g pro.

Fresh fennel blends fragrantly with fish, tomatoes, garlic, and onion. This orange-scented soup tastes as good as it smells.

7 g net carb

FISH SOUP PROVENÇALE

8	ounces fresh or frozen skinless haddock, grouper, or halibut fillets
1	small fennel bulb
3	cups vegetable broth, fish stock, or chicken broth
1	cup finely chopped onion
1	small yellow summer squash, cubed (about 1 cup)
1	cup dry white wine
1	teaspoon finely shredded orange peel or lemon peel
3	cloves garlic, minced
2	cups chopped fresh tomatoes or one 14½-ounce can diced tomatoes, undrained
2	tablespoons snipped fresh thyme
	Snipped fresh thyme (optional)

START TO FINISH:
30 minutes
MAKES:
4 servings

1 Thaw fish, if frozen. Rinse fish; pat dry with paper towels. Cut fish into 1-inch pieces; set aside.

2 Cut off and discard upper stalks of fennel. Remove any wilted outer layers; cut a thin slice from base. Wash fennel; cut in half lengthwise and thinly slice.

3 In a large saucepan stir together fennel, broth, onion, squash, wine, orange peel, and garlic. Bring to boiling; reduce heat. Simmer, covered, for 10 minutes. Stir in fish, tomatoes, and the 2 tablespoons thyme. Return to boiling; reduce heat. Simmer, covered, about 3 minutes more or until fish flakes easily when tested with a fork. If desired, garnish with additional snipped thyme.

Nutrition Facts per serving: 156 cal., 3 g total fat (0 g sat. fat), 18 mg chol., 752 mg sodium, 15 g carbo., 8 g fiber, 14 g pro.

A trio of herbs gives this hearty fish soup aromatic appeal and irresistible flavor.

6 g
net
carb

CHUNKY VEGETABLE-COD SOUP

START TO FINISH:

25 minutes

MAKES:

4 servings

1	pound fresh or frozen skinless cod fillets or steaks
½	cup chopped red sweet pepper
¼	cup chopped onion
1	tablespoon butter or margarine
3½	cups vegetable broth or chicken broth
1	cup frozen cut green beans
1	cup coarsely chopped cabbage
½	cup sliced carrot
1	teaspoon snipped fresh basil
1	teaspoon snipped fresh thyme
½	teaspoon snipped fresh rosemary
¼	teaspoon black pepper

1 Thaw fish, if frozen. Rinse fish; pat dry with paper towels. Cut fish into 1-inch pieces. In a large saucepan or Dutch oven cook sweet pepper and onion in hot butter until tender.

2 Stir in broth, green beans, cabbage, carrot, basil, thyme, rosemary, and black pepper. Bring to boiling; reduce heat. Simmer, covered, for 8 to 10 minutes or until vegetables are nearly tender.

3 Stir fish into broth mixture. Return to boiling; reduce heat. Simmer, covered, about 5 minutes or until fish flakes easily when tested with a fork, stirring once.

Nutrition Facts per serving: 201 cal., 10 g total fat (7 g sat. fat), 49 mg chol., 294 mg sodium, 7 g carbo., 1 g fiber, 21 g pro.

Although great any time of year, this fresh-tasting seafood soup is perfectly light for summer. The savory combination is embellished with a lemon-pepper accent.

SHRIMP & GREENS SOUP

12	ounces peeled and deveined fresh or frozen shrimp
1	large leek, sliced
2	cloves garlic, minced
1	tablespoon olive oil
3	14-ounce cans reduced-sodium chicken broth or vegetable broth
1	tablespoon snipped fresh Italian flat-leaf parsley or parsley
1	tablespoon snipped fresh marjoram or thyme
1/4	teaspoon lemon-pepper seasoning
2	cups shredded bok choy or spinach leaves

1 Thaw shrimp, if frozen. Rinse shrimp; pat dry with paper towels.

2 In a large saucepan cook leek and garlic in hot oil over medium-high heat about 2 minutes or until leek is tender. Carefully add chicken broth, parsley, marjoram, and lemon-pepper seasoning. Bring to boiling; add shrimp. Return to boiling; reduce heat.

3 Simmer, uncovered, for 2 minutes. Stir in bok choy. Cook about 1 minute more or until shrimp are opaque.

Nutrition Facts per serving: 147 cal., 6 g total fat (1 g sat. fat), 131 mg chol., 1,093 mg sodium, 5 g carbo., 2 g fiber, 18 g pro.

START TO FINISH:
30 minutes
MAKES:
4 servings

A dash of nutmeg brings out the best in shrimp and emphasizes the slightly sweet, nutty taste of the Gruyère cheese. For a velvety smooth soup, be sure to use process cheese.

9 g net carb

CREAMY SHRIMP & SPINACH STEW

START TO FINISH:

30 minutes

MAKES:

4 servings

8	ounces fresh or frozen, peeled, deveined small shrimp
1	cup sliced fresh button, shiitake, and/or crimini mushrooms
½	cup chopped onion
1	clove garlic, minced
2	tablespoons butter or margarine
3	tablespoons unbleached all-purpose flour
1	bay leaf
⅛	teaspoon ground nutmeg
⅛	teaspoon black pepper
1	14-ounce can vegetable or chicken broth
1	cup half-and-half, light cream, or milk
¾	cup shredded process Gruyère cheese (3 ounces)
2	cups torn fresh spinach

1 Thaw shrimp, if frozen. Rinse shrimp; pat dry with paper towels. Set aside.

2 In a medium saucepan cook mushrooms, onion, and garlic in hot butter over medium heat until tender. Stir in flour, bay leaf, nutmeg, and pepper. Add broth and half-and-half all at once. Cook and stir until mixture is thickened and bubbly.

3 Add shrimp; cook for 2 minutes more. Add Gruyère cheese and stir until cheese melts. Discard bay leaf. Stir in spinach. Serve immediately.

Nutrition Facts per serving: 326 cal., 22 g total fat (12 g sat. fat), 148 mg chol., 676 mg sodium, 11 g carbo., 2 g fiber, 23 g pro.

Lemongrass, a signature ingredient in Thai cooking, contributes lemon aroma and flavor to this simple soup. Look for lemongrass in Asian specialty markets or the produce section of larger supermarkets.

8 g net carb

THAI-STYLE SHRIMP SOUP

- 1 14-ounce can chicken broth
- 1 small zucchini, cut into matchstick-size pieces (about 1½ cups)
- 1 green onion, bias-cut into 1¼-inch slices
- 2 tablespoons grated fresh ginger
- 2 tablespoons minced fresh lemongrass or 1½ teaspoons finely shredded lemon peel
- ¼ teaspoon crushed red pepper
- 12 ounces small shrimp, peeled and deveined
- 1 14-ounce can unsweetened coconut milk
- 2 tablespoons shredded fresh basil
- 2 tablespoons toasted shaved coconut

Fresh basil sprigs (optional)

START TO FINISH:

25 minutes

MAKES:

3 or 4 servings

1 In a saucepan bring broth to boiling. Add zucchini, green onion, ginger, lemongrass, and red pepper. Return to boiling; reduce heat. Simmer, uncovered, for 3 minutes, stirring occasionally.

2 Add shrimp. Simmer, uncovered, for 1 to 3 minutes or until shrimp are opaque. Add coconut milk. Heat through but do not boil.

3 To serve, ladle into bowls. Top with shredded basil, coconut, and, if desired, basil sprigs.

Nutrition Facts per serving: 445 cal., 37 g total fat (31 g sat. fat), 115 mg chol., 708 mg sodium, 12 g carbo., 4 g fiber, 21 g pro.

Long-stemmed, tiny-capped, and slightly crunchy, enoki mushrooms play an important role in Asian cooking. These elegant mushrooms have a light, fruity flavor. Wait until the last moment to toss them in because they toughen if heated.

8 g net carb

LEMON & SCALLOP SOUP

START TO FINISH:

25 minutes

MAKES:

4 servings

12	ounces fresh or frozen bay scallops
5	cups reduced-sodium chicken broth or fish stock
½	cup dry white wine, reduced-sodium chicken broth, or fish stock
3	tablespoons snipped fresh cilantro
2	teaspoons finely shredded lemon peel
¼	teaspoon black pepper
1	pound asparagus spears, trimmed and cut into bite-size pieces
1	cup fresh enoki mushrooms or shiitake mushrooms
½	cup sliced green onions
1	tablespoon lemon juice

1 Thaw scallops, if frozen. Rinse well and drain; set aside.

2 In a large saucepan combine broth, wine, cilantro, lemon peel, and pepper. Bring to boiling.

3 Add scallops, asparagus, shiitake mushrooms (if using), and green onions. Return to boiling; reduce heat. Simmer, uncovered, for 3 to 5 minutes or until asparagus is tender and scallops are opaque.

4 Remove saucepan from heat. Stir in the enoki mushrooms (if using) and lemon juice. Serve immediately.

Nutrition Facts per serving: 153 cal., 2 g total fat (0 g sat. fat), 28 mg chol., 940 mg sodium, 10 g carbo., 2 g fiber, 20 g pro.

Chicken bouillon granules boost the flavor of this comforting soup.

8 g net carb

CREAM OF BROCCOLI SOUP

2 cups chopped broccoli

2 cups boiling water

3 tablespoons butter or margarine

¼ cup unbleached all-purpose flour

2 teaspoons instant chicken bouillon granules

Dash black pepper

2 cups half-and-half, light cream, or milk

START TO FINISH:

20 minutes

MAKES:

6 servings

1 In a large saucepan cook broccoli in the boiling water for 8 to 10 minutes or until very tender. Drain broccoli, reserving cooking liquid. (Add additional water, if necessary, to make 1½ cups liquid.)

2 In a blender container combine broccoli and the reserved cooking liquid. Cover and blend at low speed until smooth. Set aside.

3 In the same saucepan melt butter. Stir in flour, bouillon granules, and pepper. Add half-and-half all at once. Cook and stir over medium heat until thickened and bubbly. Cook and stir 1 minute more.

4 Stir in broccoli mixture; heat through.

Nutrition Facts per serving: 186 cal., 15 g total fat (10 g sat. fat), 46 mg chol., 393 mg sodium, 9 g carbo., 1 g fiber, 4 g pro.

Looking for a cooking shortcut? Grab a couple jars of roasted red sweet peppers and you'll have the beginning of a bright bowl of soup.

ROASTED RED PEPPER SOUP

START TO FINISH:

35 minutes

MAKES:

5 servings

3 cups chicken broth

2 7-ounce jars roasted red sweet peppers, drained and rinsed

1 cup chopped onion

½ cup thinly sliced celery

¼ teaspoon salt

1¼ cups half-and-half, light cream, or milk

1 In a large saucepan combine broth, roasted peppers, onion, celery, and salt. Bring to boiling; reduce heat. Simmer, uncovered, about 15 minutes or until onion and celery are very tender. Cool slightly.

2 Place half of the pepper mixture in a blender container or food processor bowl. Cover and blend or process until smooth. Repeat with remaining pepper mixture. Return all of the mixture to saucepan. Stir in half-and-half; cook over medium heat until heated through.

Nutrition Facts per serving: 229 cal., 13 g total fat (5 g sat. fat), 23 mg chol., 619 mg sodium, 12 g carbo., 3 g fiber, 6 g pro.

Serve this soup as a wonderful first course to a ham dinner or a Southern-inspired menu.

PEANUT-PUMPKIN SOUP

¼ cup finely chopped onion

¼ cup finely chopped celery

1 tablespoon butter or margarine

2½ cups chicken broth

1 15-ounce can pumpkin

¼ cup natural smooth peanut butter

¼ teaspoon black pepper

Chopped peanuts (optional)

Snipped fresh chives (optional)

START TO FINISH:

25 minutes

MAKES:

6 servings

1 In a large saucepan cook onion and celery in hot butter over medium heat for 5 minutes, stirring occasionally. Add broth and pumpkin. Bring to boiling; reduce heat. Simmer, covered, about 5 minutes or until vegetables are tender.

2 Add peanut butter and pepper. Cook and stir over medium-low heat until combined and heated through. If desired, sprinkle each serving with chopped peanuts and chives.

Nutrition Facts per serving: 121 cal., 9 g total fat (3 g sat. fat), 5 mg chol., 495 mg sodium, 9 g carbo., 3 g fiber, 4 g pro.

The glorious green color of this soup comes from spinach and watercress.
A hint of lemon provides a spring-fresh taste.

EMERALD SOUP

5	green onions, chopped (²⁄₃ cup)
4	large cloves garlic, minced
2	tablespoons butter or margarine
2	tablespoons unbleached all-purpose flour
3	cups vegetable broth
3½	cups half-and-half or light cream
1	teaspoon finely shredded lemon peel
¼	teaspoon ground white pepper
¼	teaspoon ground nutmeg
⅛	teaspoon cayenne pepper
6	cups fresh spinach leaves, chopped
1	cup watercress, chopped

1 In a large saucepan cook green onions and garlic in hot butter over medium heat for 3 to 5 minutes or until onion is tender. Stir in flour and cook for 2 minutes. Carefully stir in broth. Cook and stir about 5 minutes or until thoroughly combined and slightly thickened.

2 Add half-and-half, lemon peel, white pepper, nutmeg, cayenne pepper, spinach, and watercress. Bring to boiling; reduce heat. Simmer, covered, about 10 minutes or until spinach and watercress are tender.

3 Place half of the spinach mixture in a blender container or food processor bowl. Cover and blend or process until smooth. Repeat with remaining mixture. Return all of the mixture to the saucepan; heat through.

Nutrition Facts per serving: 263 cal., 21 g total fat (13 g sat. fat), 63 mg chol., 643 mg sodium, 11 g carbo., 2 g fiber, 9 g pro.

This satisfying Chinese-style soup is easy to make. Thickened with unbleached flour, the soup won't be quite as clear as the traditional cornstarch-thickened mixture.

5 g net carb

HOT & SOUR SOUP

4   ounces fresh shiitake mushrooms, stems removed and caps thinly sliced

2   cloves garlic, minced

2   teaspoons peanut oil or cooking oil

2   14-ounce cans reduced-sodium chicken broth

2   tablespoons white vinegar or seasoned rice vinegar

2   tablespoons reduced-sodium soy sauce

½   teaspoon crushed red pepper or 1 teaspoon chile oil

1   cup shredded cooked chicken (about 5 ounces)

2   cups packaged shredded cabbage with carrot (coleslaw mix) or shredded napa cabbage

2   tablespoons cold water

2   tablespoons unbleached all-purpose flour

1   teaspoon toasted sesame oil

Sliced green onions (optional)

START TO FINISH:
30 minutes
MAKES:
4 servings

1 In a large saucepan cook mushrooms and garlic in hot oil for 4 minutes, stirring occasionally. Stir in broth, vinegar, soy sauce, and red pepper; bring to boiling. Stir in chicken and coleslaw mix. Return to boiling; reduce heat. Simmer, uncovered, for 5 minutes.

2 In a small bowl stir together the cold water and flour. Stir into soup; simmer about 2 minutes or until slightly thickened. Remove from heat; stir in sesame oil. If desired, sprinkle with sliced green onions.

Nutrition Facts per serving: 144 cal., 7 g total fat (1 g sat. fat), 31 mg chol., 838 mg sodium, 6 g carbo., 1 g fiber, 15 g pro.

Use any combination of mushrooms to total 12 ounces for this first-course soup.

THREE-MUSHROOM SOUP

PREP:

15 minutes

COOK:

32 minutes

MAKES:

6 servings

8   ounces fresh mushrooms, sliced (3 cups)

2   ounces portobello mushroom, sliced ½ inch thick

2   ounces shiitake, porcini, or other mushrooms, sliced ½ inch thick

3   cloves garlic, minced

1   tablespoon olive oil or cooking oil

⅓   cup dry sherry (optional)

3   14½-ounce cans reduced-sodium chicken broth

½   teaspoon dried thyme, crushed, or 1 tablespoon snipped fresh thyme

1 In a large saucepan cook mushrooms and garlic in hot oil about 10 minutes or until mushrooms have softened and most of the liquid has evaporated; stir occasionally. If desired, stir in sherry. Cook for 2 minutes more.

2 Add chicken broth and dried thyme (if using). Bring to boiling; reduce heat. Simmer, covered, for 20 minutes. Stir in the fresh thyme (if using).

Nutrition Facts per serving: 58 cal., 4 g total fat (0 g sat. fat), 0 mg chol., 580 mg sodium, 4 g carbo., 1 g fiber, 3 g pro.

Rolled oats give this cream soup extra body. Leeks, Gruyère cheese, and a sprinkle of bacon establish a rich and savory base.

7 g net carb

ALPINE CHEESE SOUP

4	slices bacon, cut up
½	cup chopped onion
½	cup chopped celery
1	medium leek (white part only), halved lengthwise and sliced (⅓ cup)
2	14-ounce cans reduced-sodium chicken broth
½	cup quick-cooking rolled oats
¼	teaspoon black pepper
¾	cup shredded process Gruyère or Swiss cheese (3 ounces)
¼	cup whipping cream, half-and-half, or light cream
2	tablespoons snipped fresh parsley

1 In a large saucepan cook bacon until crisp. Remove bacon and drain on paper towels, reserving drippings in saucepan.

2 Cook onion, celery, and leek in reserved bacon drippings over medium heat about 5 minutes or until tender. Stir in broth, oats, and pepper. Bring to boiling; reduce heat. Simmer, covered, for 20 minutes. Remove from heat. Stir in cheese. Cool slightly.

3 Place half of the soup in a blender container or food processor bowl. Cover and blend or process until smooth. Repeat with remaining soup. Return all of the soup to saucepan; stir in cream. Heat through, but do not boil. Ladle into soup bowls; sprinkle with crumbled bacon and parsley.

Nutrition Facts per serving: 161 cal., 11 g total fat (6 g sat. fat), 33 mg chol., 442 mg sodium, 8 g carbo., 1 g fiber, 9 g pro.

PREP:
25 minutes
COOK:
25 minutes
MAKES:
6 servings

Blend a farmer's market crop of tomatoes, sweet peppers, and banana peppers to whip up this quick chilled summer soup.

ICED YELLOW TOMATO SOUP

PREP:

15 minutes

CHILL:

4 hours

MAKES:

8 servings

1½ pounds yellow tomatoes, peeled, seeded, and cut up (about 5 medium)

2 14-ounce cans reduced-sodium chicken broth

1 large yellow sweet pepper, seeded and cut up

2 to 3 yellow banana peppers, seeded and cut up

½ of a small onion

4 cloves garlic, chopped

1 small Roma tomato, peeled, seeded, and chopped

Fresh chives (optional)

1 In a food processor bowl or blender container, combine half of the yellow tomatoes, half of the broth, half of the sweet pepper, half of the banana peppers, half of the onion, and half of the garlic. Cover and process or blend until smooth. Transfer to a large bowl. Repeat with the remaining half. Cover and chill for 4 hours.

2 To serve, ladle soup into serving bowls and top each serving with Roma tomato and, if desired, chives.

Nutrition Facts per serving: 41 cal., 1 g total fat (0 g sat. fat), 0 mg chol., 299 mg sodium, 7 g carbo., 1 g fiber, 2 g pro.

Fit this classic French dish into your schedule by using a slow cooker for as little as 2½ hours or as long as 10 hours.

FRENCH ONION SOUP

4	to 6 large onions, thinly sliced (4 to 6 cups)
1	clove garlic, minced
3	tablespoons butter or margarine
4½	cups beef broth
1½	teaspoons Worcestershire sauce
⅛	teaspoon black pepper
½	cup shredded Swiss or Gruyère cheese

1 In a large skillet cook onions and garlic in hot butter, covered, over medium-low heat about 20 minutes or until tender, stirring occasionally.

2 Transfer onion mixture to a 3½- or 4-quart slow cooker. Add broth, Worcestershire sauce, and pepper. Cover and cook on low-heat setting for 5 to 10 hours or on high-heat setting for 2½ to 3 hours.

3 Ladle soup into bowls. Sprinkle with cheese.

Nutrition Facts per serving: 126 cal., 9 g total fat (6 g sat. fat), 25 mg chol., 719 mg sodium, 6 g carbo., 1 g fiber, 5 g pro.

PREP:

30 minutes

COOK:

5 to 10 hours (low) or 2½ to 3 hours (high)

MAKES:

6 servings

If you have time, chill the broth before using. The chilled fat rises to the top, so you can easily remove every bit of it.

CHICKEN BROTH

PREP:

25 minutes

COOK:

2½ hours

MAKES:

about 6 cups broth and 2 to 4 cups meat

3   pounds bony chicken pieces (wings, backs, and/or necks)

3   stalks celery with leaves, cut up

2   carrots, cut up

1   large onion, unpeeled and cut up

1   teaspoon salt

1   teaspoon dried thyme, sage, or basil, crushed

½   teaspoon whole black peppercorns or ¼ teaspoon ground black pepper

4   sprigs fresh parsley

2   bay leaves

2   cloves garlic, unpeeled and halved

6   cups cold water

1 If using wings, cut each wing at joints into 3 pieces. Place chicken pieces in a 6-quart kettle or stock pot. Add celery, carrots, onion, salt, thyme, peppercorns, parsley, bay leaves, and garlic. Add the water. Bring to boiling; reduce heat. Simmer, covered, for 2½ hours. Remove chicken pieces from broth.

2 Strain broth through a large sieve or colander lined with two layers of 100-percent-cotton cheesecloth. Discard vegetables and seasonings in cheesecloth. If desired, clarify broth.* If using the broth while hot, skim off fat. (If storing broth for later use, chill broth in a bowl for 6 hours. Lift off fat. Cover and chill up to 3 days or freeze up to 6 months.)

3 If desired, when bones are cool enough to handle, remove meat. Chop meat; discard bones. Place meat in an airtight container; seal. Chill up to 3 days or freeze up to 3 months.

*NOTE: To clarify hot, strained broth, in a large saucepan combine 1 beaten egg white, eggshell from 1 egg, and ¼ cup water. Add hot broth. Bring to boiling. Remove from heat; let stand for 5 minutes. Strain broth through a large sieve or colander lined with two layers of 100-percent-cotton cheesecloth.

Nutrition Facts per cup broth: 35 cal., 3 g total fat (1 g sat. fat), 3 mg chol., 401 mg sodium, 1 g carbo., 0 g fiber, 0 g pro.

Roast the soup bones first to release their rich flavor, then cook them in a slow cooker with vegetables and herbs to draw an array of flavors into the broth.

1 g net carb

BEEF BROTH

4	pounds meaty beef soup bones (beef shank crosscuts or short ribs)
½	cup water
3	carrots, cut up
2	medium onions, unpeeled and cut up
2	stalks celery with leaves, cut up
1	tablespoon dried basil or dried thyme, crushed
1½	teaspoons salt
10	whole black peppercorns
8	sprigs fresh parsley
4	bay leaves
2	cloves garlic, unpeeled and halved
8	cups water

PREP:

20 minutes

COOK:

10 to 12 hours (low) or 5 to 6 hours (high)

ROAST:

30 minutes

OVEN:

450°F

MAKES:

6 to 7 cups broth and 2 to 4 cups meat

1 Place soup bones in a large, shallow roasting pan. Roast in a 450° oven about 30 minutes or until well browned, turning once. Place soup bones in a 4- to 6-quart slow cooker. Pour the ½ cup water into the roasting pan, scraping up browned bits; add water mixture to slow cooker. Stir in carrots, onions, celery, basil, salt, peppercorns, parsley, bay leaves, and garlic. Add the 8 cups water. Cover and cook on low-heat setting for 10 to 12 hours or on high-heat setting for 5 to 6 hours.

2 Remove bones from cooker. Strain broth through a large sieve or colander lined with two layers of 100-percent-cotton cheesecloth. Discard solids in cheesecloth. If desired, clarify broth.* If using the broth while hot, skim off fat. (If storing broth for later use, chill broth in a bowl for 6 hours. Lift off fat. Cover and chill up to 3 days or freeze up to 6 months.)

3 When bones are cool enough to handle, remove meat from bones. Chop meat; discard bones. Place meat in an airtight container; seal. Chill up to 3 days or freeze up to 3 months.

*NOTE: To clarify hot, strained broth, in a large saucepan combine 1 beaten egg white, eggshell from 1 egg, and ½ cup water. Add hot broth. Bring to boiling. Remove from heat; let stand for 5 minutes. Strain broth through a large sieve or colander lined with two layers of 100-percent-cotton cheesecloth.

Nutrition Facts per cup broth: 38 cal., 3 g total fat (1 g sat. fat), 5 mg chol., 598 mg sodium, 1 g carbo., 0 g fiber, 1 g pro.

SALADS

Never before have markets offered such a variety of fresh vegetables, fruits, and greens. Packed with disease-fighting antioxidants, these versatile salad ingredients perfectly complement one another, creating nutritional masterpieces. Choose from any of the fabulous main- or side-dish selections in this chapter to add extra texture, color, nutrients, and flavor to your low-carb meals.

Chicken simmered in coconut milk joins Thai peppers and coconut chips for an enticing international-style dish.

6 g net carb

COCONUT CHICKEN SALAD

PREP:

10 minutes

COOK:

12 minutes

CHILL:

1 hour

MAKES:

4 servings

12　ounces skinless, boneless chicken breast halves and/or thighs

1　14-ounce can unsweetened coconut milk

¼　teaspoon salt

⅛　teaspoon black pepper

¼　cup thinly sliced red onion or Vidalia onion

2　tablespoons lime juice

2　Thai red chile peppers, seeded, if desired, and finely chopped*

1　cup shredded lettuce

½　cup coconut chips, toasted

　　Salt

　　Black pepper

1 In a large skillet combine chicken, coconut milk, the ¼ teaspoon salt, and ⅛ teaspoon pepper. Bring to boiling; reduce heat. Simmer, covered, for 12 to 14 minutes or until chicken is no longer pink (170°F for breasts, 180°F for thighs). Drain well; discard milk mixture. Cool chicken slightly; cut into bite-size pieces.

2 In a medium bowl combine chicken pieces, onion, lime juice, and Thai peppers. Cover and chill for 1 hour. Before serving gently stir shredded lettuce and half of the toasted coconut chips into the chicken mixture. Season to taste with additional salt and pepper. Sprinkle with remaining coconut chips.

***NOTE:** Hot peppers contain oils that can burn your eyes, lips, and skin. Wear plastic or rubber gloves while preparing hot peppers and be sure to thoroughly wash your hands and nails in hot, soapy water afterward.

Nutrition Facts per serving: 201 cal., 10 g total fat (7 g sat. fat), 49 mg chol., 294 mg sodium, 7 g carbo., 1 g fiber, 20 g pro.

Free yourself from slicing and dicing. Packaged coleslaw mix provides the crunchy base for this Eastern-inspired meal, redolent of sesame oil, red pepper, and soy sauce.

6 g net carb

CABBAGE & CHICKEN WITH SESAME DRESSING

¼	cup bottled Italian salad dressing
1	tablespoon soy sauce
1	teaspoon toasted sesame oil
⅛	to ¼ teaspoon crushed red pepper
3	cups packaged shredded cabbage with carrot (coleslaw mix)
2	cups chopped cooked chicken (10 ounces)
2	tablespoons snipped fresh cilantro
1	head Boston or Bibb lettuce, separated into leaves
¼	cup slivered almonds, toasted

START TO FINISH:

20 minutes

MAKES:

4 servings

1 For dressing, in a small bowl stir together salad dressing, soy sauce, sesame oil, and crushed red pepper. Set aside.

2 In a bowl combine cabbage, chicken, and cilantro. Drizzle with dressing; toss lightly to coat. Line 4 plates with lettuce leaves. Divide chicken mixture among plates. Sprinkle with almonds.

Nutrition Facts per serving: 298 cal., 18 g total fat (3 g sat. fat), 68 mg chol., 457 mg sodium, 9 g carbo., 3 g fiber, 25 g pro.

Prepare this easy, fresh-tasting salad with your favorite combination of greens or make it even easier by using packaged greens.

 9 g net carb

CHICKEN & NECTARINE SALAD

START TO FINISH:

15 minutes

MAKES:

4 servings

4   cups torn mixed greens

2   cups chopped, cooked chicken

2   medium nectarines or peeled peaches, pitted and sliced

2   green onions, thinly sliced

½   cup low-carb vinaigrette

1 In a large bowl combine greens, chicken, fruit, and green onions. Drizzle with vinaigrette; toss to mix.

Nutrition Facts per serving: 326 cal., 22 g total fat (4 g sat. fat), 62 mg chol., 218 mg sodium, 11 g carbo., 2 g fiber, 22 g pro.

Still haven't shaken your collegiate penchant for ramen noodles? Try them in this colorful salad.

7 g net carb

ORIENTAL CHICKEN NOODLE SALAD

1   3-ounce package chicken-flavored ramen noodles

1   cup fresh pea pods or ½ of a 6-ounce package frozen pea pods, thawed

1½ cups chopped, cooked chicken breast

1½ cups shredded Chinese (napa) cabbage or cabbage

1   8¾-ounce can whole baby corn, drained and halved

¼   cup bottled Italian salad dressing

1   tablespoon soy sauce

1   tablespoon toasted sesame seeds

START TO FINISH:

20 minutes

MAKES:

4 servings

1 Reserve flavoring packet from noodles for another use. Cook noodles according to package directions; drain. Rinse with cold water; drain again.

2 Meanwhile, if using fresh pea pods, trim ends and remove strings. In a large salad bowl combine fresh or thawed pea pods, chicken, cabbage, corn, and cooked noodles.

3 For dressing, in a screw-top jar combine salad dressing, soy sauce, and sesame seeds. Cover and shake well. Pour over salad; toss to coat.

Nutrition Facts per serving: 235 cal., 13 g total fat (2 g sat. fat), 54 mg chol., 507 mg sodium, 9 g carbo., 2 g fiber, 19 g pro.

Traditional Greek salads often don't include lettuce. True to that tradition, this sprightly salad makes a great dish when you want something tangy, crunchy, and full of vegetables.

7 g net carb

GREEK SALAD

START TO FINISH:

15 minutes

MAKES:

4 servings

3	medium tomatoes, cut into wedges
1	medium cucumber, halved lengthwise and thinly sliced
1	small red onion, cut into thin wedges
1	recipe Greek Vinaigrette (see below)
8	to 10 pitted kalamata olives
½	cup crumbled feta cheese (2 ounces)

1 In a medium bowl combine tomatoes, cucumber, and red onion. Pour Greek Vinaigrette over tomato mixture; toss gently to coat. Sprinkle with olives and feta cheese.

GREEK VINAIGRETTE: In a screw-top jar combine 2 tablespoons olive oil or salad oil; 2 tablespoons lemon juice; 2 teaspoons snipped fresh oregano or ½ teaspoon dried oregano, crushed; ⅛ teaspoon salt; and ⅛ teaspoon black pepper. Cover and shake well.

Nutrition Facts per serving: 154 cal., 12 g total fat (4 g sat. fat), 17 mg chol., 369 mg sodium, 9 g carbo., 2 g fiber, 4 g pro.

The peppery kick of coarsely ground papaya seeds in the dressing contrasts with the soothing sweetness of the fresh fruit.

4g net carb

CRIMSON GREENS & PAPAYA SALAD

1	large papaya
7	cups torn red-tip leaf lettuce and/or mixed salad greens
1	cup shredded radicchio
1	small red onion, thinly sliced and separated into rings
¼	cup snipped fresh cilantro
3	tablespoons salad oil
1	tablespoon toasted sesame oil*
2	tablespoons lemon juice
2	tablespoons rice vinegar or white wine vinegar
1	tablespoon no-calorie, heat-stable granular sugar substitute
⅛	teaspoon salt

START TO FINISH:
25 minutes
MAKES:
8 servings

1 Peel, seed, and slice the papaya, reserving 1 tablespoon of the seeds for the dressing.

2 In a large salad bowl combine papaya slices, lettuce, radicchio, red onion, and cilantro; toss gently to mix.

3 For dressing, in a blender container or food processor bowl combine salad oil, sesame oil, lemon juice, vinegar, sugar substitute, and salt. Cover and blend or process until smooth. Add reserved papaya seeds; blend or process until the seeds are the consistency of coarsely ground pepper. Pour dressing over salad. Toss lightly to coat.

*NOTE: If toasted sesame oil is unavailable, increase the salad oil to ¼ cup.

Nutrition Facts per serving: 86 cal., 7 g total fat (1 g sat. fat), 0 mg chol., 44 mg sodium, 5 g carbo., 1 g fiber, 1 g pro.

Leftover grilled or deli-sliced meats add substance to this refreshing salad. To carry through with the Asian flavors, include Chinese cabbage as part of the greens mixture.

THAI COBB SALAD

START TO FINISH:

25 minutes

MAKES:

4 servings

½ cup bottled Italian salad dressing

1 tablespoon soy sauce

1 to 1½ teaspoons grated fresh ginger

¼ to ½ teaspoon crushed red pepper

8 cups torn mixed salad greens

1½ cups coarsely chopped cooked pork, beef, or chicken (8 ounces)

1 avocado, seeded, peeled, and cut into ½-inch pieces

1 cup coarsely shredded carrots

¼ cup fresh cilantro leaves

¼ cup thinly sliced green onions

¼ cup honey-roasted peanuts

1 For dressing, in a large bowl stir together salad dressing, soy sauce, ginger, and crushed red pepper. Add mixed salad greens; toss lightly to coat.

2 Divide salad greens among 4 dinner plates. Top with meat, avocado, carrots, cilantro, green onions, and peanuts.

Nutrition Facts per serving: 255 cal., 15 g total fat (4 g sat. fat), 52 mg chol., 743 mg sodium, 11 g carbo., 4 g fiber, 19 g pro.

Serve this easy wilted salad as a companion to broiled fish and chicken. Keep your cooked entrée warm while you quickly toss together this fanciful medley.

3 g net carb

WARM WINTER SALAD

2 cups torn romaine

2 cups coarsely shredded radicchio and/or Belgian endive

2 cups torn escarole

1 medium onion, thinly sliced and separated into rings

3 tablespoons olive oil or salad oil

2 tablespoons pine nuts or slivered almonds

2 cloves garlic, minced

¼ teaspoon dried tarragon, crushed

Freshly ground black pepper

Lemon wedges

START TO FINISH:

20 minutes

MAKES:

4 servings

1 In a large bowl toss together romaine, radicchio, and escarole; set aside. In a 10-inch skillet cook and stir onion in hot oil about 5 minutes or until onion is tender. Add pine nuts. Cook and stir for 1 to 2 minutes more or until nuts are toasted.

2 Add garlic, tarragon, and greens to skillet. Toss for 30 to 60 seconds or just until greens are wilted (do not overcook). Sprinkle with pepper. Pass lemon wedges to squeeze over salad.

Nutrition Facts per serving: 138 cal., 13 g total fat (2 g sat. fat), 0 mg chol., 13 mg sodium, 5 g carbo., 2 g fiber, 3 g pro.

Gorgonzola, a full-flavored blue-veined cheese, provides a cool and creamy counterpoint to succulent sirloin.

BEEF & BLUE CHEESE SALAD

7 g net carb

PREP:
15 minutes

GRILL:
14 minutes

MAKES:
4 servings

3 tablespoons balsamic vinegar

2 tablespoons olive oil

1 clove garlic, minced

½ teaspoon salt

½ teaspoon black pepper

12 ounces boneless beef top sirloin steak, cut 1 inch thick

1 tablespoon snipped fresh thyme

2 teaspoons snipped fresh rosemary

4 ¼-inch slices red onion

6 cups lightly packed mesclun or torn mixed salad greens

8 yellow and/or red pear-shaped tomatoes, halved

2 tablespoons crumbled Gorgonzola or other blue cheese

1 For vinaigrette, in a screw-top jar stir together vinegar, oil, garlic, salt, and pepper; cover and shake well. Trim fat from steak. Brush 1 tablespoon of the vinaigrette evenly onto each side of steak. Press thyme and rosemary onto both sides of steak. Brush both sides of onion slices with some of the remaining vinaigrette, reserving the rest; set aside.

2 For a charcoal grill, place steak on the rack of an uncovered grill directly over medium coals. Grill to desired doneness, turning once halfway through grilling. Allow 14 to 18 minutes for medium rare (145°F) or 18 to 22 minutes for medium (160°F). While the steak is grilling, add onion slices to grill. Grill for 6 to 8 minutes or until tender. Remove onions from grill when done. (For a gas grill, preheat grill. Reduce heat to medium. Place steak, then onions on the grill rack over heat. Cover and grill as above.)

3 Divide the mesclun among 4 dinner plates. To serve, thinly slice the steak across the grain. Separate onion slices into rings. Arrange warm steak slices and onion rings on top of mesclun. Drizzle with the reserved vinaigrette. Top with tomatoes and cheese.

Nutrition Facts per serving: 266 cal., 16 g total fat (5 g sat. fat), 59 mg chol., 373 mg sodium, 9 g carbo., 2 g fiber, 22 g pro.

Quickly stir-fry the steak slices and sweet pepper strips, then toss with bottled salad dressing for a savory and satisfying dinner salad.

HOT ITALIAN BEEF SALAD

12 ounces beef flank steak or beef top round steak, cut 1 inch thick

6 cups torn mixed salad greens

1 medium red or green sweet pepper, cut into bite-size strips

3 teaspoons olive oil or cooking oil

½ cup bottled Italian salad dressing or red wine vinegar and oil salad dressing

Coarsely ground black pepper

1 Trim fat from steak. Cut steak into thin, bite-size strips. Arrange salad greens on 4 salad plates; set aside.

2 In a large skillet cook and stir sweet peppers in 2 teaspoons of the oil for 1 to 2 minutes or until nearly crisp-tender.

3 Add remaining 1 teaspoon oil to the skillet; add steak strips. Cook and stir for 2 to 3 minutes or until desired doneness. Add salad dressing to skillet. Cook and stir until heated through. Spoon beef mixture over salad greens. Sprinkle with black pepper.

Nutrition Facts per serving: 318 cal., 24 g total fat (5 g sat. fat), 41 mg chol., 348 mg sodium, 7 g carbo., 2 g fiber, 19 g pro.

START TO FINISH:

20 minutes

MAKES:

4 servings

So many flavors and textures come together in so little time! If your market doesn't offer bay scallops, you can substitute the larger sea scallops. Cut them in half crosswise before cooking.

SCALLOP STIR-FRY SALAD

START TO FINISH:

30 minutes

MAKES:

4 servings

2	tablespoons orange juice
2	tablespoons reduced-sodium soy sauce
1	tablespoon rice vinegar or white wine vinegar
1	teaspoon toasted sesame oil
12	ounces bay scallops
1	cup fresh snow pea pods, strings and tips removed
2	tablespoons cooking oil
1	medium red sweet pepper, coarsely chopped
½	cup sliced green onions
1	8-ounce jar baby corn, rinsed and drained
2	cups shredded Chinese (napa) cabbage
2	cups shredded fresh spinach or romaine

1 In a small bowl stir together orange juice, soy sauce, vinegar, and sesame oil; set aside. Rinse scallops; pat dry. Halve pea pods lengthwise. Pour 1 tablespoon of the cooking oil into a wok or large skillet. Heat over medium-high heat. Cook and stir scallops in hot oil for 3 to 4 minutes or until scallops are opaque. Remove scallops from wok.

2 Add remaining 1 tablespoon cooking oil to wok. Cook and stir pea pods, sweet pepper, and green onions for 2 to 3 minutes or until crisp-tender. Add cooked scallops, corn, and orange juice mixture to wok. Cook and stir about 1 minute or until heated through. Remove from heat.

3 In a large salad bowl combine cabbage and spinach. Top with scallop mixture, tossing lightly to combine.

Nutrition Facts per serving: 171 cal., 9 g total fat (1 g sat. fat), 26 mg chol., 421 mg sodium, 10 g carbo., 3 g fiber, 15 g pro.

Beat the clock with a quick salad of cooked shrimp, crisp greens, and a spicy dressing.

SHRIMP WITH CHIPOTLE VINAIGRETTE

12	ounces peeled, deveined medium shrimp
1	tablespoon cooking oil
1	tablespoon lime juice
½	to 1 teaspoon crushed dried chipotle pepper
⅓	cup tomato juice
1	tablespoon salad oil
1	clove garlic, minced
8	cups torn mixed salad greens, romaine, or spinach
½	cup sliced red onion

START TO FINISH:
30 minutes
MAKES:
4 servings

1 In a large skillet cook and stir shrimp in hot oil for 3 to 4 minutes or until shrimp turn opaque. Remove from heat; squeeze lime juice over shrimp. Set shrimp aside to cool slightly.

2 Meanwhile, for vinaigrette, in a small bowl stir together chipotle pepper, tomato juice, salad oil, and garlic.

3 To serve, divide salad greens among 4 plates. Top with shrimp and onion. Drizzle with vinaigrette.

Nutrition Facts per serving: 159 cal., 8 g total fat (1 g sat. fat), 131 mg chol., 253 mg sodium, 6 g carbo., 3 g fiber, 16 g pro.

Boiling shrimp is quicker than buying fast food. It's also a healthful change of pace, particularly when heaped over fresh spinach leaves.

TOSSED SALAD WITH SHRIMP & ORANGES

START TO FINISH:

30 minutes

MAKES:

4 servings

12 ounces fresh or frozen peeled, deveined shrimp

2 oranges

Orange juice

1 teaspoon snipped fresh rosemary

2 tablespoons white wine vinegar

2 tablespoons salad oil

6 cups torn fresh spinach or torn mixed salad greens

1 small red onion, thinly sliced and separated into rings

1 Thaw shrimp, if frozen. Finely shred 1 teaspoon orange peel; set orange peel aside. Peel and section oranges over a bowl to catch juices; set orange sections aside. Measure juices and add additional orange juice to equal $^1/_3$ cup; set orange juice aside.

2 Rinse shrimp; pat dry with paper towels. Cook shrimp in boiling, salted water for 1 to 3 minutes or until shrimp turn opaque; drain. Rinse with cold water; drain again. Set shrimp aside.

3 For dressing, in a small saucepan bring reserved orange juice and rosemary to boiling. Remove from heat; stir in reserved orange peel, vinegar, and salad oil.

4 In a large bowl toss together spinach, onion rings, orange sections, and shrimp. Pour dressing over salad. Toss lightly to coat.

Nutrition Facts per serving: 174 cal., 8 g total fat (1 g sat. fat), 131 mg chol., 216 mg sodium, 10 g carbo., 3 g fiber, 17 g pro.

Firm-fleshed swordfish or tuna slices well after cooking for easy arrangement on top of arugula and other greens. Complete this salad with a generous drizzle of roasted sweet pepper dressing.

GARDEN GREENS WITH SWORDFISH

1	pound fresh or frozen swordfish or tuna steaks, cut 1 inch thick
1	tablespoon lemon juice
1	teaspoon dried Italian seasoning, crushed
¼	teaspoon garlic salt
⅛	teaspoon black pepper
6	cups torn mixed salad greens
12	red and/or yellow baby pear tomatoes or cherry tomatoes, halved
1	recipe Roasted Pepper Dressing (see below)

START TO FINISH:
30 minutes
MAKES:
4 servings

❶ Thaw fish, if frozen. Rinse fish; pat dry with paper towels. Brush fish with lemon juice. For rub, stir together Italian seasoning, garlic salt, and pepper. Sprinkle over fish; rub in with your fingers. Place fish on the greased, unheated rack of a broiler pan.

❷ Broil 4 inches from heat for 5 minutes. Using a wide spatula, carefully turn over fish. Broil 3 to 7 minutes more or until fish flakes easily when tested with a fork. Cool; cut fish into thin bite-size strips.

❸ Divide salad greens among 4 plates. Top with fish and tomatoes. Drizzle Roasted Pepper Dressing over salads.

ROASTED PEPPER DRESSING: In a blender container or food processor bowl combine ½ of a 7-ounce jar roasted red sweet peppers, drained (½ cup); ¼ cup salad oil; 3 tablespoons vinegar; ¼ teaspoon salt; and dash cayenne pepper. Cover and blend or process until nearly smooth. Cover and chill up to 24 hours. Makes about ¾ cup.

Nutrition Facts per serving: 282 cal., 18 g total fat (3 g sat. fat), 45 mg chol., 374 mg sodium, 6 g carbo., 2 g fiber, 24 g pro.

Smoked salmon is the height of elegance. Paired with a shallot-and-chive vinaigrette and fancy baby greens, it's great company fare.

SALMON SALAD WITH CHIVE VINAIGRETTE

PREP:

20 minutes

SOAK:

1 hour

GRILL:

22 minutes

MAKES:

4 servings

2   cups alder or hickory wood chips

1   1½-pound fresh or frozen skinless, boneless salmon fillet, ¾ to 1 inch thick

2   shallots, chopped

¼   cup rice vinegar

2   tablespoons lime juice

4   teaspoons no-calorie, heat-stable granular sugar substitute (Splenda)

½   teaspoon salt

½   cup olive oil

2   tablespoons snipped fresh chives

1   tablespoon snipped fresh dill

½   teaspoon salt

½   teaspoon black pepper

8   ounces mesclun or torn mixed salad greens (6 cups)

1 At least 1 hour before grilling, soak wood chips in enough water to cover. Drain before using.

2 Thaw fish, if frozen. Rinse fish; pat dry with paper towels. For vinaigrette, in a food processor bowl or blender container combine shallots, vinegar, lime juice, sugar substitute, and ½ teaspoon salt. With machine running, slowly add oil. Add chives; process or blend with one or two on-off pulses just to mix. Set aside.

3 Sprinkle fish with dill, ½ teaspoon salt, and the pepper. Cut several slits in a piece of heavy foil large enough to hold fish. Grease foil; place fish on foil, tucking under any thin edges.

4 For a charcoal grill, arrange medium-hot coals around a drip pan. Test for medium heat above the pan. Sprinkle drained wood chips over the coals. Cover and heat about 10 minutes or until chips begin to smoke. Place fish on foil on grill rack over drip pan. Cover and grill just until fish flakes easily when tested with a fork. Allow 15 to 18 minutes per ½-inch thickness of fish. (For a gas grill, preheat grill. Reduce heat to medium. Adjust for indirect cooking. Add soaked wood chips according to manufacturer's directions. Place fish on foil over unlit burner. Grill as above.) Remove from grill.

5 Stir vinaigrette. In a large bowl pour half of the vinaigrette over mesclun; toss to coat. Divide mesclun among 4 dinner plates. Cut fish into 4 serving-size pieces and arrange on top of mesclun. If desired, pass remaining vinaigrette. To store any leftover vinaigrette, cover and refrigerate for up to 1 week.

Nutrition Facts per serving: 577 cal., 45 g total fat (7 g sat. fat), 99 mg chol., 690 mg sodium, 5 g carbo., 1 g fiber, 35 g pro.

If you like food peppery hot, this combination of tuna and Cajun flavors is sure to ignite your appetite.

2 g net carb

CAJUN TUNA SPREAD

1	3-ounce package cream cheese, softened
3	tablespoons mayonnaise or salad dressing
1	teaspoon paprika
¼	teaspoon black pepper
1	clove garlic, minced
⅛	teaspoon cayenne pepper
1	6½-ounce can tuna, drained and broken into chunks
¼	cup finely chopped red or green sweet pepper
1	green onion, thinly sliced
	Lettuce leaves (optional)

1 In a small mixing bowl beat cream cheese, mayonnaise, paprika, black pepper, garlic, and cayenne pepper with an electric mixer on medium speed until well combined. Stir in tuna, sweet pepper, and green onion. Cover; chill for 3 to 24 hours. If desired, serve on lettuce-lined plates.

Nutrition Facts per serving: 280 cal., 22 g total fat (8 g sat. fat), 55 mg chol., 367 mg sodium, 3 g carbo., 1 g fiber, 18 g pro.

PREP:
15 minutes
CHILL:
3 to 24 hours
MAKES:
3 servings (1½ cups)

Use a variety of tomato colors and shapes to create an eye-catching mixture. Cut larger tomatoes into slices or wedges; halve cherry or pear varieties.

5 g net carb

TOMATO-CRAB SALAD

START TO FINISH:

15 minutes

MAKES:

6 servings

2 pounds ripe tomatoes, such as Brandywine, Green Zebra, and/or yellow cherry

3 tablespoons tarragon vinegar or cider vinegar

2 tablespoons extra-virgin olive oil

¼ cup snipped fresh tarragon

¾ teaspoon salt

½ teaspoon cracked black pepper

½ cup cooked lump crabmeat (about 3 ounces)

Fresh tarragon sprigs (optional)

1 Arrange tomatoes on a platter. For dressing, in a screw-top jar combine vinegar, oil, and 3 tablespoons of the snipped tarragon. Cover and shake well. Drizzle dressing over tomatoes. Sprinkle with remaining 1 tablespoon snipped tarragon. Serve immediately or cover and chill up to 8 hours.

2 Just before serving, sprinkle salt and pepper over salad. Top with crabmeat. If desired, garnish with tarragon sprigs.

Nutrition Facts per serving: 89 cal., 5 g total fat (1 g sat. fat), 8 mg chol., 166 mg sodium, 7 g carbo., 2 g fiber, 4 g pro.

Ground curry in this egg salad moves it from ordinary to "eggstraordinary."

CURRIED EGG SALAD

2 g
net
carb

8	hard-cooked eggs, chopped
½	cup mayonnaise or salad dressing
¼	cup finely chopped pitted ripe olives
2	tablespoons finely chopped green onion
½	to 1 teaspoon curry powder
¼	teaspoon salt

1 In a bowl stir together eggs, mayonnaise, olives, green onion, curry powder, and salt. Cover and chill for 4 to 24 hours.

Nutrition Facts per serving: 243 cal., 22 g total fat (4 g sat. fat), 294 mg chol., 333 mg sodium, 2 g carbo., 0 g fiber, 9 g pro.

PREP:
15 minutes
CHILL:
4 hours
MAKES:
12 (¼-cup) servings

Beautiful layered vegetables in glass jars often grace counters at Italian groceries. Those artful creations come to mind with this striking mixture of vegetables, beans, and prosciutto bound together with a creamy dressing.

5 g net carb

ITALIAN ZUCCHINI SALAD

PREP:
30 minutes

CHILL:
2 hours

MAKES:
8 servings

2   large zucchini and/or yellow summer squash, cut into $1/4$-inch slices (4 cups)

1    $15^{1}/_{2}$-ounce can white kidney beans (cannellini beans), rinsed and drained

1   7-ounce jar roasted red sweet peppers, drained and cut into thin strips

4   ounces prosciutto, cut into thin strips (1 cup)

6   cups torn fresh spinach

2   cups torn arugula

$1/3$ cup bottled creamy Italian salad dressing

$1/4$ cup mayonnaise or salad dressing

1   cup shredded provolone or fontina cheese (4 ounces)

$1/2$ cup fresh Italian parsley leaves

1 In a large bowl combine zucchini, beans, pepper strips, and prosciutto. Cover and chill for 2 to 24 hours.

2 Just before serving, add spinach and arugula to zucchini mixture; toss to combine.

3 For dressing, stir together Italian dressing and mayonnaise; pour over zucchini mixture. Toss lightly to coat. Add cheese and parsley; toss to combine.

Nutrition Facts per serving: 213 cal., 15 g total fat (4 g sat. fat), 22 mg chol., 827 mg sodium, 11 g carbo., 6 g fiber, 12 g pro.

Tangy mustard greens with a mustardy vinaigrette and crunchy walnuts is a perfect side dish for spicy grilled meats and poultry.

MUSTARD GREENS SALAD

1   small red sweet pepper, seeded and cut into thin strips

1   tablespoon cooking oil

2   tablespoons seasoned rice vinegar

4   teaspoons green peppercorn mustard, tarragon mustard, or Dijon-style mustard

4   cups shredded mustard greens

3   tablespoons chopped walnuts

1 In a large skillet cook and stir peppers in hot oil over medium heat for 2 minutes. Stir in vinegar and mustard. Cook and stir just until bubbly; remove from heat. In a large salad bowl combine greens and walnuts. Toss warm pepper mixture with greens and walnuts. Serve immediately.

Nutrition Facts per serving: 96 cal., 8 g total fat (1 g sat. fat), 0 mg chol., 43 mg sodium, 5 g carbo., 3 g fiber, 3 g pro.

START TO FINISH:

10 minutes

MAKES:

4 to 6 servings

Tender asparagus spears combine with shredded cabbage and red onion tossed in a sesame oil dressing.

ASIAN-STYLE ASPARAGUS SLAW

PREP:

10 minutes

COOK:

4 minutes

MAKES:

6 servings

1	pound asparagus
4	cups very finely shredded green cabbage
1	cup very finely shredded red cabbage
1	small carrot, very finely shredded
¼	cup snipped fresh parsley
¼	small red onion, thinly sliced
1	tablespoon toasted sesame oil
2	tablespoons seasoned rice vinegar
¼	teaspoon white pepper

1 Snap off and discard fibrous stem ends of asparagus. Rinse asparagus; drain. In a medium saucepan bring 1 inch of water to boiling. Place asparagus in steamer basket; cover and steam for 4 minutes or until asparagus is crisp-tender. Drain. Gently rinse with cool water.

2 In a large bowl combine green cabbage, red cabbage, carrot, parsley, and onion. Toss gently with sesame oil, vinegar, and pepper.

3 Divide asparagus spears among 6 salad plates; top with cabbage mixture.

Nutrition Facts per serving: 54 cal., 3 g total fat (0 g sat. fat), 0 mg chol., 70 mg sodium, 6 g carbo., 2 g fiber, 2 g pro.

Here's a salad that should be eaten with your fingers. Serve each salad in a paper cup, perfect for a spring picnic or patio meal.

ASPARAGUS FINGER SALAD

8	ounces asparagus spears
⅓	cup dairy sour cream
1	tablespoon snipped fresh chives
2	teaspoons lemon juice
1	teaspoon snipped fresh tarragon
⅛	teaspoon salt
⅛	teaspoon black pepper
4	large butterhead lettuce or romaine leaves
1	small carrot, halved lengthwise
2	teaspoons finely shredded lemon peel

PREP:

15 minutes

COOK:

2 minutes

MAKES:

4 servings

1 Snap off and discard woody bases from asparagus. If desired, scrape off scales from asparagus spears. Cook asparagus, covered, in a small amount of boiling water for 2 to 4 minutes or until crisp-tender. Transfer asparagus to a bowl filled with ice water. Set aside.

2 For dipping sauce, in a small bowl stir together sour cream, chives, lemon juice, tarragon, salt, and pepper. Cover and chill until serving time.

3 To serve, cut center vein from each lettuce leaf, keeping each leaf in one piece. Place lettuce leaves on a serving plate. Pat asparagus dry with paper towels. Cut each carrot half into 4 equal lengthwise strips. Divide asparagus and carrot strips evenly across middle of lettuce leaves. Sprinkle each serving with lemon peel. Wrap lettuce around asparagus. If desired, place each asparagus salad upright in a small cup. Serve or drizzle with dipping sauce.

Nutrition Facts per serving: 49 cal., 3 g total fat (2 g sat. fat), 8 mg chol., 93 mg sodium, 5 g carbo., 2 g fiber, 2 g pro.

Fresh mozzarella, also called buffalo mozzarella, has a sweet flavor and soft texture. Find it in Italian markets, cheese shops, and specialty delis.

5 g net carb

FRESH MOZZARELLA SALAD

START TO FINISH:

20 minutes

MAKES:

4 servings

4   cups torn mixed greens (such as radicchio, spinach, arugula, and/or chicory)

1   cup yellow and/or red cherry tomatoes, halved

¼   cup snipped fresh basil

½   cup Greek olives

1   recipe Italian Vinaigrette (see below)

3   ounces thinly sliced fresh mozzarella cheese

1 In a large mixing bowl toss together the mixed greens, tomatoes, snipped basil, and olives. Drizzle Italian Vinaigrette over salad; then toss to coat. Top with mozzarella cheese. Makes 4 servings.

ITALIAN VINAIGRETTE: In a screw-top jar combine 2 tablespoons olive oil or salad oil, 2 tablespoons balsamic vinegar, 2 teaspoons snipped fresh oregano or basil, ⅛ teaspoon salt, and ⅛ teaspoon pepper. Cover the jar and shake well. Serve immediately or cover and store in refrigerator up to 2 weeks. Shake before serving. Makes about ¼ cup.

Nutrition Facts per serving: 169 cal., 14 g total fat (4 g sat. fat), 16 mg chol., 255 mg sodium, 7 g carbo., 2 g fiber, 6 g pro.

Balsamic vinegar, made from white Trebbiano grape juice, is aged in wooden barrels for several years to develop the unique flavor starring in this salad.

MARINATED VEGETABLE SALAD

2	medium ripe fresh tomatoes or 4 Roma tomatoes
1	medium green sweet pepper
1	small zucchini or yellow summer squash, thinly sliced (1¼ cups)
¼	cup thinly sliced red onion
2	tablespoons snipped fresh parsley
3	tablespoons olive oil
3	tablespoons balsamic vinegar or wine vinegar
1	tablespoon snipped fresh thyme or basil or 1 teaspoon dried thyme or basil, crushed
1	clove garlic, minced
1	tablespoon pine nuts, toasted

PREP:

15 minutes

STAND:

30 minutes

MAKES:

6 to 8 servings

1 Cut tomatoes into wedges. Cut green pepper into small squares. In a large bowl combine tomatoes, green pepper, zucchini, onion, and parsley.

2 For dressing, in a screw-top jar combine oil, vinegar, thyme, and garlic. Cover and shake well. Pour dressing over vegetable mixture. Toss lightly to coat.

3 Let mixture stand at room temperature for 30 to 60 minutes, stirring occasionally. Stir in the pine nuts. Serve with a slotted spoon.

Nutrition Facts per serving: 41 cal., 2 g total fat (0 g sat. fat), 0 mg chol., 6 mg sodium, 5 g carbo., 1 g fiber, 1 g pro.

The tomato pieces shrink in size as they dry slightly, intensifying their flavor.

2 g net carb

MELTED TOMATO SALAD

PREP:

10 minutes

BAKE:

1 1/2 hours

OVEN:

300°F

MAKES:

6 servings

4 cups quartered medium tomatoes (about 2 pounds) or halved cherry tomatoes

3 tablespoons olive oil

1/4 cup snipped fresh basil

1/4 teaspoon salt

1/4 teaspoon black pepper

6 cups baby spinach

1 In a large shallow glass baking dish place tomatoes in an even layer. Drizzle with oil; sprinkle with basil, salt, and pepper. Bake, uncovered, in a 300° oven for 1 1/2 to 2 hours or until tomatoes are slightly dried and charred. Cool slightly (15 minutes).

2 On a large serving platter arrange spinach. Spoon tomatoes and the pan juices over spinach.

Nutrition Facts per serving: 89 cal., 7 g total fat (1 g sat. fat), 0 mg chol., 146 mg sodium, 6 g carbo., 4 g fiber, 2 g pro.

A bag of frozen mixed vegetables delivers a garden of color without all the cleaning and cooking. These ready-to-go vegetables are the secret to this step-saving salad.

ITALIAN VEGETABLE SALAD

1 16-ounce package loose-pack frozen zucchini, carrots, cauliflower, lima beans, and Italian beans

½ cup cubed provolone or mozzarella cheese (2 ounces)

¼ cup sliced pitted ripe olives

2 green onions, sliced

⅓ cup bottled clear Italian salad dressing

2 tablespoons grated Parmesan cheese

1 In a medium bowl combine frozen vegetables, provolone cheese, olives, and onions. Add dressing; toss to coat. Cover and chill for 8 to 24 hours.

2 To serve, sprinkle Parmesan cheese over salad; toss to coat.

Nutrition Facts per serving: 156 cal., 12 g total fat (4 g sat. fat), 10 mg chol., 319 mg sodium, 7 g carbo., 2 g fiber, 6 g pro.

PREP:
10 minutes

CHILL:
8 hours

MAKES:
5 or 6 servings

BEEF, VEAL & LAMB

Americans are crazy about meat—sizzling steaks, juicy burgers, savory chops, and unpretentious roasts. Fortunately, our ranchers and farmers produce some of the best meats in the world. The cuts are flavorful, lean, juicy, and tender, making these luscious entrées enticing choices for anyone, whether or not they're on a low-carb diet.

BEEF, VEAL & LAMB 135

Melt-in-your-mouth beef tenderloin enhanced with fresh herbs and mustard makes this a perfect entrée for entertaining.

2 g net carb

MUSTARD & HERB BEEF TENDERLOIN

PREP:

10 minutes

ROAST:

35 minutes

OVEN:

425°F

STAND:

15 minutes

MAKES:

8 servings

2   tablespoons Dijon-style mustard

1   tablespoon snipped fresh rosemary or ½ teaspoon dried rosemary, crushed

1   tablespoon snipped fresh thyme or ½ teaspoon dried thyme, crushed

1   tablespoon snipped fresh basil or 1 teaspoon dried basil, crushed

1   2-pound beef tenderloin

¾   cup soft bread crumbs (1 slice)

1   tablespoon butter or margarine, melted

1 In a small bowl stir together mustard and half of the rosemary, half of the thyme, and half of the basil. Place meat on a rack in a shallow roasting pan. Spread mustard-herb mixture over meat. Insert a meat thermometer into center of meat. Roast, uncovered, in a 425° oven for 30 to 35 minutes or until the thermometer registers 135°F.

2 Meanwhile, combine bread crumbs, butter, and remaining herbs. Remove meat from oven; sprinkle with crumb mixture, pressing lightly into mustard-herb mixture. Roast for 5 to 10 minutes more or until thermometer registers 140°F. Cover meat with foil; let stand for 15 minutes before slicing. (The meat's temperature will rise 5°F during standing.)

Nutrition Facts per serving: 211 cal., 11 g total fat (4 g sat. fat), 74 mg chol., 177 mg sodium, 2 g carbo., 0 g fiber, 24 g pro.

Although this marinade contains several intensely flavored ingredients, they blend harmoniously.

MARINATED FLANK STEAK

1	1½-pound beef flank steak
½	cup reduced-sodium soy sauce
¼	cup orange juice
¼	cup dry red wine, dry sherry, or orange juice
3	tablespoons Dijon-style mustard
3	tablespoons olive oil or cooking oil
2	tablespoons grated fresh ginger or 1 teaspoon ground ginger
2	tablespoons tomato paste
1	teaspoon ground cumin
½	teaspoon freshly ground black pepper
2	small cloves garlic, minced

1 Place flank steak in a large self-sealing plastic bag set in a shallow dish. For marinade, stir together soy sauce, orange juice, wine, mustard, oil, ginger, tomato paste, cumin, pepper, and garlic. Pour marinade over steak; seal bag. Marinate in refrigerator for 4 to 8 hours. Drain, discarding marinade.

2 For a charcoal grill, place steak on the rack of an uncovered grill directly over medium coals. Grill 17 to 21 minutes for medium doneness (160°F). (For a gas grill, preheat grill. Reduce heat to medium. Place steak on grill rack over heat. Cover and grill as above.)

3 To serve, thinly slice meat diagonally across the grain.

Nutrition Facts per serving: 313 cal., 18 g total fat (7 g sat. fat), 87 mg chol., 255 mg sodium, 1 g carbo., 0 g fiber, 34 g pro.

PREP:

15 minutes

MARINATE:

4 hours

GRILL:

17 minutes

MAKES:

4 servings

Give the seasoning rub a chance to penetrate the tender meat by chilling it for at least 8 hours, just as you would when marinating.

1 g net carb

FAVORITE BEEF TENDERLOIN

PREP:

15 minutes

CHILL:

8 hours

ROAST:

50 minutes

OVEN:

425°F

STAND:

15 minutes

MAKES:

12 to 15 servings

1 tablespoon dried thyme, crushed

1 teaspoon ground white pepper

1 teaspoon garlic salt

1 teaspoon seasoned salt

¼ teaspoon dried oregano, crushed

1 4- to 5-pound beef tenderloin

2 tablespoons Worcestershire sauce

1 In a small bowl stir together thyme, pepper, garlic salt, seasoned salt, and oregano. Sprinkle mixture over all sides of meat; rub in with your fingers. Place meat in a self-sealing plastic bag; seal bag. Chill for 8 to 24 hours.

2 Remove meat from bag and place on a rack in a foil-lined roasting pan. Insert a meat thermometer into center of meat. Drizzle with Worcestershire sauce. Roast in a 425° oven for 50 to 60 minutes or until meat thermometer registers 135°F. Cover with foil and let stand 15 minutes before slicing. (The meat's temperature will rise 5°F to 10°F during standing.)

Nutrition Facts per serving: 237 cal., 11 g total fat (4 g sat. fat), 92 mg chol., 304 mg sodium, 1 g carbo., 0 g fiber, 31 g pro.

Marinate the flank steak several hours ahead so it's full of flavor by broiling time. Also make the relish ahead of time to allow the flavors to blend.

FLANK STEAK WITH CORN RELISH

1	8¾-ounce can whole kernel corn, drained
¾	cup green or regular salsa
1	medium tomato, chopped (about ⅔ cup)
¾	cup bottled Italian salad dressing
2	tablespoons cracked black pepper
1	tablespoon Worcestershire sauce
1	teaspoon ground cumin
1	1¼- to 1½-pound beef flank steak
	Fresh cilantro (optional)

1 In a storage container combine corn, salsa, and tomato. Chill, covered, for up to 2 days. (Bring to room temperature before serving.)

2 For marinade, in a bowl stir together salad dressing, pepper, Worcestershire sauce, and cumin.

3 Score flank steak on both sides by making shallow cuts at 1-inch intervals in a diamond pattern. Place steak in a self-sealing plastic bag set in a shallow dish. Pour marinade over steak; seal bag. Marinate in the refrigerator for 6 to 24 hours, turning bag once. Drain steak, discarding marinade.

4 Place the steak on the unheated rack of a broiler pan. Broil 3 to 4 inches from heat for 15 to 18 minutes or until medium doneness (160°F), turning once halfway through broiling.

5 To serve, thinly slice the meat diagonally across the grain. Spoon corn relish over meat. If desired, garnish with cilantro.

Nutrition Facts per serving: 232 cal., 12 g total fat (4 g sat. fat), 38 mg chol., 309 mg sodium, 10 g carbo., 1 g fiber, 22 g pro.

9 g net carb

PREP:
15 minutes

MARINATE:
6 hours

BROIL:
15 minutes

MAKES:
6 servings

Tenderloin is one of the leanest cuts of beef. To keep these prized steaks at their juicy best, don't overcook them.

PEPPERED STEAK WITH MUSHROOM SAUCE

PREP:

20 minutes

COOK:

10 minutes

MAKES:

6 servings

6	beef tenderloin steaks or 3 boneless beef top sirloin steaks, cut 1 inch thick (about 1½ pounds total)
1½	teaspoons dried whole green peppercorns, crushed, or ½ teaspoon coarsely ground black pepper
½	teaspoon dried thyme, crushed
½	teaspoon dried oregano, crushed
¼	teaspoon salt
	Nonstick cooking spray
⅓	cup water
½	teaspoon instant beef bouillon granules
¾	cup sliced fresh shiitake or other mushrooms
¾	cup milk
2	tablespoons unbleached all-purpose flour
½	teaspoon dried thyme, crushed
⅔	cup dairy sour cream
	Fresh thyme sprigs (optional)

1 Trim fat from steaks. In a small bowl stir together peppercorns, ½ teaspoon dried thyme, oregano, and salt. Sprinkle mixture over both sides of steaks; rub in with your fingers.

2 Lightly coat a large nonstick skillet with cooking spray. Heat over medium-high heat. Add meat; reduce heat to medium. Cook until desired doneness, turning once. Allow about 10 minutes for medium rare (145°F) or about 15 minutes for medium doneness (160°F). Remove meat from skillet; cover and keep warm.

3 For sauce, add water and bouillon granules to skillet. Bring to boiling. Add mushrooms; cook about 2 minutes or until mushrooms are tender. In a small bowl stir together milk, flour, and ½ teaspoon dried thyme; add to mushroom mixture. Cook and stir until thickened and bubbly. Stir in sour cream; heat through but do not boil. Serve the meat with sauce. If desired, garnish with fresh thyme.

Nutrition Facts per serving: 268 cal., 14 g total fat (6 g sat. fat), 81 mg chol., 252 mg sodium, 8 g carbo., 1 g fiber, 26 g pro.

The essence of summertime sophistication, this soaked steak picks up the pleasantly piney taste of the gin in the marinade.

GRILLED STEAK WITH MARTINI TWIST

4	boneless beef top loin steaks, cut 1 inch thick (1¾ to 2 pounds total)
¼	cup finely chopped green onions
¼	cup gin
1	tablespoon olive oil
1	teaspoon finely shredded lemon peel
1	teaspoon multicolor peppercorns, crushed
	Salt
2	tablespoons sliced pimiento-stuffed green olives
	Lemon peel strips

PREP:
10 minutes

MARINATE:
30 minutes

GRILL:
11 minutes

MAKES:
4 servings

1 Trim fat from steaks. Place steaks in a self-sealing plastic bag set in a shallow dish. For marinade, in a small bowl stir together green onions, gin, olive oil, and lemon peel. Pour over steaks; seal bag. Marinate in the refrigerator for 30 minutes, turning bag once. Drain steaks, discarding marinade. Press the crushed peppercorns onto both sides of the steaks.

2 For a charcoal grill, place steaks on the rack of an uncovered grill directly over medium coals. Grill until desired doneness, turning once halfway through grilling. Allow 11 to 15 minutes for medium rare (145°F) or 14 to 18 minutes for medium doneness (160°F). (For a gas grill, preheat grill. Reduce heat to medium. Place steaks on grill rack over heat. Cover and grill as above.)

3 Season steaks to taste with salt. Garnish with sliced olives and lemon peel strips.

Nutrition Facts per serving: 264 cal., 8 g total fat (2 g sat. fat), 93 mg chol., 201 mg sodium, 1 g carbo., 0 g fiber, 43 g pro.

Fresh lemon flavors this super-lean flank steak or top sirloin.

6 g
net
carb

LEMONY FLANK STEAK

PREP:

15 minutes

MARINATE:

2 hours

BROIL:

15 minutes

MAKES:

6 servings

1	1½-pound beef flank steak or boneless beef top sirloin steak
1	teaspoon finely shredded lemon peel
½	cup lemon juice
2	tablespoons no-calorie, heat-stable granular sugar substitute
2	tablespoons reduced-sodium soy sauce
2	teaspoons snipped fresh oregano or ½ teaspoon dried oregano, crushed
⅛	teaspoon black pepper

1 Trim fat from steak. Score steak on both sides by making shallow cuts at 1-inch intervals in a diamond pattern. Place steak in a self-sealing plastic bag set in a shallow dish. For marinade, stir together lemon peel, lemon juice, sugar substitute, soy sauce, oregano, and pepper. Pour over steak; seal bag. Marinate in the refrigerator for 2 to 24 hours. Drain steak, reserving marinade.

2 Place steak on the unheated rack of a broiler pan. Broil 4 to 5 inches from heat for 15 to 18 minutes for medium doneness (160°F), turning and brushing once with marinade halfway through broiling. Discard any remaining marinade.

3 To serve, thinly slice meat diagonally across the grain.

Nutrition Facts per serving: 201 cal., 8 g total fat (3 g sat. fat), 46 mg chol., 367 mg sodium, 6 g carbo., 0 g fiber, 26 g pro.

Cuts other than strip steaks will benefit from this peppy seasoning. Rub the mixture on T-bone or sirloin steaks, too. If you're cooking fewer steaks, simply halve the mixture.

KANSAS CITY STRIP STEAKS

4	8-ounce beef top loin steaks, cut 1 inch thick
2	tablespoons prepared horseradish
2	tablespoons lemon juice
4	teaspoons sugar
2	teaspoons paprika
2	teaspoons bottled minced garlic (4 cloves)
1	teaspoon salt
1	teaspoon black pepper
½	teaspoon instant beef bouillon granules

1 Trim fat from steaks. In a small bowl stir together horseradish, lemon juice, sugar, paprika, garlic, salt, pepper, and bouillon granules. Sprinkle mixture over both sides of each steak; rub in with your fingers. Cover and chill for 1 hour.

2 For a charcoal grill, place steaks on the rack of an uncovered grill directly over medium coals. Grill until desired doneness, turning once halfway through grilling. Allow 11 to 15 minutes for medium rare (145°F) or 14 to 18 minutes for medium doneness (160°F). (For a gas grill, preheat grill. Reduce heat to medium. Place steaks on grill rack over heat. Cover and grill as above.)

Nutrition Facts per serving: 276 cal., 19 g total fat (8 g sat. fat), 74 mg chol., 400 mg sodium, 8 g carbo., 0 g fiber, 22 g pro.

PREP:
10 minutes
CHILL:
1 hour
GRILL:
11 minutes
MAKES:
8 servings

Strong brewed coffee contributes to the mellow flavor of this slow-cooked steak.

JAVA SWISS STEAK

PREP:

20 minutes

COOK:

8 to 10 hours (low) or 4 to 5 hours (high)

MAKES:

6 servings

2	pounds boneless beef round steak, cut ¾ inch thick
1	tablespoon cooking oil
3	medium onions, cut into wedges
4	teaspoons quick-cooking tapioca
2	tablespoons soy sauce
1	teaspoon bottled minced garlic or 2 cloves garlic, minced
2	bay leaves
½	teaspoon dried oregano, crushed
1	cup strong brewed coffee

1 Trim fat from steak. Cut steak into serving-size pieces. In a 12-inch skillet brown meat on both sides in hot oil (add more oil, if necessary). Drain off fat.

2 Place onions in a 3½- or 4-quart slow cooker. Add meat. Sprinkle meat with tapioca. Add soy sauce, garlic, bay leaves, and oregano. Pour coffee over all.

3 Cover and cook on low-heat setting for 8 to 10 hours or on high-heat setting for 4 to 5 hours. Remove meat and onions to serving platter. Discard bay leaves. Spoon some of the cooking juices over meat and onions.

Nutrition Facts per serving: 256 cal., 9 g total fat (3 g sat. fat), 72 mg chol., 399 mg sodium, 6 g carbo., 1 g fiber, 35 g pro.

Fresh rosemary adds a distinctive sweet, pinelike essence to this marinade fitting for the king of beef cuts.

0 g net carb

MARINATED PRIME RIB

¾ cup dry red wine

½ cup chopped onion

¼ cup water

¼ cup lemon juice

1 tablespoon Worcestershire sauce

1½ teaspoons snipped fresh rosemary or ½ teaspoon dried rosemary, crushed

½ teaspoon dried marjoram, crushed

¼ teaspoon garlic salt

1 4- to 6-pound beef rib roast

1 For marinade, in a small bowl stir together wine, onion, the water, lemon juice, Worcestershire sauce, rosemary, marjoram, and garlic salt. Place roast in a self-sealing plastic bag set in a shallow dish. Pour marinade over meat; seal bag. Marinate in the refrigerator for 6 to 24 hours, turning occasionally. Drain meat, discarding marinade.

2 Place meat, fat side up, in a large roasting pan. Insert a meat thermometer into center without touching bone.

3 Roast in a 325° oven until desired doneness. Allow 1¾ to 2¼ hours for medium rare (135°F) or 2 ¼ to 2 ¾ hours for medium doneness (150°F). Transfer meat to a cutting board. Cover with foil and let stand for 15 minutes before carving. (The meat's temperature will rise 10°F during standing.)

Nutrition Facts per serving: 162 cal., 9 g total fat (4 g sat. fat), 53 mg chol., 67 mg sodium, 0 g carbo., 0 g fiber, 18 g pro.

PREP:
10 minutes
MARINATE:
6 hours
ROAST:
1¾ hours
OVEN:
325°F
STAND:
15 minutes
MAKES:
12 to 16 servings

This sirloin steak wears a coat of ground coffee, a familiar complement to the balsamic vinegar-spiced sauce.

COFFEE-CRUSTED SIRLOIN

PREP:

15 minutes

GRILL:

14 minutes

STAND:

15 minutes

MAKES:

4 servings

1	pound boneless beef top sirloin steak, cut 1 inch thick
¼	cup balsamic vinegar
2	teaspoons finely ground coffee beans
¼	teaspoon salt
2	teaspoons finely chopped shallot
1	tablespoon butter or margarine
2	teaspoons unbleached all-purpose flour
½	cup reduced-sodium chicken broth
¼	cup half-and-half or light cream
⅛	teaspoon black pepper

1 Trim fat from steak. Place steak in a shallow dish. Pour 2 tablespoons of the balsamic vinegar over steak. Cover and let stand at room temperature for 15 minutes, turning once. In a small bowl combine ground coffee beans and salt. Drain steak, discarding vinegar. Press coffee mixture into both sides of the steak.

2 For a charcoal grill, place steak on the rack of an uncovered grill directly over medium coals. Grill until desired doneness, turning once. Allow 14 to 18 minutes for medium rare (145°F) or 18 to 22 minutes for medium doneness (160°F). (For a gas grill, preheat grill. Reduce heat to medium. Place steaks on grill rack over heat. Cover and grill as above.)

3 Meanwhile, in a small saucepan cook shallot in hot butter for 2 to 3 minutes or until tender. Stir in flour. Add chicken broth. Cook and stir until thickened and bubbly. Cook and stir for 1 minute more. Remove from heat. Stir in half-and-half and pepper. Stir in the remaining 2 tablespoons balsamic vinegar.

4 Slice meat; serve with sauce.

Nutrition Facts per serving: 213 cal., 9 g total fat (4 g sat. fat), 83 mg chol., 319 mg sodium, 7 g carbo., 0 g fiber, 25 g pro.

An elegant cut such as tenderloin deserves an equally upscale sauce. Don't stop at steak—this versatile sauce is also tasty over grilled pork or chicken.

FILET MIGNON WITH COGNAC SAUCE

4	beef tenderloin steaks, cut 1 inch thick (about 1 pound total)
3	tablespoons Cognac or brandy
½	teaspoon coarsely ground black pepper
1	cup sliced fresh mushrooms
1	tablespoon finely chopped shallot
1	tablespoon butter or margarine
½	cup beef broth
¼	cup half-and-half or light cream
2	tablespoons Dijon-style mustard
1	tablespoon unbleached all-purpose flour

1 Trim fat from steaks. Place steaks in a shallow dish. Pour 2 tablespoons of the Cognac over the steaks. Cover and let stand at room temperature for 15 minutes, turning once. Drain steaks, discarding Cognac in dish. Sprinkle pepper over both sides of each steak.

2 For a charcoal grill, place steaks on the rack of an uncovered grill directly over medium coals. Grill until desired doneness, turning once. Allow 11 to 15 minutes for medium rare (145°F) or 14 to 18 minutes for medium doneness (160°F). (For a gas grill, preheat grill. Reduce heat to medium. Place steaks on grill rack over heat. Cover and grill as above.)

3 Meanwhile, in a small saucepan cook mushrooms and shallot in hot butter for 3 to 4 minutes or until tender. Stir in broth and remaining 1 tablespoon Cognac. Bring to boiling; reduce heat. Boil gently, uncovered, for 5 minutes.

4 In a small bowl stir together half-and-half, mustard, and flour until smooth. Stir into broth mixture. Cook and stir until thickened and bubbly. Cook and stir for 1 minute more. Serve sauce over steaks.

Nutrition Facts per serving: 258 cal., 11 g total fat (5 g sat. fat), 65 mg chol., 375 mg sodium, 4 g carbo., 0 g fiber, 25 g pro.

PREP:
10 minutes
GRILL:
11 minutes
STAND:
15 minutes
MAKES:
4 servings

Fresh garlic chives give this marinade a pleasant herb flavor. If you can't find them at a farmer's market or grocery store, use regular chives plus with some minced garlic.

PEPPERCORN BEEF

PREP:

15 minutes

GRILL:

11 minutes

MARINATE:

8 hours

MAKES:

4 servings

4   beef tenderloin steaks (about 1½ pounds total) or 1- to 1½-pound boneless beef top loin steak, cut 1¼ inches thick

⅓   cup bottled oil and vinegar salad dressing

⅓   cup dry red wine

¼   cup snipped fresh garlic chives or ¼ cup snipped fresh chives plus 1 teaspoon bottled minced garlic

1   teaspoon cracked multicolor or black peppercorns

1 Place steaks in a large self-sealing plastic bag set in a shallow dish. For marinade, in a small bowl stir together salad dressing, wine, garlic chives, and peppercorns. Pour marinade over steaks; seal bag. Turn to coat steaks. Marinate in the refrigerator for 8 to 12 hours, turning bag occasionally. Drain steaks, reserving marinade.

2 For a charcoal grill, place steaks on the rack of an uncovered grill directly over medium coals. Grill to desired doneness, turning once halfway through grilling and brushing once with reserved marinade after 8 minutes of grilling. Allow 11 to 15 minutes for medium rare (145°F) or 14 to 18 minutes for medium doneness (160°F). (For a gas grill, preheat grill. Reduce heat to medium. Place steaks on grill rack over heat. Cover and grill as above.)

3 Discard any remaining marinade. If using top loin steak, cut into 4 serving-size pieces.

Nutrition Facts per serving: 287 cal., 16 g total fat (5 g sat. fat), 96 mg chol., 218 mg sodium, 1 g carbo., 0 g fiber, 32 g pro.

Anyone who has marinated a flank steak knows how tender it becomes—and how flavorful. Hoisin and soy sauces, sherry, ginger, and garlic combine for this Asian-inspired marinade.

2 g net carb

ASIAN FLANK STEAK

1   1¼-pound beef flank steak

½   cup beef broth

⅓   cup hoisin sauce

¼   cup reduced-sodium soy sauce

¼   cup sliced green onions

3   tablespoons dry sherry or apple, orange, or pineapple juice

1   tablespoon no-calorie, heat-stable granular sugar substitute (Splenda)

1   teaspoon grated fresh ginger

4   cloves garlic, minced

     Nonstick cooking spray

1 Trim fat from steak. Place steak in a self-sealing plastic bag set in a shallow dish. For marinade, in a small bowl stir together broth, hoisin sauce, soy sauce, green onions, sherry, sugar substitute, ginger, and garlic. Pour over steak; seal bag. Marinate in the refrigerator for 4 to 24 hours, turning bag occasionally. Drain steak, discarding marinade.

2 Lightly coat the unheated rack of a broiler pan with cooking spray. Place steak on the prepared rack. Broil 3 to 4 inches from heat for 15 to 18 minutes for medium doneness (160°F), turning once halfway through broiling.

3 To serve, thinly slice meat diagonally across the grain.

Nutrition Facts per serving: 164 cal., 7 g total fat (3 g sat. fat), 38 mg chol., 323 mg sodium, 2 g carbo., 0 g fiber, 21 g pro.

PREP:
15 minutes

MARINATE:
4 hours

BROIL:
15 minutes

MAKES:
6 servings

Combine the ease of 5-ingredient preparation and the convenience of slow cooking for an entrée that's a busy cook's dream come true.

8g net carb

BEEF WITH MUSHROOMS

PREP:

10 minutes

COOK:

*8 to 10 hours (low) or
4 to 5 hours (high)*

MAKES:

4 servings

1 pound boneless beef round steak, cut 1 inch thick

2 medium onions, sliced

2 4$\frac{1}{2}$-ounce jars whole mushrooms, drained

1 12-ounce jar beef gravy

$\frac{1}{4}$ cup dry red wine or apple juice

1 Trim fat from steak. Cut steak into 4 serving-size pieces. Place onion slices in a 3$\frac{1}{2}$- or 4-quart slow cooker. Arrange mushrooms over onions; add meat. Stir together gravy and wine. Pour over meat.

2 Cover and cook on low-heat setting for 8 to 10 hours or on high-heat setting for 4 to 5 hours.

Nutrition Facts per serving: 220 cal., 4 g total fat (2 g sat. fat), 51 mg chol., 814 mg sodium, 11 g carbo., 3 g fiber, 31 g pro.

A Scotch bonnet pepper, one of the hottest varieties available, adds sizzle to this jerk-marinated steak.

2 g net carb

JERK LONDON BROIL

4	green onions
¼	cup lime juice
1	1-inch piece fresh ginger, sliced
1	Scotch bonnet chile pepper, seeded and finely chopped (optional)*
2	tablespoons cooking oil
3	cloves garlic
2	teaspoons Jamaican jerk seasoning
1	1¼- to 1½-pound beef flank steak

PREP:
10 minutes

MARINATE:
4 hours

GRILL:
17 minutes

MAKES:
6 servings

1 For marinade, in a blender container combine green onions, lime juice, ginger, Scotch bonnet pepper (if desired), oil, garlic, and jerk seasoning; cover and blend until smooth. Score steak on both sides by making shallow cuts at 1-inch intervals in a diamond pattern. Place steak in a glass dish; spread marinade over the steak. Cover dish with plastic wrap and marinate in the refrigerator for 4 to 24 hours. Drain steak, discarding marinade.

2 For a charcoal grill, place steak on the rack of an uncovered grill directly over medium coals. Grill for 17 to 21 minutes or until medium doneness (160°F), turning once halfway through grilling. (For a gas grill, preheat grill. Reduce heat to medium. Place steak on grill rack over heat. Cover and grill as above.)

3 To serve, thinly slice meat diagonally across the grain.

*NOTE: Hot chile peppers contain oils that can burn your eyes, lips, and skin. Wear plastic or rubber gloves while preparing hot peppers and be sure to thoroughly wash your hands and nails in hot, soapy water afterward.

Nutrition Facts per serving: 187 cal., 11 g total fat (3 g sat. fat), 44 mg chol., 117 mg sodium, 2 g carbo., 0 g fiber, 18 g pro.

You've heard of camp coffee—the kind cowboys enjoy around the fire with a good, fresh steak. Somebody put the two together, and the result is this great-tasting piece of beef.

STAY-AWAKE STEAK

PREP:

10 minutes

SOAK:

1 hour

MARINATE:

2 hours

GRILL:

22 minutes

MAKES:

6 servings

1   boneless beef top sirloin steak, cut 1 inch thick (about 1½ pounds)

1   medium onion, chopped (½ cup)

½   cup bottled steak sauce or low-carb barbecue sauce

¼   to ⅓ cup strong brewed espresso or coffee

2   tablespoons Worcestershire sauce

2   cups wood chips (hickory, pecan, or oak)

2   12-ounce cans beer or 3 cups water

1 Trim fat from meat. Place steak in a self-sealing plastic bag set in a shallow dish. For marinade, in a small bowl stir together onion, steak sauce, espresso, and Worcestershire sauce. Pour over steak; seal bag. Marinate in the refrigerator for 2 to 24 hours, turning bag occasionally. Drain steak, discarding marinade.

2 At least 1 hour before grilling, soak wood chips in the beer. Drain before using.

3 For a charcoal grill, arrange medium-hot coals around a drip pan; test for medium heat above drip pan. Add soaked wood chips to coals. Place steaks on grill rack over drip pan; cover grill and cook until desired doneness. Allow 22 to 26 minutes for medium rare (145°F) or 26 to 30 minutes for medium (160°F). (For a gas grill, preheat grill. Reduce heat to medium. Adjust for indirect cooking. Add soaked wood chips according to manufacturer's directions. Cover and heat about 10 minutes or until chips begin to smoke. Place steak on the grill rack over unlit burner. Smoke as directed.)

4 To serve, thinly slice meat across the grain.

Nutrition Facts per serving: 251 cal., 17 g total fat (7 g sat. fat), 74 mg chol., 138 mg sodium, 2 g carbo., 0 g fiber, 22 g pro.

Kosher salt is a coarse salt with no additives. Many cooks prefer it because it has a light, flaky texture and clean taste. Look for it next to the regular salt in your supermarket.

7 g net carb

BEEF WITH PORTOBELLO RELISH

4   beef tenderloin steaks, cut 1 inch thick
     (about 1¼ pounds total)

     Kosher salt

     Cracked black pepper

1   medium yellow onion, cut into ½-inch slices

8   ounces fresh portobello mushrooms, stems removed

4   Roma tomatoes, halved lengthwise

3   tablespoons snipped fresh basil

2   tablespoons minced garlic

2   tablespoons olive oil

1   teaspoon kosher salt

1   teaspoon cracked black pepper

PREP:

15 minutes

GRILL:

15 minutes

MAKES:

4 servings

1 Trim fat from steaks. Season steaks with salt and pepper. For a charcoal grill, place steaks on the rack of an uncovered grill directly over medium coals. Grill until desired doneness, turning once. Allow 11 to 15 minutes for medium rare (145°F) or 14 to 18 minutes for medium doneness (160°F).

2 Meanwhile, for relish, grill onion, mushrooms, and tomatoes directly over medium coals until tender, turning once halfway through grilling. Allow 15 minutes for onion and 10 minutes for mushrooms and tomatoes. (For a gas grill, preheat grill. Reduce heat to medium. Place steaks, then vegetables on grill rack over heat. Cover and grill as above.)

3 Cut onion, mushrooms, and tomato halves into 1-inch pieces. In a medium bowl stir together basil, garlic, olive oil, the 1 teaspoon kosher salt, and the 1 teaspoon cracked black pepper; stir in grilled vegetables. To serve, spoon warm relish over steaks.

Nutrition Facts per serving: 329 cal., 18 g total fat (5 g sat. fat), 87 mg chol., 617 mg sodium, 9 g carbo., 2 g fiber, 33 g pro.

Beef rib roast is company fare, especially when seasoned with a generous dose of black pepper, shallots, basil, and thyme.

PEPPERED RIB ROAST

PREP:

10 minutes

GRILL:

2¹/₄ hours

STAND:

15 minutes

MAKES:

10 to 12 servings

4   teaspoons coarsely ground black pepper

2   tablespoons finely chopped shallots

1   teaspoon coarse salt

1   teaspoon dried basil, crushed

1   teaspoon dried thyme, crushed

1   6-pound beef rib roast

1   tablespoon olive oil

① For rub, in a small bowl stir together pepper, shallots, salt, basil, and thyme; set aside. Trim fat from meat. Brush meat with oil. Sprinkle rub over meat; rub in with your fingers. Insert a meat thermometer into center of meat without touching bone.

② For a charcoal grill, arrange medium coals around a drip pan. Test for medium-low heat above pan. Place roast, bone side down, on grill rack over pan. Cover and grill until meat thermometer registers 135°F for medium rare (2¹/₄ to 2³/₄ hours) or 150°F for medium (2³/₄ to 3¹/₄ hours). (For a gas grill, preheat grill. Reduce heat to medium-low. Adjust for indirect cooking. Grill as above, except place meat in a roasting pan.)

③ Remove meat from grill. Cover with foil; let stand for 15 minutes before carving. (The meat's temperature will rise 10°F during standing.)

Nutrition Facts per serving: 310 cal., 18 g total fat (7 g sat. fat), 100 mg chol., 305 mg sodium, 1 g carbo., 0 g fiber, 34 g pro.

A good long soak in this lime-salsa marinade will make a semitough cut of beef, such as flank steak, tender and terrific.

2 g net carb

FAJITA-STYLE FLANK STEAK

1	1½-pound beef flank steak
¼	cup bottled Italian salad dressing
¼	cup bottled salsa
½	teaspoon finely shredded lime peel
1	tablespoon lime juice
1	tablespoon snipped fresh cilantro or parsley
⅛	teaspoon bottled hot pepper sauce

1 Trim fat from steak. Place steak in a self-sealing plastic bag set in a shallow dish. For marinade, in a small bowl stir together salad dressing, salsa, lime peel, lime juice, cilantro, and hot pepper sauce. Pour over steak; seal bag. Marinate in the refrigerator for 8 to 24 hours, turning the bag occasionally. Drain steak, reserving marinade.

2 Place steak on the unheated rack of a broiler pan. Broil 3 to 4 inches from the heat for 15 to 18 minutes for medium doneness (160°F), turning once and brushing occasionally with marinade up to the last 5 minutes of broiling.

3 Pour any remaining marinade into a small saucepan; bring to boiling. Boil 1 minute. Thinly slice steak across the grain. Serve steak with hot marinade.

Nutrition Facts per serving: 224 cal., 12 g total fat (4 g sat. fat), 45 mg chol., 207 mg sodium, 2 g carbo., 0 g fiber, 25 g pro.

PREP:

15 minutes

MARINATE:

8 hours

BROIL:

15 minutes

MAKES:

6 servings

Yes, it's slow, but long oven-braising rewards the patient cook with a meat that's incredibly tender and full-flavored.

OVEN-BARBECUED BEEF BRISKET

PREP:

15 minutes

BAKE:

3 hours

OVEN:

325°F

MAKES:

10 to 12 servings

1	3- to 3½-pound fresh beef brisket
¾	cup water
1	medium onion, chopped (½ cup)
3	tablespoons Worcestershire sauce
2	tablespoons cider vinegar or white wine vinegar
1	tablespoon chili powder
1	teaspoon instant beef bouillon granules
⅛	teaspoon cayenne pepper
2	cloves garlic, minced
⅔	cup low-carb catsup
1	tablespoon unbleached all-purpose flour

1 Trim fat from meat. Place meat in a 13×9×2-inch baking pan. In a bowl stir together the water, onion, Worcestershire sauce, vinegar, chili powder, bouillon granules, cayenne pepper, and garlic. Pour over meat. Cover with foil.

2 Bake in a 325° oven about 3 hours or until tender, turning once. Remove meat, reserving juices. Thinly slice meat. Place on a serving platter. Keep warm.

3 For sauce, pour juices into a measuring cup; skim fat. If necessary, add enough water to equal ¾ cup. In a saucepan stir together catsup and flour. Stir in reserved juices. Cook and stir over medium heat until thickened and bubbly. Cook and stir for 1 minute more. Serve sauce with meat.

Nutrition Facts per serving: 206 cal., 7 g total fat (2 g sat. fat), 78 mg chol., 386 mg sodium, 4 g carbo., 0 g fiber, 29 g pro.

If it's more convenient to oven-roast the beef, use a shallow roasting pan and roast in a 325°F oven for 30 to 45 minutes.

8 g net carb

BEEF TENDERLOIN WITH CABERNET SAUCE

1	2½-pound beef tenderloin roast
¼	cup olive oil
	Salt
	Black pepper
1	large onion, chopped (1 cup)
2	stalks celery, chopped (1 cup)
2	medium carrots, chopped (1 cup)
4	cloves garlic, thinly sliced
1½	cups Cabernet Sauvignon
1½	cups beef broth
½	cup balsamic vinegar
2	bay leaves
1	tablespoon butter or margarine
½	teaspoon snipped fresh rosemary

PREP:
15 minutes
GRILL:
1 hour
STAND:
15 minutes
MAKES:
8 to 10 servings

1 For a charcoal grill, arrange hot coals around a drip pan. Test for medium-high heat above drip pan. Lightly coat beef with 2 tablespoons of the olive oil and season with salt and pepper. Insert a meat thermometer into the center of the meat. Place meat on grill rack over pan. Cover and grill about 1 hour or until thermometer registers 135°F (medium rare). Cover and let stand 15 minutes before slicing. (The meat's temperature will rise 10°F during standing.) (For a gas grill, preheat grill. Reduce heat to medium. Adjust for indirect cooking. Place meat on grill rack. Grill as above.)

2 Meanwhile, for sauce, heat the remaining 2 tablespoons olive oil in a large saucepan over medium-high heat. Add onion, celery, carrots, and garlic; cook and stir about 10 minutes or until vegetables are brown. Add wine, broth, vinegar, and bay leaves. Simmer, uncovered, for 10 minutes. Strain, reserving liquid. Discard solids. Continue to boil the liquid gently, uncovered, for 25 to 30 minutes or until reduced to ½ cup and slightly thickened. (Watch the sauce closely during the final 5 minutes of cooking, as it will reduce more rapidly.)

3 To serve, stir butter and rosemary into the sauce. Season to taste with salt and pepper. Thinly slice the beef; serve immediately with the sauce.

Nutrition Facts per serving : 335 cal., 17 g total fat (5 g sat. fat), 84 mg chol., 345 mg sodium, 9 g carbo., 1 g fiber, 28 g pro.

Beef short ribs are rubbed with spices and herbs then slow-roasted until the meat is falling-off-the-bone tender. This recipe is not only irresistible, but also practical and easy.

8 g net carb

SIZZLING SOUTHWEST SHORT RIBS

PREP:

10 minutes

BAKE:

2 hours

OVEN:

450°F/350°F

MAKES:

6 servings

2	teaspoons ground cumin
2	teaspoons ground coriander
1	to 2 teaspoons chili powder
1	teaspoon dried thyme, crushed
1	teaspoon dried oregano, crushed
½	teaspoon salt
¼	teaspoon cayenne pepper
6	boneless beef short ribs (1¾ pounds)
1	medium onion, chopped (½ cup)
1½	cups salsa or picante sauce
¼	cup red wine vinegar
2	cloves garlic, minced
¼	cup snipped fresh cilantro (optional)

1 Line a 13×9×2-inch baking pan with foil. For rub, stir together cumin, coriander, chili powder, thyme, oregano, salt, and cayenne pepper. Sprinkle over both sides of ribs; rub in with your fingers. Place ribs in prepared baking pan. Cover with foil; bake in a 450° oven for 1 hour.

2 Carefully pour off fat and juices. Sprinkle ribs with onion. Stir together salsa, vinegar, and garlic. Spoon over ribs. Reduce oven temperature to 350°. Bake, covered, for 1 hour more or until tender. Transfer ribs to serving platter. Spoon sauce from pan over ribs. If desired, sprinkle with cilantro.

Nutrition Facts per serving: 367 cal., 21 g total fat (8 g sat. fat), 112 mg chol., 509 mg sodium, 8 g carbo., 0 g fiber, 39 g pro.

Lemon and garlic shine in a marinade that's just right for tender cubes of beef.

0 g net carb

MEDITERRANEAN BEEF KABOBS

1	1½-pound boneless beef sirloin steak
3	green onions, sliced
¼	cup olive oil
3	tablespoons lemon juice
1½	teaspoons bottled minced garlic
2	teaspoons dried tarragon, crushed
½	teaspoon dried oregano, crushed
¼	teaspoon freshly ground black pepper

PREP:

15 minutes

MARINATE:

4 hours

BROIL:

10 minutes

MAKES:

6 servings

1 Trim fat from meat. Cut meat into 1½-inch cubes. Place meat cubes in a self-sealing plastic bag set in a shallow dish.

2 For marinade, in a small bowl stir together green onions, olive oil, lemon juice, garlic, tarragon, oregano, and pepper. Pour over meat; seal bag. Marinate in the refrigerator for 4 to 24 hours, turning bag occasionally. Drain meat, discarding marinade.

3 Thread meat cubes onto six 12-inch metal skewers, leaving a ¼-inch space between pieces. Place kabobs on the unheated rack of a broiler pan. Broil 4 to 5 inches from the heat for 10 to 12 minutes or until meat is slightly pink in the center, turning occasionally to brown evenly.

Nutrition Facts per serving: 165 cal., 7 g total fat (2 g sat. fat), 69 mg chol., 56 mg sodium, 0 g carbo., 0 g fiber, 24 g pro.

Japanese teriyaki sauce is a natural partner for sweet pineapple. Use the leftover marinade as a sauce for the meat when serving.

7 g net carb

PINEAPPLE-TERIYAKI BEEF

PREP:

15 minutes

MARINATE:

6 hours

BROIL:

18 minutes

MAKES:

6 to 8 servings

1   2-pound boneless beef top round steak, cut 1½ inches thick
1   8-ounce can crushed pineapple (juice pack)
2   tablespoons finely chopped green onion
2   tablespoons reduced-sodium teriyaki sauce
1   teaspoon bottled minced garlic
1   teaspoon grated fresh ginger

1 Trim fat from steak. Place steak in a self-sealing plastic bag set in a shallow dish. Drain pineapple, reserving juice. Cover and refrigerate pineapple for sauce.

2 For marinade, in a small bowl stir together reserved pineapple juice, green onion, teriyaki sauce, garlic, and ginger. Pour marinade over steak; seal bag. Marinate in the refrigerator for 6 to 24 hours, turning bag occasionally. Drain steak, reserving marinade.

3 Place steak on the unheated rack of a broiler pan. Broil 4 to 5 inches from the heat until desired doneness, turning once halfway through broiling. Allow 18 to 21 minutes for medium-rare (145°F) or 22 to 27 minutes for medium doneness (160°F).

4 Meanwhile, for sauce, in a small saucepan combine reserved marinade and pineapple. Bring to boiling; reduce heat. Simmer, uncovered, for 5 minutes. Remove from heat.

5 Cut steak into serving-size pieces. Top with sauce.

Nutrition Facts per serving: 186 cal., 4 g total fat (1 g sat. fat), 62 mg chol., 183 mg sodium, 7 g carbo., 0 g fiber, 29 g pro.

Grilled vegetables are the best accompaniment to a grilled steak. Not only are the flavors complementary, but cooking them all together allows the cook to be part of the fun, not stuck in the kitchen.

8g net carb

CITRUS GRILLED SIRLOIN STEAK

1	teaspoon finely shredded lemon peel
¼	cup lemon juice
2	tablespoons olive oil
3	cloves garlic, minced
1	teaspoon cracked black pepper
¾	teaspoon salt
3	large yellow sweet peppers, quartered
3	medium zucchini, sliced lengthwise into 3 planks
1	1¾-pound boneless beef sirloin steak, cut 1 to 1¼ inches thick

PREP:

25 minutes

GRILL:

15 minutes

MAKES:

6 servings

1 For dressing, in a small bowl stir together lemon peel, lemon juice, oil, garlic, pepper, and salt. In a glass baking dish toss 2 tablespoons of the dressing with sweet peppers and zucchini; set aside. Reserve 2 tablespoons dressing. Brush steak with some of the remaining dressing.

2 For a charcoal grill, place steak on the rack of an uncovered grill directly over medium coals. Grill until desired doneness, turning once and brushing with dressing halfway through grilling. Allow 15 to 20 minutes for medium rare (145°F) or 18 to 26 minutes for medium (160°F).

3 Place vegetables on grill around meat for the last 10 minutes of grilling time. Grill vegetables, turning once. (For a gas grill, preheat grill. Reduce heat to medium. Place steaks, then vegetables on grill rack over heat. Cover and grill as above.)

4 With kitchen shears, cut zucchini into bite-size pieces. In a bowl toss vegetables with reserved 2 tablespoons dressing. Slice steak; serve with vegetables.

Nutrition Facts per serving: 245 cal., 9 g total fat (2 g sat. fat), 80 mg chol., 361 mg sodium, 10 g carbo., 2 g fiber, 30 g pro.

Ground meats need to be cooked to 160°F to be safe to eat. To check the temperature of meat loaf, insert the tip of an instant-read thermometer about ¹/₄ inch into the loaf for 10 seconds.

5 g net carb

CHEESY MEAT LOAF

PREP:

15 minutes

BAKE:

45 minutes

OVEN:

350°F

STAND:

5 minutes

MAKES:

4 servings

1 slightly beaten egg

³/₄ cup soft rye bread crumbs (1 slice)

³/₄ cup shredded provolone or mozzarella cheese (3 ounces)

3 tablespoons beer, milk, or water

2 tablespoons purchased basil pesto

¹/₄ teaspoon ground nutmeg

¹/₄ teaspoon black pepper

1 pound lean ground beef

Sliced provolone or mozzarella cheese (optional)

1 In a large bowl stir together egg, bread crumbs, cheese, beer, pesto, nutmeg, and pepper. Add ground beef; mix well. Form into a loaf; place in an 8×4×3-inch loaf pan.

2 Bake in a 350° oven for 45 to 50 minutes or until meat is done (160°F).

3 Transfer loaf to a platter. If desired, diagonally halve slices of provolone cheese. Place three cheese triangles on top of meat loaf. Let stand for 5 minutes before slicing.

Nutrition Facts per serving: 341 cal., 22 g total fat (9 g sat. fat), 141 mg chol., 338 mg sodium, 6 g carbo., 1 g fiber, 29 g pro.

Your favorite Italian flavors are wrapped up in this cheese-topped meat loaf.

4 g
net
carb

SICILIAN MEAT ROLL

2	beaten eggs
½	cup tomato juice
¾	cup soft bread crumbs (1 slice)
2	tablespoons snipped fresh parsley
1	small clove garlic, minced
½	teaspoon dried oregano, crushed
¼	teaspoon salt
¼	teaspoon black pepper
2	pounds lean ground beef
6	thin slices cooked ham (6 ounces)
1¾	cups shredded mozzarella cheese (7 ounces)

PREP:
30 minutes
BAKE:
80 minutes
OVEN:
350°F
MAKES:
8 to 10 servings

1 In a large bowl, stir together eggs and tomato juice; stir in bread crumbs, parsley, garlic, oregano, salt, and pepper. Add ground beef; mix well.

2 On a piece of foil, lightly pat meat mixture into a 12×10-inch rectangle. Arrange the ham slices on top of meat mixture to within ¾ inch of edges. Sprinkle 1½ cups of the cheese over ham. Starting from a short side, carefully roll up meat mixture, using foil to lift. Seal edge and ends. Place meat roll, seam side down, in a 13×9×2-inch baking pan.

3 Bake in a 350° oven about 1¼ hours or until done (160°F). (Center of meat roll will be pink because of ham.) Sprinkle top of meat roll with remaining ¼ cup cheese. Bake about 5 minutes more or until cheese is melted.

Nutrition Facts per serving: 323 cal., 19 g total fat (8 g sat. fat), 152 mg chol., 604 mg sodium, 4 g carbo., 0 g fiber, 33 g pro.

Off-the-shelf herbs combine with dry bread crumbs to form a savory crust for this roast. The simple cream sauce makes it extra flavorful.

4 g net carb

VEAL ROAST WITH HERB CRUST

PREP:

15 minutes

ROAST:

2¹/₂ hours

OVEN:

325°F

MAKES:

10 to 12 servings

1   3-pound boneless veal leg round roast

¹/₄ cup fine dry bread crumbs

2   tablespoons water

1   tablespoon Dijon-style mustard

1   tablespoon lemon juice

1   teaspoon dried basil, crushed

1   teaspoon dried thyme, crushed

¹/₂ teaspoon coarsely ground black pepper

1   cup beef broth

2   tablespoons unbleached all-purpose flour

¹/₄ cup half-and-half or light cream

1 Place meat on a rack in a shallow roasting pan. In a small bowl stir together bread crumbs, the water, mustard, lemon juice, basil, thyme, and pepper. Spread mixture over surface of meat.

2 Insert a meat thermometer into the center of the meat. Roast in a 325° oven for 2¹/₂ to 3 hours or until thermometer registers 155°F. (If crust becomes too dry, cover meat loosely with foil after 1¹/₂ to 2 hours.) Cover with foil; let stand 15 minutes before carving. (The meat's temperature will rise 5°F during standing.)

3 For sauce, skim fat from pan drippings. In a small saucepan stir beef broth into flour; add meat drippings. Cook and stir until thickened and bubbly. Cook and stir for 1 minute more. Stir in half-and-half; heat through but do not boil. Pass the sauce with meat.

Nutrition Facts per serving: 200 cal., 6 g total fat (2 g sat. fat), 111 mg chol., 214 mg sodium, 4 g carbo., 0 g fiber, 31 g pro.

Short on time tonight? Briefly marinate tender veal chops in a white wine-sage mixture and toss them on the grill. Short on time tomorrow? Marinate the meat overnight.

VEAL WITH PESTO-STUFFED MUSHROOMS

4	veal loin chops, cut ¾ inch thick (about 1¼ pounds)
¼	cup dry white wine
3	large cloves garlic, minced
1	tablespoon snipped fresh sage or thyme
1	tablespoon white wine Worcestershire sauce
1	tablespoon olive oil
	Freshly ground black pepper
8	large fresh mushrooms (2 to 2½ inches in diameter)
2	to 3 tablespoons purchased basil pesto

PREP:
10 minutes

MARINATE:
15 minutes

GRILL:
12 minutes

MAKES:
4 servings

1 Place chops in a self-sealing plastic bag set in a shallow dish. For marinade, in a small bowl stir together wine, garlic, sage, Worcestershire sauce, and oil. Pour marinade over chops; seal bag. Marinate at room temperature for 15 minutes. (Or marinate in refrigerator for up to 24 hours, turning bag occasionally.) Drain chops, reserving marinade.

2 Sprinkle chops with pepper. For a charcoal grill, place chops on the rack of an uncovered grill directly over medium heat. Grill for 12 to 15 minutes for medium doneness (160°F), turning and brushing with marinade halfway through cooking.

3 Meanwhile, carefully remove stems from mushrooms; chop stems for another use or discard. Brush mushroom caps with reserved marinade; place mushrooms stem sides down on grill rack. Grill for 4 minutes. Turn stem sides up; spoon some pesto into each. Grill about 4 minutes more or until heated through. (For a gas grill, preheat grill. Reduce heat to medium. Place chops, then mushrooms on grill rack over heat. Cover and grill as above.)

4 Serve mushrooms with chops.

Nutrition Facts per serving: 285 cal., 16 g total fat (2 g sat. fat), 100 mg chol., 157 mg sodium, 4 g carbo., 1 g fiber, 28 g pro.

3 g net carb

Pick up your special order from the butcher, then everything else about this elegant roast is surprisingly simple.

ROSEMARY-MUSTARD LAMB ROAST

PREP:

15 minutes

ROAST:

45 minutes

OVEN:

325°F

STAND:

15 minutes

MAKES:

4 servings

2 1- to 1½-pound lamb rib roasts (6 to 8 ribs each)

¼ cup coarse-grain brown mustard

1 tablespoon snipped fresh rosemary

1 to 2 cloves garlic, minced

½ teaspoon black pepper

¾ cup soft bread crumbs (1 slice)

¼ cup finely chopped pecans

1 Trim fat from meat. In a small bowl stir together mustard, rosemary, garlic, and pepper; brush onto meat. Toss together bread crumbs and nuts. Gently press the crumb mixture onto the roasts on all sides.

2 Place roasts on a rack in a shallow roasting pan. Insert a meat thermometer into the center of the meat without touching bone. Roast in a 325° oven until desired doneness. Allow 45 minutes to 1 hour for medium-rare (140°F) or 1 to 1½ hours for medium (155°F).

3 Cover with foil; let stand for 15 minutes before carving. (The meat's temperature will rise 5°F during standing.)

Nutrition Facts per serving: 269 cal., 16 g total fat (4 g sat. fat), 74 mg chol., 311 mg sodium, 7 g carbo., 1 g fiber, 25 g pro.

Sour cream, Dijon mustard, garlic, and thyme create a wonderful crust that has a twofold purpose—to provide flavor and to seal in the juices of the succulent lamb.

2g net carb

DIJON-CRUSTED LAMB RIB ROAST

1	2½-pound lamb rib roast (8 ribs)
3	tablespoons Dijon-style mustard
1	tablespoon olive oil
2	cloves garlic, minced
1	teaspoon snipped fresh thyme or ½ teaspoon dried thyme, crushed
¼	teaspoon salt
¼	teaspoon black pepper
¼	cup dairy sour cream

PREP:
10 minutes
GRILL:
50 minutes
STAND:
15 minutes
MAKES:
4 servings

1 Trim fat from meat. In a bowl stir together mustard, oil, garlic, thyme, salt, and pepper. Set aside 2 tablespoons of the mustard mixture; cover and chill. Brush meat with remaining mustard mixture. Insert a meat thermometer into meat without touching bone.

2 For a charcoal grill, arrange medium-hot coals around a drip pan. Test for medium heat above pan. Place meat bone side down on grill rack over drip pan. Cover and grill until desired doneness. Allow 50 to 60 minutes for medium rare (140°F) or 1 to 1½ hours for medium doneness (155°F). (For a gas grill, preheat grill. Reduce heat to medium. Adjust for indirect cooking. Grill as above, except place meat bone side down in a roasting pan.)

3 Remove meat from grill. Cover with foil; let stand for 15 minutes before carving. (The meat's temperature will rise 5°F during standing.) Meanwhile, for sauce, in a bowl stir together sour cream and reserved mustard mixture. To serve, cut meat into four 2-rib portions. Pass sauce with meat.

Nutrition Facts per serving: 404 cal., 26 g total fat (9 g sat. fat), 126 mg chol., 539 mg sodium, 2 g carbo., 0 g fiber, 38 g pro.

The combination of coriander, cumin, and pepper is common in Moroccan meat dishes, especially mixed as it is here with garlic and lemon.

MOROCCAN LAMB ROAST

PREP:

15 minutes

MARINATE:

2 hours

ROAST:

1³/₄ hours

OVEN:

350°F

STAND:

15 minutes

MAKES:

10 servings

1   5-pound bone-in leg of lamb

4   to 8 cloves garlic, peeled and cut into slivers

2   tablespoons coriander seed, crushed

2   tablespoons finely shredded lemon peel

1   tablespoon olive oil

1   teaspoon cumin seed, crushed

¹/₂   teaspoon salt

¹/₂   teaspoon whole black peppercorns, crushed

1 Trim excess fat from meat. Cut several ¹/₂-inch-wide slits randomly into top and sides of roast. Insert garlic slivers into slits. In a small bowl stir together coriander seed, lemon peel, olive oil, cumin seed, salt, and pepper. Sprinkle over all sides of meat; rub in with your fingers. Cover and chill for 2 to 24 hours.

2 Insert a meat thermometer in the thickest portion of the meat without touching bone. Place lamb on a rack in a shallow roasting pan. Roast lamb in a 350° oven until desired doneness. Allow 1³/₄ to 2¹/₄ hours for medium-rare (140°F) or 2¹/₄ to 2³/₄ hours for medium doneness (155°F).

3 Remove meat from oven. Cover with foil and let stand for 15 minutes. (The meat's temperature will rise about 5°F during standing.)

Nutrition Facts per serving: 235 cal., 10 g total fat (3 g sat. fat), 101 mg chol., 185 mg sodium, 1 g carbo., 0 g fiber, 32 g pro.

Fresh mint in this marinade is a welcome change from the traditional mint jelly.

2 g net carb

LAMB CHOPS WITH MINT MARINADE

8	lamb loin chops, cut 1 inch thick (about 2 pounds)
2	tablespoons lemon juice
2	tablespoons olive oil
3	cloves garlic, minced
¼	cup snipped fresh mint
¼	teaspoon black pepper
¼	teaspoon salt

PREP:
10 minutes

MARINATE:
30 minutes

GRILL:
12 minutes

MAKES:
4 servings

1 Trim fat from chops. Place chops in a self-sealing plastic bag set in a shallow dish. For marinade, stir together lemon juice, oil, garlic, 3 tablespoons of the mint, and the pepper. Pour marinade over chops; seal bag. Turn bag to coat chops. Marinate in the refrigerator for 30 minutes to 24 hours. Drain chops, discarding marinade.

2 Sprinkle chops with the salt. For a charcoal grill, grill chops on the rack of an uncovered grill directly over medium coals until desired doneness, turning once. Allow 12 to 14 minutes for medium rare (145°F) or 15 to 17 minutes for medium doneness (160°F). (For a gas grill, preheat grill. Reduce heat to medium. Place chops on grill rack over heat. Cover and grill as above.) To serve, sprinkle with remaining 1 tablespoon mint.

Nutrition Facts per serving: 310 cal., 18 g total fat (5 g sat. fat), 107 mg chol., 229 mg sodium, 2 g carbo., 0 g fiber, 34 g pro.

PORK

Whether grilled chops, perfectly done tenderloins, slow-cooked ribs, or robustly flavored patties, lean, juicy pork is a palate pleaser. Adding subtle herbs, bold sauces, easy marinades, or spicy rubs can change pork cuts from ordinary main dishes into center-of-the-plate sensations. Peruse the following recipes and find a bevy of delightful, low-carb entrées.

6

This pair of chops is ideal for dinner when the kids are away; double the recipe and you'll be ready to impress the hungriest quartet.

6 g net carb

WEDNESDAY NIGHT PORK CHOPS

PREP:
10 minutes
COOK:
23 minutes
MAKES:
2 servings

2 pork loin or rib chops, cut 1¼ to 1½ inches thick (about 1½ pounds total)

¼ teaspoon coarsely ground black pepper

⅛ teaspoon salt

1 tablespoon cooking oil

1 cup baby summer squash, such as green or yellow pattypan and zucchini

¾ cup half-and-half or light cream

½ teaspoon coriander seed, coarsely crushed

1 Season chops with pepper and salt. In a large skillet cook chops in hot oil over medium heat for 18 to 20 minutes or until done (160°F) and juices run clear, turning once. If necessary, cut larger squash pieces into slices or halves. Add squash to skillet during the last 5 minutes of cooking. Remove chops and squash; keep warm.

2 Discard drippings from skillet. Add cream and coriander to skillet, stirring to scrape up brown bits. Bring to boiling; reduce heat. Simmer, uncovered, for 5 to 7 minutes or until sauce is slightly thickened and reduced to about ¼ cup. Spoon sauce over chops.

Nutrition Facts per serving: 758 cal., 44 g total fat (17 g sat. fat), 254 mg chol., 388 mg sodium, 8 g carbo., 2 g fiber, 76 g pro.

In Jamaica, jerk, seasoned with a blend of herbs and spices, is smoked over the wood of the allspice tree. This method skips the smoking but offers the same great taste that made jerk a favorite in the States.

 3 g net carb

JERK PORK

6	boneless pork loin chops, cut ¾ inch thick
4	medium green onions, cut up
2	tablespoons cooking oil
1	tablespoon molasses
1	tablespoon rum
1	tablespoon lime juice
1	fresh jalapeño pepper, seeded and cut up*
1	2-inch piece fresh ginger, cut up
2	large cloves garlic, cut up
¾	teaspoon ground allspice
½	teaspoon dried thyme, crushed
¼	teaspoon salt

PREP:
10 minutes

MARINATE:
2 hours

GRILL:
20 minutes

MAKES:
6 servings

1 Trim fat from chops. Place chops in a self-sealing plastic bag set in a shallow dish. For marinade, in a blender container or food processor bowl combine green onions, oil, molasses, rum, lime juice, jalapeño pepper, ginger, garlic, allspice, thyme, and salt. Cover and blend or process until nearly smooth. Pour over chops; seal bag. Marinate in the refrigerator for 2 to 24 hours, turning bag occasionally. Drain chops, discarding marinade.

2 For a charcoal grill, place chops on the rack of an uncovered grill directly over medium heat. Grill for 20 to 24 minutes or until done (160°F) and juices run clear, turning once halfway through grilling. (For a gas grill, preheat grill. Reduce heat to medium. Place chops on grill rack over heat. Cover and grill as above.)

***NOTE:** Hot peppers contain oils that can burn your eyes, lips, and skin. Wear plastic or rubber gloves while preparing hot peppers and be sure to thoroughly wash your hands in hot, soapy water afterward.

Nutrition Facts per serving: 174 cal., 8 g total fat (2 g sat. fat), 55 mg chol., 90 mg sodium, 3 g carbo., 0 g fiber, 20 g pro.

Satay, an Indonesian snack food, enjoys main-course treatment in these tender pork skewers.

7 g net carb

THAI PORK SATAY

PREP:

15 minutes

MARINATE:

2 hours

GRILL:

8 minutes

MAKES:

6 servings

1½ pounds pork tenderloin or boneless pork loin roast

2 tablespoons fish sauce

2 tablespoons lime juice

2 tablespoons finely chopped lemongrass or 1 teaspoon finely shredded lemon peel

1 tablespoon cooking oil

1 large clove garlic, minced

1 recipe Satay Sauce (see below)

Chinese (napa) cabbage leaves

1 Trim fat from meat. Cut meat across the grain into ¼-inch-thick slices. If using loin roast, cut slices to make 3×1-inch strips. Place meat in a self-sealing plastic bag set in a shallow dish. For marinade, in a small bowl stir together fish sauce, lime juice, lemongrass, oil, and garlic. Pour over meat; seal bag. Marinate in the refrigerator for 2 hours, turning bag occasionally.

2 Meanwhile, prepare Satay Sauce. Cover and chill until ready to serve. Soak twelve 8-inch bamboo skewers in warm water for 1 to 2 hours. Drain bamboo skewers. Drain meat, discarding marinade. Thread meat onto skewers accordion-style, leaving a ¼-inch space between pieces.

3 For a charcoal grill, place kabobs on the rack of an uncovered grill directly over medium coals. Grill for 8 to 10 minutes or until juices run clear, turning once halfway through grilling. (For a gas grill, preheat grill. Reduce heat to medium. Place kabobs on the grill rack. Cover and grill as above.)

4 Serve kabobs on cabbage leaves with Satay Sauce.

SATAY SAUCE: In a food processor bowl or blender container combine ¾ cup purchased unsweetened coconut milk; ⅓ cup natural peanut butter; 2 tablespoons no-calorie, heat-stable granular sugar substitute; 2 tablespoons lime juice; 2 tablespoons grated fresh ginger; 1 tablespoon fish sauce; and ½ teaspoon crushed red pepper or ¼ teaspoon cayenne pepper. Cover and process or blend until smooth; transfer to a small bowl.

Nutrition Facts per serving: 333 cal., 19 g total fat (9 g sat. fat), 66 mg chol., 813 mg sodium, 9 g carbo., 2 g fiber, 32 g pro.

Just three ingredients make a fast sauce for juicy broiled pork chops.
From start-to-finish, this appealing entrée takes just 15 minutes.

PORK WITH ORANGE-DIJON SAUCE

4 g net carb

<table>
<tr><td>6</td><td>boneless pork sirloin chops, cut ½ inch thick (about 2 pounds)</td></tr>
<tr><td></td><td>Salt</td></tr>
<tr><td></td><td>Black pepper</td></tr>
<tr><td>¼</td><td>cup sugar-free orange marmalade or sugar-free apricot preserves</td></tr>
<tr><td>2</td><td>tablespoons Dijon-style mustard</td></tr>
<tr><td>½</td><td>teaspoon dried thyme, crushed</td></tr>
</table>

PREP:
10 minutes

BROIL:
5 minutes

MAKES:
6 servings

1 Trim fat from meat. Sprinkle both sides of chops lightly with salt and pepper. In a small bowl stir together orange marmalade, mustard, and thyme; set aside.

2 Place chops on the unheated rack of a broiler pan. Broil 3 to 4 inches from the heat for 5 to 7 minutes or until done (160°F) and juices run clear, turning once. To serve, spoon sauce over chops.

Nutrition Facts per serving: 183 cal., 5 g total fat (2 g sat. fat), 84 mg chol., 187 mg sodium, 4 g carbo., 0 g fiber, 29 g pro.

Ground coriander tastes like a blend of lemon and sage. Don't confuse it with the leaves of the coriander plant, also known as cilantro. The flavor of the latter is different, and the two are not interchangeable.

0 g net carb

SHREDDED SAVORY PORK

PREP:

15 minutes

COOK:

2¹/₂ hours

MAKES:

8 servings

1 2-pound boneless pork blade roast
   Water
2 large onions, quartered
3 fresh jalapeño peppers, cut up*
8 cloves garlic, minced
2 teaspoons ground coriander
2 teaspoons ground cumin
2 teaspoons dried oregano, crushed
¹/₂ teaspoon salt
¹/₂ teaspoon black pepper

1 Trim fat from meat. Place roast in a large saucepan or pot; add enough water to nearly cover. Stir in onions, jalapeño peppers, garlic, coriander, cumin, oregano, salt, and black pepper. Bring to boiling; reduce heat. Simmer, covered, for 2¹/₂ to 3 hours or until very tender.

2 Remove meat from liquid with a slotted spoon; discard cooking liquid. When cool enough to handle, shred the meat, pulling through it with 2 forks in opposite directions. Use meat to fill tacos or burritos or in taco salad.

*NOTE: Hot peppers contain oils that can burn your eyes, lips, and skin. Wear plastic or rubber gloves while preparing hot peppers and be sure to thoroughly wash your hands in hot, soapy water afterward.

Nutrition Facts per serving: 188 cal., 12 g total fat (4 g sat. fat), 74 mg chol., 192 mg sodium, 0 g carbo., 0 g fiber, 20 g pro.

This elegant-looking dish is far easier to prepare than it looks. The stuffing makes a swirl of color in each slice and provides a sweet, nutty counterpoint to the tender pork.

PORK WITH NUTTY PEAR STUFFING

½   cup chopped pear

¼   cup chopped hazelnuts (filberts) or almonds, toasted

¼   cup finely shredded carrot

¼   cup soft bread crumbs

2   tablespoons finely chopped onion

1   teaspoon grated fresh ginger

¼   teaspoon salt

¼   teaspoon black pepper

1   12-ounce pork tenderloin

1   teaspoon cooking oil

2   tablespoons sugar-free orange marmalade

PREP:

20 minutes

ROAST:

35 minutes

OVEN:

425°F

MAKES:

4 servings

1 For stuffing, in a small bowl stir together pear, nuts, carrot, bread crumbs, onion, ginger, salt, and black pepper; set aside.

2 Trim any fat from meat. Butterfly meat by making a lengthwise slit down the center to within ½ inch of the underside. Open flat; pound with the flat side of a meat mallet to about ¼-inch thickness.

3 Spread stuffing over meat. Fold in ends. Starting from a long side, roll up meat. Secure with 100-percent-cotton string or wooden toothpicks. Place meat roll on a rack in a shallow roasting pan. Brush lightly with oil. Insert a meat thermometer into center of meat.

4 Roast in a 425° oven for 30 to 40 minutes or until meat thermometer registers 155°F. Brush orange marmalade over top of meat. Roast about 5 minutes more or until meat thermometer registers 160°F.

Nutrition Facts per serving: 198 cal., 9 g total fat (1 g sat. fat), 55 mg chol., 193 mg sodium, 10 g carbo., 2 g fiber, 20 g pro.

Marinating these peppery chops the night before you plan to serve them makes quick work of a great dinner.

1 g net carb

PEPPERY PORK CHOPS

PREP:

15 minutes

MARINATE:

6 hours

GRILL:

11 minutes

MAKES:

4 servings

4	center-cut loin pork chops, cut 1 inch thick
¼	cup dry sherry
2	tablespoons soy sauce
2	tablespoons cooking oil
2	tablespoons grated fresh ginger
1	tablespoon no-calorie, heat-stable granular sugar substitute (Splenda)
1	tablespoon rice vinegar or lemon juice
1	large clove garlic, minced
¾	teaspoon coarsely ground black pepper

1 Trim fat from chops. Place chops in a self-sealing plastic bag set in a shallow dish. For marinade, in a small bowl stir together sherry, soy sauce, oil, ginger, sugar substitute, rice vinegar, garlic, and pepper. Pour over chops; seal bag. Marinate in the refrigerator for 6 to 24 hours, turning bag occasionally. Drain pork chops, discarding marinade.

2 For a charcoal grill, place chops on the rack of an uncovered grill directly over medium coals. Grill for 11 to 14 minutes or until done (160°F) and juices run clear, turning once halfway through grilling. (For a gas grill, preheat grill. Reduce heat to medium. Place chops on grill rack. Cover and grill as above.)

Nutrition Facts per serving: 269 cal., 11 g total fat (3 g sat. fat), 92 mg chol., 184 mg sodium, 1 g carbo., 0 g fiber, 38 g pro.

While the pork loin grills, add a couple of jalapeños to the rack. Chopped and stirred into gravy, their smoky heat gives the sauce real spunk.

PORK LOIN WITH JALAPEÑO GRAVY

8 g
net
carb

PREP:
15 minutes
GRILL:
1 hour
STAND:
15 minutes
MAKES:
4 servings

1   2- to 2½-pound pork boneless top loin roast (single loin)

1   teaspoon garlic powder

1   teaspoon paprika

½   teaspoon salt

½   teaspoon black pepper

2   jalapeño peppers, halved, seeded, and stemmed*

    Cooking oil

2   tablespoons unbleached all-purpose flour

1⅔   cups half-and-half or milk

① Trim fat from meat. In a bowl stir together garlic powder, paprika, salt, and black pepper. Sprinkle over all sides of meat; rub in with your fingers. Insert a meat thermometer into center of meat.

② For a charcoal grill, arrange medium-hot coals around outside edge of grill. Test for medium heat above center of grill. Place meat on rack in a roasting pan; place pan in center of grill. Cover and grill for 1 to 1½ hours or until meat thermometer registers 155°F. Remove meat from grill. Reserve drippings in roasting pan. Cover meat and let stand 15 minutes before slicing. (The meat's temperature will rise 5°F during standing.)

③ Meanwhile, lightly brush jalapeño peppers with oil. Add peppers to grill skin side down (lay peppers perpendicular to wires on the grill rack so they won't fall into the coals). Grill about 5 minutes or until soft and slightly charred. Cool slightly; finely chop. (For a gas grill, preheat grill. Reduce heat to medium. Adjust for indirect cooking. Place meat in roasting pan on grill. Grill pork and peppers as above.)

④ For gravy, pour 2 tablespoons reserved drippings into a saucepan (add oil, if necessary, to make 2 tablespoons); add flour. Stir until smooth. Add half-and-half. Cook and stir until bubbly; add peppers. Cook and stir for 1 minute more. Serve with meat.

*NOTE: Hot peppers contain oils that can burn your eyes, lips, and skin. Wear plastic or rubber gloves while preparing hot peppers and be sure to thoroughly wash your hands and nails in hot, soapy water afterward.

Nutrition Facts per serving: 431 cal., 28 g total fat (12 g sat. fat), 139 mg chol., 386 mg sodium, 8 g carbo., 0 g fiber, 36 g pro.

This fiery tenderloin takes its inspiration from the high desert cooking of the Southwest.

5 g net carb

SMOKY CHIPOTLE TENDERLOIN

PREP:

15 minutes

MARINATE:

1 hour

GRILL:

40 minutes

STAND:

15 minutes

MAKES:

6 to 8 servings

6	cloves garlic, minced
1	teaspoon ground cumin
1	teaspoon dried oregano, crushed
¼	teaspoon ground cinnamon
1	tablespoon cooking oil
1	8-ounce can tomato sauce
½	cup water
¼	cup cider vinegar
2	teaspoons no-calorie, heat-stable granular sugar substitute
½	teaspoon salt
2	12- to 16-ounce pork tenderloins
3	to 5 canned chipotle peppers in adobo sauce

1 For marinade, in a medium skillet cook garlic, cumin, oregano, and cinnamon in hot oil for 1 minute. Stir in tomato sauce, the water, vinegar, sugar substitute, and salt. Bring to boiling. Remove skillet from heat; cool mixture.

2 Meanwhile, trim fat from meat. Place meat in a self-sealing plastic bag set aside in a shallow dish. Set aside. In a food processor bowl or blender container combine the tomato mixture and chipotle peppers. Cover and process or blend until smooth. Pour over meat in bag; seal bag. Marinate in the refrigerator 1 to 4 hours, turning bag occasionally. Drain, reserving marinade.

3 For a charcoal grill, arrange medium-hot coals around a drip pan. Test for medium heat above the pan. Place meat on grill rack over drip pan. Insert a meat thermometer into thickest portion of one of the tenderloins. Cover and grill for 40 to 50 minutes or until thermometer registers 155°F, brushing occasionally with marinade during the first 20 minutes of grilling. (For a gas grill, preheat grill. Reduce heat to medium. Adjust for indirect cooking. Grill as above, except place meat on a rack in a roasting pan.)

4 Remove meat from grill. Cover with foil and let stand for 15 minutes before slicing. (The meat's temperature will rise 5°F during standing.) To serve, slice meat diagonally across the grain.

Nutrition Facts per serving: 181 cal., 6 g total fat (2 g sat. fat), 73 mg chol., 499 mg sodium, 6 g carbo., 1 g fiber, 24 g pro.

Demi-glace (DEHM-ee glahs) is a thick, meat-flavored gel that is a wonderful foundation for soups and sauces. To cut down on preparation, you can buy prepared demi-glace at a gourmet shop. To use prepared demi-glace, reconstitute it with water, using the proportions on the package.

4 g net carb

PORK LOIN WITH SHIITAKE DEMI-GLACE

1	3- to 5-pound pork loin center rib roast, backbone loosened
2	teaspoons coarsely ground black pepper
1	teaspoon dried thyme, crushed
1	cup chopped leeks (white part only)
1	cup thinly sliced shiitake mushrooms (stems removed)
1	tablespoon olive oil
1	cup reconstituted prepared demi-glace
1	tablespoon rice vinegar
1	tablespoon soy sauce
$\frac{1}{2}$	teaspoon ground ginger
$\frac{1}{2}$	teaspoon dry mustard

PREP:
15 minutes
ROAST:
1$\frac{1}{4}$ hours
OVEN:
325°F
STAND:
15 minutes
MAKES:
8 servings

1 Trim fat from meat. For rub, stir together pepper and thyme. Sprinkle over roast; rub into meat with your fingers. Place roast rib side down in a shallow roasting pan. Insert a meat thermometer into the center of the roast without touching bone. Roast in a 325° oven for 1$\frac{1}{4}$ to 2 hours or until thermometer registers 155°F. Transfer meat to a serving platter. Cover with foil; let stand for 15 minutes. (The meat's temperature will rise 5°F during standing.)

2 Meanwhile, for sauce, in a medium saucepan cook leeks and mushrooms in hot oil until tender. Stir in demi-glace, vinegar, soy sauce, ginger, and mustard; heat through. Slice roast between ribs; serve immediately with sauce.

Nutrition Facts per serving: 382 cal., 23 g total fat (7 g sat. fat), 112 mg chol., 338 mg sodium, 4 g carbo., 0 g fiber, 37 g pro.

There's a surprise inside the pocket of these quick-cooking boneless pork chops—a mouthwatering mushroom stuffing. Instead of white button mushrooms, try using crimini mushrooms for even more mushroom flavor.

PORK CHOPS WITH MUSHROOM STUFFING

PREP:

15 minutes

GRILL:

20 minutes

MAKES:

4 servings

2   tablespoons thinly sliced green onions

2   teaspoons olive oil

1   8-ounce package fresh mushrooms, coarsely chopped

2   teaspoons snipped fresh rosemary or fresh oregano

⅛   teaspoon salt

⅛   teaspoon black pepper

4   boneless pork loin chops, cut 1 inch thick

2   teaspoons Worcestershire sauce

     Salt

     Black pepper

1 For stuffing, in a large skillet cook green onions in hot oil over medium heat for 1 minute. Stir in mushrooms, rosemary, the ⅛ teaspoon salt, and the ⅛ teaspoon pepper. Cook and stir for 2 to 3 minutes more or until mushrooms are tender. Remove from heat.

2 Trim fat from chops. Make a pocket in each chop by cutting from fat side almost to, but not through, the opposite side. Spoon stuffing into pockets in chops. If necessary, secure with wooden toothpicks. Brush chops with Worcestershire sauce. Season chops lightly with additional salt and pepper.

3 For a charcoal grill, place chops on the rack of an uncovered grill directly over medium coals. Grill about 20 minutes or until done (160°F) and juices run clear, turning once. (For a gas grill, preheat grill. Reduce heat to medium. Place chops on grill rack. Cover and grill as above.) To serve, remove wooden toothpicks.

Nutrition Facts per serving: 241 cal., 14 g total fat (4 g sat. fat), 77 mg chol., 218 mg sodium, 4 g carbo., 1 g fiber, 25 g pro.

Fruit and pork have been a dynamic duet for centuries because of the way the fruit enhances the taste of the pork.

PEACHY PORK TENDERLOIN

1   12-ounce pork tenderloin

⅓   cup peach nectar

3   tablespoons reduced-sodium teriyaki sauce

2   tablespoons snipped fresh rosemary

1   tablespoon olive oil

1 Trim fat from pork. Place pork in a self-sealing plastic bag set in a shallow dish. For marinade, in a small bowl stir together peach nectar, teriyaki sauce, rosemary, and oil. Pour over pork; seal bag. Marinate in refrigerator for 4 to 24 hours, turning bag occasionally. Drain pork, discarding marinade.

2 For a charcoal grill, arrange medium-hot coals around a drip pan. Test for medium heat above the pan. Place tenderloin on grill rack over pan. Insert a meat thermometer into thickest portion of the tenderloin. Cover and grill for 40 to 50 minutes or until thermometer registers 155°F. (For a gas grill, preheat grill. Reduce heat to medium. Adjust for indirect cooking. Place tenderloin on rack. Grill as above.)

3 Remove meat from grill. Cover with foil and let stand for 15 minutes before slicing. (The meat's temperature will rise 5°F during standing.)

Nutrition Facts per serving: 162 cal., 7 g total fat (2 g sat. fat), 60 mg chol., 285 mg sodium, 6 g carbo., 0 g fiber, 19 g pro.

PREP:

10 minutes

MARINATE:

4 hours

GRILL:

40 minutes

STAND:

15 minutes

MAKES:

4 servings

This express-lane dinner gives you time to slow down as soon as you walk in the door. Simply mix up the marinade and pour it over the pork. Let it sit in the refrigerator while you unwind. Grill about 40 minutes and dinner's done.

GRILLED MUSTARD-GLAZED PORK

PREP:

10 minutes

MARINATE:

30 minutes

GRILL:

40 minutes

STAND:

15 minutes

MAKES:

6 servings

2	12- to 14-ounce pork tenderloins
½	cup apple juice
¼	cup cider vinegar
2	large shallots, minced
¼	cup coarse-grain brown mustard
2	tablespoons olive oil
1½	teaspoons soy sauce
	Dash black pepper

1 Trim fat from meat. Place tenderloins in a self-sealing plastic bag set in a shallow dish. For marinade, stir together apple juice, vinegar, shallots, mustard, oil, soy sauce, and pepper. Pour over meat; seal bag. Marinate in refrigerator for 30 minutes, turning bag occasionally. Drain tenderloins, reserving marinade.

2 For a charcoal grill, arrange medium-hot coals around a drip pan. Test for medium heat above pan. Insert a meat thermometer into thickest portion of one of the tenderloins. Cover and grill for 40 to 50 minutes or until meat thermometer registers 155°F. (For a gas grill, preheat grill. Reduce heat to medium. Adjust for indirect cooking. Place tenderloins on grill rack. Grill as above.)

3 Remove meat from grill. Cover with foil and let stand for 15 minutes before slicing. (The meat's temperature will rise 5°F during standing.)

4 Meanwhile, for sauce, pour reserved marinade into a medium saucepan. Bring to boiling; reduce heat. Simmer, uncovered, about 8 minutes or until reduced to ⅔ cup. Slice tenderloins across the grain. Serve with the sauce.

Nutrition Facts per serving: 149 cal., 5 g total fat (1 g sat. fat), 73 mg chol., 100 mg sodium, 1 g carbo., 0 g fiber, 24 g pro.

Mexican in origin, dark red adobo sauce is made with hot spices, herbs, and vinegar. It's especially tasty as a seasoning for pork.

1 g net carb

ADOBO PORK CHOPS

6	boneless pork loin chops, cut ¾ inch thick
2	tablespoons no-calorie, heat-stable granular sugar substitute (Splenda)
2	tablespoons orange juice
2	tablespoons olive oil
1	tablespoon red wine vinegar or cider vinegar
2	teaspoons hot chili powder
1	teaspoon ground cumin
1	teaspoon dried oregano, crushed
½	teaspoon salt
¼	teaspoon cayenne pepper (optional)
¼	teaspoon ground cinnamon
3	cloves garlic, minced
2	tablespoons snipped fresh cilantro

PREP:
15 minutes

MARINATE:
2 hours

GRILL:
12 minutes

MAKES:
6 servings

1 Trim fat from chops. Place chops in a self-sealing plastic bag set in a shallow dish. For marinade, in a small bowl stir together sugar substitute, orange juice, oil, vinegar, chili powder, cumin, oregano, salt, cayenne pepper (if desired), cinnamon, garlic, and cilantro. Pour over chops; seal bag. Marinate in the refrigerator for 2 to 24 hours, turning bag occasionally. Drain chops, discarding marinade.

2 For a charcoal grill, place chops on the rack of an uncovered grill directly over medium coals. Grill for 12 to 15 minutes or until done (160°F) and juices run clear, turning once halfway through grilling. (For a gas grill, preheat grill. Reduce heat to medium. Place chops on grill rack over heat. Cover and grill as above.)

Nutrition Facts per serving: 231 cal., 10 g total fat (3 g sat. fat), 77 mg chol., 160 mg sodium, 1 g carbo., 0 g fiber, 32 g pro.

Thick, bone-in pork chops are sold in the Midwest as Iowa chops. Elsewhere, look for a boneless version known as America's cut.

SMOKED IOWA PORK CHOPS

PREP:

10 minutes

SOAK:

1 hour

GRILL:

35 minutes

MAKES:

4 servings

2   cups oak or pecan wood chips

4   pork loin or rib chops, cut 1¼ inches thick
    (about 3 pounds total)

1   tablespoon dry mustard

1½   teaspoons salt

1½   teaspoons paprika

1½   teaspoons dried basil, crushed

1   to 1½ teaspoons freshly ground black pepper

½   teaspoon garlic powder

1 At least 1 hour before grilling, soak wood chips in enough water to cover.

2 Trim fat from chops. For rub, in a small bowl stir together dry mustard, salt, paprika, basil, pepper, and garlic powder. Sprinkle evenly over chops; rub in with your fingers.

3 Drain wood chips. For a charcoal grill, arrange medium-hot coals around a drip pan. Test for medium heat above the pan. Sprinkle drained wood chips over coals. Place chops on grill rack over drip pan. Cover and grill for 35 to 40 minutes or until done (160°F) and meat juices run clear. (For a gas grill, preheat grill. Reduce heat to medium. Adjust for indirect cooking. Add drained wood chips according to manufacturer's directions. Place chops on grill rack. Grill as above.)

Nutrition Facts per serving: 356 cal., 14 g total fat (5 g sat. fat), 139 mg chol., 975 mg sodium, 1 g carbo., 0 g fiber, 52 g pro.

This recipe relies on apple wood chips or chunks to infuse an herb-rubbed pork roast with a sweet, smoky flavor. Look for a variety of wood chips or chunks—including orange, cherry, hickory, maple, mesquite, and pecan—where grilling supplies are sold.

APPLE-SMOKED PORK LOIN

3 cups apple wood or orange wood chips or 6 to 8 apple wood or orange wood chunks

1 2- to 2½-pound boneless pork top loin pork roast (single loin)

2 teaspoons dried oregano, crushed

½ teaspoon salt

½ teaspoon coarsely ground black pepper

4 cloves garlic, minced

PREP:
10 minutes

SOAK:
1 hour

GRILL:
1 hour

STAND:
15 minutes

MAKES:
8 servings

1 At least 1 hour before cooking, soak wood chips or chunks in enough water to cover.

2 Meanwhile, trim fat from roast. Place roast in a shallow dish. For rub, in a small bowl stir together oregano, salt, pepper, and garlic. Sprinkle mixture evenly over all sides of roast; rub in with your fingers.

3 Drain wood chips. For a charcoal grill, arrange medium coals around a drip pan. Test for medium-low heat above pan. Sprinkle half of the drained wood chips over the coals. Place roast on grill rack over drip pan. Cover and grill for 1 to 1¼ hours or until an instant-read thermometer registers 155°F. Add more coals and wood chips as needed during grilling. (For a gas grill, preheat grill. Reduce heat to medium. Adjust for indirect cooking. Place roast on grill rack. Grill as above, following manufacturer's directions for use of chips.)

4 Remove roast from grill. Cover with foil; let stand for 15 minutes. (The meat's temperature will rise 5°F during standing.)

Nutrition Facts per serving: 163 cal., 6 g total fat (2 g sat. fat), 66 mg chol., 193 mg sodium, 1 g carbo., 0 g fiber, 24 g pro.

When grilling, for best results don't buy pork chops thinner than ¾ inch. At this thickness they grill quickly but remain moist and tender.

2g net carb

ROSEMARY PORK CHOPS

PREP:

10 minutes

MARINATE:

2 hours

GRILL:

20 minutes

MAKES:

4 servings

4   pork chops, cut ¾ inch thick (about 1¾ pounds total)

2   tablespoons Dijon-style mustard

2   tablespoons balsamic vinegar

2   tablespoons lemon juice

2   tablespoons olive oil

3   cloves garlic, minced

4   teaspoons snipped fresh rosemary or 1 teaspoon dried rosemary, crushed

½   teaspoon salt

½   teaspoon black pepper

1 Place meat in a self-sealing plastic bag set in a shallow dish. For marinade, in a small bowl stir together mustard, vinegar, lemon juice, oil, garlic, rosemary, salt, and pepper. Pour over meat; seal bag. Marinate in refrigerator for 2 to 4 hours, turning frequently. Drain meat, discarding marinade.

2 For a charcoal grill, arrange medium-hot coals around a drip pan. Test for medium heat above pan. Place chops on rack over drip pan. Cover and grill for 20 to 24 minutes or until done (160°F) and juices run clear. (For a gas grill, preheat grill. Reduce heat to medium. Adjust grill for indirect cooking. Place chops on grill rack. Grill as above.)

Nutrition Facts per serving: 300 cal., 14 g total fat (4 g sat. fat), 105 mg chol., 244 mg sodium, 2 g carbo., 0 g fiber, 39 g pro.

These grilled ribs marinate in a spicy and gingery coconut milk sauce that will send your taste buds to Thailand.

2g net carb

THAI-COCONUT RIBS

4	pounds pork loin back ribs
1	cup purchased unsweetened coconut milk
3	tablespoons no-calorie, heat-stable granular sugar substitute (Splenda)
3	tablespoons soy sauce
1	tablespoon grated fresh ginger
1	teaspoon finely shredded lime peel
1	tablespoon lime juice
4	cloves garlic, minced
1	teaspoon crushed red pepper

1 Trim fat from ribs. Cut ribs into 6 serving-size pieces. Place ribs in a self-sealing plastic bag set in a shallow dish. For marinade, in a small bowl stir together coconut milk, sugar substitute, soy sauce, ginger, lime peel, lime juice, garlic, and red pepper. Pour over ribs; seal bag. Marinate in the refrigerator for 8 to 24 hours, turning bag occasionally. Drain ribs, reserving marinade.

2 For a charcoal grill, arrange medium-hot coals around a drip pan. Test for medium heat above the pan. Place ribs, bone side down, on grill rack over drip pan. Cover and grill for 1½ to 1¾ hours or until ribs are tender, brushing frequently with marinade during the first hour of grilling. Discard any remaining marinade. (For a gas grill, preheat grill. Reduce heat to medium. Adjust for indirect cooking. Grill as above, except place the ribs in a roasting pan.)

Nutrition Facts per serving: 339 cal., 16 g total fat (8 g sat. fat), 89 mg chol., 313 mg sodium, 2 g carbo., 0 g fiber, 43 g pro.

PREP:

15 minutes

MARINATE:

8 hours

GRILL:

1½ hours

MAKES:

6 servings

Dry rubs are sensational on pork ribs—especially when the ribs are cooked slowly enough to soak up loads of smoky flavor. For extra flavor, this recipe adds apple juice.

3 g net carb

BARBECUED BABY BACK RIBS

PREP:

15 minutes

GRILL:

1 1/2 hours

MAKES:

8 servings

3½	to 4 pounds pork loin back ribs
1	tablespoon paprika
1½	teaspoons garlic salt
1	teaspoon onion powder
1	teaspoon dried sage, crushed
½	teaspoon celery seed
¼	teaspoon cayenne pepper
½	cup apple juice

1 Trim fat from ribs. In a small bowl stir together paprika, garlic salt, onion powder, sage, celery seed, and cayenne pepper. Sprinkle mixture over both sides of ribs; rub in with your fingers.

2 For a charcoal grill, arrange medium-hot coals around a drip pan. Test for medium heat above drip pan. Place ribs on grill rack over drip pan. Cover and grill for 1½ to 1¾ hours or until ribs are tender and no pink remains, brushing occasionally with apple juice after the first 45 minutes of cooking. (For a gas grill, preheat grill. Reduce heat to medium. Adjust for indirect cooking. Place ribs on grill rack. Grill as above.)

Nutrition Facts per serving: 324 cal., 14 g total fat (5 g sat. fat), 94 mg chol., 253 mg sodium, 3 g carbo., 0 g fiber, 43 g pro.

Some Texans would start this marinade only with Shiner Bock, but any good, flavorful beer will do. The ancho pepper gives these Lone Star ribs a bold border flair.

TEXAS BEER-SMOKED RIBS

6	pounds meaty pork spareribs or loin back ribs
1	12-ounce bottle beer
2	tablespoons chili powder
2	tablespoons lime juice
1	teaspoon ground cumin
3	cloves garlic, minced
¾	teaspoon salt
4	to 6 mesquite or hickory wood chunks
3	dried ancho or other dried large chile peppers (optional)

PREP:
10 minutes

MARINATE:
24 hours

SOAK:
1 hour

GRILL:
3 hours

MAKES:
6 servings

1 Trim fat from ribs. Cut ribs into 8-rib portions. Place ribs in a large self-sealing plastic bag set in a large shallow dish. For marinade, in a medium bowl stir together beer, chili powder, lime juice, cumin, garlic, and salt. Pour over ribs; seal bag. Marinate in the refrigerator for 24 hours, turning bag occasionally. Drain ribs, reserving marinade.

2 At least 1 hour before smoke-cooking, soak wood chunks in enough water to cover.

3 Drain wood chunks. In the smoker arrange preheated coals, drained wood chunks, and the lined water pan according to the manufacturer's directions. Pour the marinade into pan; if desired, add the dried peppers. Place ribs on grill rack over pan. Cover and smoke for 3 to 4 hours or until ribs are tender. Add more coals, wood chunks, and water as needed.

Nutrition Facts per serving: 580 cal., 43 g total fat (17 g sat. fat), 133 mg chol., 232 mg sodium, 1 g carbo., 0 g fiber, 43 g pro.

Seven different seasonings give meaty pork ribs flavor to spare.

9 g
net
carb

MARINATED BARBECUED SPARERIBS

PREP:

15 minutes

MARINATE:

6 hours

GRILL:

1¹/₂ hours

MAKES:

6 servings

1   cup chili sauce

¹/₄   cup low-carb catsup

¹/₄   cup soy sauce

2   tablespoons coarse German mustard

1   tablespoon balsamic vinegar

1   tablespoon lemon juice or lime juice

2   teaspoons grated fresh ginger

1   3¹/₂- to 4-pound slab meaty pork spareribs

1 For marinade, in a small bowl stir together chili sauce, catsup, soy sauce, mustard, vinegar, lemon juice, and ginger. Line a roasting pan with plastic wrap; coat ribs with marinade and place on plastic wrap (cut ribs to fit into pan, if necessary). Cover and marinate in the refrigerator for 6 to 24 hours. Remove ribs, reserving marinade.

2 For a charcoal grill, arrange medium-hot coals around a drip pan. Test for medium heat above pan. Place ribs on grill rack over pan. Cover and grill for 1¹/₂ to 1³/₄ hours or until the ribs are tender and no pink remains. Brush with reserved marinade occasionally during the first hour of grilling. (For a gas grill, preheat grill. Reduce heat to medium. Adjust for indirect cooking. Place ribs on grill rack. Grill as above.) Discard any remaining marinade.

Nutrition Facts per serving: 501 cal., 35 g total fat (14 g sat. fat), 124 mg chol., 1,419 mg sodium, 12 g carbo., 3 g fiber, 31 g pro.

For best flavor, coat all sides of the roast with the orange peel and zippy spice mixture.

1 g net carb

ORANGE-RUBBED PORK ROAST

1   2- to 2½-pound boneless pork top loin roast (single loin)

1   tablespoon finely shredded orange peel

1   teaspoon ground coriander

1   teaspoon paprika

½   teaspoon ground ginger

½   teaspoon salt

¼   teaspoon black pepper

1 Trim fat from meat. Rub orange peel onto all sides of roast. In a small bowl stir together coriander, paprika, ginger, salt, and pepper. Sprinkle evenly over meat. Place meat on a rack in a shallow roasting pan. Insert a meat thermometer into center of meat.

2 Roast in a 325° oven for 1 to 1½ hours or until thermometer registers 155°F. Remove roast from oven. Cover with foil and let stand for 15 minutes before carving. (The meat's temperature will rise 5°F during standing.)

Nutrition Facts per serving: 171 cal., 6 g total fat (2 g sat. fat), 66 mg chol., 238 mg sodium, 1 g carbo., 0 g fiber, 27 g pro.

PREP:

15 minutes

ROAST:

1 hour

OVEN:

325°F

STAND:

15 minutes

MAKES:

6 to 8 servings

These pork chops are marinated in a spunky combo of brown mustard, curry powder, and crushed red pepper.

CURRIED MUSTARD PORK CHOPS

PREP:

15 minutes

MARINATE:

6 hours

GRILL:

20 minutes

MAKES:

4 servings

½ cup spicy brown mustard

¼ cup dry white wine

1 tablespoon curry powder

1 tablespoon olive oil

¼ to ½ teaspoon crushed red pepper

1 green onion, sliced

1 clove garlic, minced

4 boneless pork loin chops, cut 1 inch thick
(about 1 pound total)

1 For marinade, in a small bowl stir together mustard, wine, curry powder, oil, red pepper, green onion, and garlic.

2 Place pork in a self-sealing plastic bag set in a shallow dish. Pour marinade over pork; seal bag. Marinate in the refrigerator for 6 to 24 hours, turning bag occasionally. Drain pork, reserving marinade.

3 For a charcoal grill, arrange preheated coals around a drip pan. Test for medium heat above pan. Place pork chops on grill rack over drip pan. Cover and grill for 20 to 24 minutes or until done (160°F) and juices run clear, turning once and brushing with marinade halfway through grilling. (For a gas grill, preheat grill. Reduce heat to medium. Adjust for indirect cooking. Place chops on grill rack. Grill as above.) Discard any remaining marinade.

Nutrition Facts per serving: 191 cal., 12 g total fat (3 g sat. fat), 51 mg chol., 343 mg sodium, 2 g carbo., 1 g fiber, 18 g pro.

With as little as 4 hours marinating time, these juicy chops take on a delectable citrus and coriander flavor.

CORIANDER PORK CHOPS

¼	cup frozen orange juice concentrate, thawed
1	tablespoon lemon juice
1	tablespoon reduced-sodium soy sauce
1	teaspoon ground coriander
¼	teaspoon black pepper
1	clove garlic, minced
4	pork rib or loin chops, cut ¾ inch thick (about 1½ pounds total)

1 Trim fat from chops. For marinade, in a small bowl stir together orange juice concentrate, lemon juice, soy sauce, coriander, pepper, and garlic. Place chops in a self-sealing plastic bag set in a shallow dish. Pour marinade over chops; seal bag. Marinate in the refrigerator for 4 to 6 hours, turning bag occasionally. Drain chops, discarding marinade.

2 Place chops on the unheated rack of a broiler pan. Broil 3 to 4 inches from heat for 9 to 12 minutes or until done (160°F) and juices run clear, turning once.

Nutrition Facts per serving: 263 cal., 9 g total fat (3 g sat. fat), 92 mg chol., 141 mg sodium, 4 g carbo., 0 g fiber, 38 g pro.

PREP:
10 minutes
MARINATE:
4 hours
BROIL:
9 minutes
MAKES:
4 servings

Why bother making your own sausage? Because you can tailor the seasonings precisely to your liking.

1 g net carb

HOMEMADE PORK SAUSAGE

PREP:

15 minutes

GRILL:

14 minutes

MAKES:

4 servings

3	tablespoons finely snipped fresh basil
2	cloves garlic, minced
1	teaspoon fennel seed
1	teaspoon crushed red pepper
¾	teaspoon salt
½	teaspoon black pepper
1½	pounds lean ground pork

1 In a large bowl stir together basil, garlic, fennel seed, red pepper, salt, and black pepper. Add ground pork; mix well. Divide the meat mixture into 4 equal portions. Shape each portion around a flat-sided metal skewer into a 6-inch-long log.

2 For a charcoal grill, place meat on the rack of an uncovered grill directly over medium coals. Grill for 14 to 18 minutes or until done (160°F) and juices run clear, turning once halfway through grilling. (For a gas grill, preheat grill. Reduce heat to medium. Place meat on grill rack. Cover and grill as above.)

3 To serve, use the tines of a fork to push the meat from skewers.

Nutrition Facts per serving: 442 cal., 35 g total fat (13 g sat. fat), 121 mg chol., 532 mg sodium, 1 g carbo., 0 g fiber, 30 g pro.

Where there's smoke, there's rich, mellow flavor, as in this deliciously seasoned pork.

ROSEMARY & GARLIC SMOKED PORK ROAST

4	cups apple or hickory wood chips
1	2- to 3-pound boneless pork top loin roast (single loin)
2	tablespoons snipped fresh rosemary
1	tablespoon olive oil
4	cloves garlic, minced
½	teaspoon black pepper
¼	teaspoon salt
4	sprigs fresh rosemary
½	of a lemon or lime

1 At least 1 hour before grilling, soak wood chips in enough water to cover.

2 Trim fat from meat. For rub, stir together snipped rosemary, oil, garlic, pepper, and salt. Sprinkle rub evenly over meat; rub in with your fingers. Insert a meat thermometer into the center of meat.

3 Drain wood chips. For a charcoal grill, arrange medium coals around a drip pan. Pour 1 inch of water into drip pan. Test for medium-low heat above the pan. Sprinkle half of the wood chips over the coals; sprinkle rosemary sprigs over chips. Place meat on grill rack over drip pan. Cover and grill for 1 to 1½ hours or until meat thermometer registers 155°F. Add remaining wood chips halfway through grilling. (For a gas grill, preheat grill. Reduce heat to medium-low. Adjust for indirect cooking. Grill as above, except place meat on a rack in a roasting pan.)

4 Remove meat from grill. Squeeze juice from lemon over meat. Cover with foil and let stand for 15 minutes. (The meat's temperature will rise 5°F during standing.)

Nutrition Facts per serving: 174 cal., 7 g total fat (2 g sat. fat), 62 mg chol., 114 mg sodium, 1 g carbo., 0 g fiber, 25 g pro.

PREP:
15 minutes
SOAK:
1 hour
GRILL:
1 hour
STAND:
15 minutes
MAKES:
8 to 10 servings

1 g net carb

Lemon peel makes this mixture just moist enough to rub easily. The rub is exactly the right amount to cover four thick chops.

LEMON-&-HERB RUBBED PORK CHOPS

PREP:

15 minutes

GRILL:

35 minutes

MAKES:

4 servings

4	pork loin chops, cut 1¼ inches thick
4	teaspoons minced garlic (about 8 cloves)
1½	teaspoons finely shredded lemon peel
1	teaspoon dried rosemary, crushed
½	teaspoon salt
½	teaspoon dried sage, crushed
½	teaspoon black pepper

1 Trim fat from meat. For rub, in a small bowl stir together garlic, lemon peel, rosemary, salt, sage, and pepper. Sprinkle mixture over both sides of each chop; rub in with your fingers.

2 For a charcoal grill, arrange medium-hot coals around a drip pan. Test for medium heat above pan. Place chops on grill rack over pan. Cover and grill for 35 to 40 minutes or until done (160°F) and juices run clear, turning once. (For a gas grill, preheat grill. Reduce heat to medium. Adjust for indirect cooking. Place chops on rack. Grill as above.)

Nutrition Facts per serving: 351 cal., 19 g total fat (7 g sat. fat), 116 mg chol., 374 mg sodium, 3 g carbo., 0 g fiber, 41 g pro.

This tender pork roast is rubbed with a mixture of garlic, rosemary, and olive oil.
For the most flavor, use the rub on all sides of the roast.

ITALIAN PORK ROAST

5 g net carb

2	teaspoons snipped fresh rosemary or 1 teaspoon dried rosemary, crushed
1	clove garlic, minced
1	teaspoon olive oil or cooking oil
1	1½- to 2-pound boneless pork top loin roast (single loin)
1	cup chicken broth
⅓	cup sliced leek or chopped onion
1	small Golden Delicious or Granny Smith apple, cored and chopped
4	teaspoons unbleached all-purpose flour
2	tablespoons white wine vinegar
¼	teaspoon salt
⅛	teaspoon black pepper

PREP:
15 minutes
ROAST:
1 hour
OVEN:
325°F
STAND:
15 minutes
MAKES:
6 to 8 servings

1 In a small bowl stir together rosemary, garlic, and oil. Drizzle mixture over all sides of roast; rub in with your fingers. Place roast on rack in a shallow roasting pan. Insert a meat thermometer into center of roast. Roast, uncovered, in a 325° oven for 1 to 1½ hours or until meat thermometer registers 155°F. Cover with foil and let stand 15 minutes before slicing. (The meat's temperature will rise 5°F during standing.) Reserve 2 tablespoons of the pan drippings.

2 In a medium saucepan bring ¾ cup of the broth to boiling. Add leek and apple; reduce heat. Cover and simmer for 4 minutes or just until tender. Stir together remaining ¼ cup broth and the flour. Stir into leek mixture. Stir in reserved pan drippings, vinegar, salt, and pepper. Cook and stir until thickened and bubbly. Cook and stir for 2 minutes more.

3 To serve, slice roast and pass sauce with roast.

Nutrition Facts per serving: 226 cal., 10 g total fat (3 g sat. fat), 74 mg chol., 326 mg sodium, 6 g carbo., 1 g fiber, 25 g pro.

A savory blend of five herbal seeds creates a crustlike coating for this ultratender pork roast. The cooking liquid contains apple juice, which lends a bit of sweetness.

SEEDED PORK ROAST

PREP:

25 minutes

COOK:

9 to 11 hours (low) or 4½ to 5½ hours (high); plus 10 minutes

MAKES:

8 servings

1 2½- to 3-pound boneless pork shoulder roast

1 tablespoon soy sauce

2 teaspoons anise seeds, crushed

2 teaspoons fennel seeds, crushed

2 teaspoons caraway seeds, crushed

2 teaspoons dillseeds, crushed

2 teaspoons celery seeds, crushed

1⅓ cups beef broth

2 tablespoons unbleached all-purpose flour

1 Remove netting from roast, if present. If necessary, cut roast to fit into a 3½- to 5-quart slow cooker. Trim fat from meat. Brush soy sauce over surface of roast. On a large piece of foil combine anise seeds, fennel seeds, caraway seeds, dillseeds, and celery seeds. Roll roast in seeds to coat evenly.

2 Place roast in cooker. Pour 1 cup of the broth around roast.

3 Cover and cook on low-heat setting for 9 to 11 hours or on high-heat setting for 4½ to 5½ hours.

4 Transfer roast to a serving platter. For gravy, strain cooking juices and skim fat; transfer juices to small saucepan. Combine remaining ⅓ cup broth and the flour; add to juices in saucepan. Cook and stir until thickened and bubbly. Cook and stir 2 minutes more. Pass gravy with roast.

Nutrition Facts per serving: 227 cal., 10 g total fat (3 g sat. fat), 94 mg chol., 361 mg sodium, 3 g carbo., 1 g fiber, 29 g pro.

Pork tenderloin is the perfect special-occasion meat. It's lean, cooks fast, and tastes great.

0 g net carb

GRILLED PORK TENDERLOIN

1½   pounds pork tenderloin

½   cup cooking oil

⅓   cup soy sauce

2   tablespoons Worcestershire sauce

1   tablespoon dry mustard

¼   teaspoon black pepper

1 Place meat in a self-sealing plastic bag set in a deep bowl. In a small bowl stir together oil, soy sauce, Worcestershire sauce, mustard, and pepper. Pour over meat; seal bag. Marinate in the refrigerator for 4 to 6 hours, turning occasionally. Drain meat, reserving marinade.

2 For a charcoal grill, arrange medium-hot coals around a drip pan. Test for medium heat above pan. Place meat on grill rack over drip pan. Insert a meat thermometer into thickest portion of tenderloin. Cover and grill for 40 to 50 minutes or until thermometer registers 155°F. Brush with marinade twice during first half of grilling. (For a gas grill, preheat grill. Reduce heat to medium. Adjust for indirect cooking. Place tenderloin on grill rack. Grill as above.)

3 Discard marinade. Remove meat from grill. Cover with foil and let stand for 15 minutes. (The meat's temperature will rise 5°F during standing.)

Nutrition Facts per serving: 181 cal., 8 g total fat (2 g sat. fat), 81 mg chol., 222 mg sodium, 0 g carbo., 0 g fiber, 24 g pro.

PREP:
10 minutes

MARINATE:
4 hours

GRILL:
40 minutes

STAND:
15 minutes

MAKES:
6 servings

CHICKEN & TURKEY

Few foods are as popular with Americans as chicken and turkey. They are great for cooks because they provide the perfect canvas for intriguing ingredients. This multitude of recipes explores dozens of ways to prepare poultry—all sure to please your palate while meeting the requirements of low-carb dining.

7

Cut into strips and served over greens, these tangy chicken breasts make a refreshing dinner or lunch.

BALSAMIC CHICKEN OVER GREENS

PREP:

15 minutes

MARINATE:

1 hour

GRILL:

12 minutes

MAKES:

4 servings

4   skinless, boneless chicken breast halves
    (about 1¼ pounds total)

1   cup bottled balsamic vinaigrette salad dressing

3   cloves garlic, minced

¼   teaspoon crushed red pepper

8   cups torn mixed greens

1 Place chicken breast halves in a self-sealing plastic bag set in a shallow dish. For marinade, in a small bowl combine ½ cup of the salad dressing, the garlic, and crushed red pepper. Pour marinade over the chicken in bag; seal bag. Turn to coat chicken. Marinate in the refrigerator for 1 to 4 hours, turning bag occasionally.

2 Drain chicken, reserving marinade. For a charcoal grill, place chicken on the rack of an uncovered grill directly over medium coals. Grill for 12 to 15 minutes or until chicken is no longer pink (170°F), turning and brushing with marinade halfway through grilling. (For a gas grill, preheat grill. Reduce heat to medium. Place chicken on grill rack over heat. Cover and grill as above.) Discard any remaining marinade.

3 Arrange greens on serving plates. Cut chicken into strips. Place chicken on top of greens. Serve with remaining ½ cup vinaigrette.

BROILING DIRECTIONS: Place chicken breasts on the unheated rack of a broiler pan. Broil 4 to 5 inches from heat for 12 to 15 minutes or until chicken is no longer pink (170°F), turning and brushing with marinade halfway through broiling. Discard any remaining marinade.

Nutrition Facts per serving: 284 cal., 13 g total fat (2 g sat. fat), 82 mg chol., 525 mg sodium, 7 g carbo., 1 g fiber, 34 g pro.

Save half of the robust mustard marinade to heat and serve as a sauce for the grilled chicken. Keep this flavorful marinade in mind when grilling steaks and chops, too.

0 g net carb

HERBED MUSTARD BARBECUED CHICKEN

1	8-ounce jar Dijon-style mustard (1 cup)
¼	cup olive oil
2	tablespoons dry red wine
2	cloves garlic, minced
1	teaspoon dried rosemary, crushed
1	teaspoon dried basil, crushed
½	teaspoon dried oregano, crushed
½	teaspoon dried thyme, crushed
¼	teaspoon black pepper
1	3-pound broiler-fryer chicken, quartered

PREP:
15 minutes
MARINATE:
8 hours
GRILL:
45 minutes
MAKES:
4 servings

1 In a small bowl stir together mustard, oil, wine, garlic, rosemary, basil, oregano, thyme, and pepper. Arrange chicken in a 3-quart glass baking dish. Spread ½ cup of the mustard mixture evenly over chicken. Cover and refrigerate chicken and remaining mustard mixture for 8 to 24 hours.

2 Drain chicken, discarding any marinade. For a charcoal grill, arrange medium-hot coals around a drip pan. Test for medium heat above the pan. Place chicken bone sides down on grill rack over pan. Cover and grill for 45 to 55 minutes or until chicken is no longer pink (170°F for breast portions; 180°F for thigh and drumstick portions). (For a gas grill, preheat grill. Reduce heat to medium. Adjust grill for indirect cooking. Place chicken bone sides down on grill rack over unlit burner. Grill as above.)

3 Meanwhile, in a small saucepan heat reserved mustard mixture; serve with grilled chicken.

Nutrition Facts per serving: 512 cal., 32 g total fat (7 g sat. fat), 118 mg chol., 1,415 mg sodium, 1 g carbo., 1 g fiber, 37 g pro.

You can substitute herbed feta cheese for the plain feta and dried oregano.

1 g net carb

OLYMPIA CHICKEN

PREP:

15 minutes

ROAST:

1 1/4 hours

STAND:

10 minutes

OVEN:

375°F

MAKES:

6 servings

1	cup crumbled feta cheese (about 4 ounces)
1	tablespoon dried oregano, crushed
1	lemon
1	tablespoon olive oil
1/4	teaspoon coarsely ground black pepper
1	3- to 4-pound whole broiler-fryer chicken
	Lemon wedges (optional)

1 Combine feta and oregano; set aside. Halve lemon; squeeze 2 tablespoons lemon juice. Quarter squeezed lemon; set aside. In a small bowl stir together lemon juice, oil, and pepper. Set aside.

2 Rinse inside of chicken; pat dry with paper towels. Starting at the edge of the breast, slip your fingers between the skin and meat, loosening the skin as you work toward the neck end. With your entire hand under the skin, carefully free the skin around the thigh and leg area up to, but not around, the tip of the drumsticks.

3 Using your hands or a tablespoon, carefully stuff the cheese mixture under skin, filling the drumstick-thigh area first, working up to the breast. Press gently to distribute the feta cheese mixture throughout the space underneath the chicken skin.

4 Place lemon quarters inside the chicken cavity. Skewer the neck skin to the back. Tie the legs to the tail. Twist wings under back. Rub the lemon-oil mixture over entire bird. Place chicken breast side up on a rack in a shallow pan. Insert a meat thermometer into the center of an inside thigh muscle. Do not allow thermometer tip to touch bone.

5 Roast, uncovered, in a 375° oven for 1 1/4 to 1 3/4 hours or until drumsticks move easily in their sockets, meat is no longer pink, and thermometer registers 180°F. Remove chicken from oven. Cover chicken loosely with foil. Let stand 10 minutes before carving. If desired, serve with lemon wedges.

Nutrition Facts per serving: 192 cal., 13 g total fat (5 g sat. fat), 61 mg chol., 259 mg sodium, 1 g carbo., 0 g fiber, 16 g pro.

Ground coffee adds a rich color and robust flavor to this grilled chicken.

GARLICKY GRILLED CHICKEN

1   2½- to 3-pound whole roasting chicken

1   tablespoon cooking oil

2   cloves garlic, minced

     Salt

     Freshly ground black pepper

1   teaspoon dark roast ground coffee

PREP:

15 minutes

GRILL:

1 hour

STAND:

10 minutes

MAKES:

4 servings

1 Rinse inside of chicken; pat dry with paper towels. Skewer neck skin to back. Tie legs to tail. Twist wing tips under back. In a small bowl stir together oil and garlic. Brush chicken with garlic mixture. Sprinkle with salt, pepper, and ground coffee. Insert a meat thermometer into center of an inside thigh muscle. Do not allow thermometer tip to touch bone.

2 For a charcoal grill, arrange medium-hot coals around a drip pan. Test for medium heat above the pan. Place chicken breast side up on grill rack over drip pan. Cover and grill for 1 to 1¼ hours or until drumsticks move easily in their sockets, meat is no longer pink, and thermometer registers 180°F. (For a gas grill, preheat grill. Reduce heat to medium. Adjust for indirect cooking. Place chicken breast side up on grill rack over unlit burner. Grill as above.)

3 Remove chicken from grill. Cover chicken loosely with foil and let stand for 10 minutes before carving.

Nutrition Facts per serving: 200 cal., 12 g total fat (3 g sat. fat), 66 mg chol., 110 mg sodium, 0 g carbo., 0 g fiber, 20 g pro.

Rosemary grows abundantly in the Mediterranean area and is one of the region's favorite herbs for seasoning roast chicken.

0 g net carb

ROSEMARY CHICKEN

PREP:

15 minutes

MARINATE:

6 hours

GRILL:

35 minutes

MAKES:

6 servings

2   to 2½ pounds meaty chicken pieces
     (breasts, thighs, and drumsticks)

½   cup dry white wine

2   tablespoons olive oil

4   cloves garlic, minced

4   teaspoons snipped fresh rosemary

1   tablespoon finely shredded lemon peel

¼   teaspoon salt

¼   teaspoon black pepper

     Rosemary sprigs (optional)

1 If desired, skin chicken. Place chicken in a self-sealing plastic bag set in a shallow dish. For marinade, in a blender or food processor combine wine, oil, garlic, snipped rosemary, lemon peel, salt, and pepper. Cover and blend or process about 15 seconds or until well mixed. Pour over chicken; seal bag. Turn to coat chicken. Marinate in the refrigerator for 6 to 24 hours, turning bag occasionally.

2 Drain chicken, reserving marinade. For a charcoal grill, grill chicken on the rack of an uncovered grill directly over medium coals for 35 to 45 minutes or until chicken is no longer pink (170°F for breasts; 180°F for thighs and drumsticks), turning once and brushing with marinade halfway through grilling. (For a gas grill, preheat grill. Reduce heat to medium. Place chicken on grill rack over heat. Cover and grill as above.) Discard any remaining marinade. Remove the chicken from the grill to a serving platter. If desired, garnish with rosemary sprigs.

Nutrition Facts per serving: 192 cal., 10 g total fat (3 g sat. fat), 69 mg chol., 93 mg sodium, 0 g carbo., 0 g fiber, 22 g pro.

This easy marinade is also good for fish and seafood. If you like, serve the chicken on a bed of mixed greens.

TANGY LEMON CHICKEN

4   medium skinless, boneless chicken breast halves (about 1 pound total)

½   cup bottled creamy Italian salad dressing

1   tablespoon finely shredded lemon peel

¼   cup lemon juice

    Dash black pepper

1 Place the chicken in a self-sealing plastic bag set in a shallow bowl. For marinade, in a small bowl stir together the salad dressing, lemon peel, lemon juice, and pepper. Pour over chicken; seal bag. Turn to coat chicken. Marinate in the refrigerator for 2 to 4 hours, turning bag occasionally.

2 Drain chicken, reserving marinade. For a charcoal grill, grill chicken on the rack of an uncovered grill directly over medium coals for 12 to 15 minutes or until chicken is no longer pink (170°F). Turn and brush with marinade halfway through grilling. (For a gas grill, preheat grill. Reduce heat to medium. Place chicken on grill rack over heat. Cover and grill as above.) Discard any remaining marinade.

Nutrition Facts per serving: 177 cal., 6 g total fat (1 g sat. fat), 66 mg chol., 179 mg sodium, 2 g carbo., 0 g fiber, 26 g pro.

PREP:
10 minutes

MARINATE:
2 hours

GRILL:
12 minutes

MAKES:
4 servings

Grilled or roasted, the flavorful juices locked in the meat make this chicken tender and moist.

2 g net carb

HERBED CHICKEN

PREP:
15 minutes

COOK:
1 to 1¼ hours

MAKES:
4 to 6 servings

1   2½- to 3-pound whole broiler-fryer chicken
2   tablespoons butter
3   tablespoons lemon juice
1   teaspoon dried thyme, savory, or sage, crushed
3   cloves garlic, minced
¼   teaspoon salt
¼   teaspoon black pepper
    Fresh thyme (optional)

1 Rinse inside of chicken; pat dry with paper towels. Skewer neck skin to back. Tie legs to tail. Twist wing tips under back. Insert a meat thermometer into the center of an inside thigh muscle. Do not allow thermometer tip to touch bone.

2 In a small saucepan melt butter; stir in lemon juice, dried herb, garlic, salt, and pepper. Brush butter mixture onto chicken. Grill or roast as directed below. Brush occasionally with remaining herb mixture during the first 45 minutes of cooking. To serve, cut into pieces. If desired, garnish with fresh thyme.

TO GRILL: For a charcoal grill, arrange medium-hot coals around a drip pan. Test for medium heat above the pan. Place chicken breast side up on the grill rack over the drip pan. Cover and grill for 1 to 1¼ hours or until the drumsticks move easily in their sockets, meat is no longer pink, and thermometer registers 180°F. Add more coals to maintain heat as necessary. (For a gas grill, preheat grill. Reduce heat to medium. Place chicken breast side up on grill rack over unlit burner. Adjust for indirect cooking. Grill as above.)

TO ROAST: Place chicken breast side up on a rack in a shallow roasting pan. Roast, uncovered, in a 375°F oven for 1¼ to 1½ hours or until the drumsticks move easily in their sockets, meat is no longer pink, and thermometer registers 180°F.

Nutrition Facts per serving: 333 cal., 21 g total fat (8 g sat. fat), 115 mg chol., 299 mg sodium, 2 g carbo., 0 g fiber, 31 g pro.

Roast chicken is a traditional springtime main course. This version is basted with a lemony blend of oil and garlic.

CHICKEN À LA SPRING

3	tablespoons cooking oil
2	cloves garlic, minced
1	tablespoon finely shredded lemon peel
6	to 8 leaves fresh sorrel (optional)
1	lemon, cut into wedges
1	3- to 3½-pound whole broiler-fryer chicken
⅔	cup reduced-sodium chicken broth
1	tablespoon unbleached all-purpose flour
1	tablespoon lemon juice
	Salt
	Black pepper
2	tablespoons coarsely shredded fresh sorrel or spinach leaves

PREP:
15 minutes

STAND:
40 minutes

ROAST:
1 hour

OVEN:
375°F

MAKES:
6 servings

1 In a small saucepan cook and stir oil and garlic over low heat for 2 minutes. Remove from heat. Stir in lemon peel; set oil mixture aside.

2 Rinse inside of chicken; pat dry with paper towels. Place the 6 to 8 sorrel leaves (if using) and lemon wedges in the cavity of the bird. Loosen and lift skin above breast. Brush a little of the garlic-oil mixture under the breast skin. Skewer neck skin to back. Tie legs to tail. Twist wing tips under back. Brush a little more of the oil mixture over the skin of the bird. Cover and chill remaining oil mixture. Cover chicken; let stand at room temperature for 30 minutes or refrigerate up to 24 hours.

3 Place chicken breast side up on a rack in a shallow roasting pan. Insert a meat thermometer into center of an inside thigh muscle. Do not allow thermometer tip to touch bone.

4 Roast, uncovered, in a 375° oven for 1 to 1¼ hours or until drumsticks move easily in their sockets, meat is no longer pink, and thermometer registers 180°F. Baste with remaining oil mixture halfway through roasting. Remove chicken from oven. Remove sorrel leaves (if using) and lemon wedges from cavity. Cover chicken loosely with foil; let stand 10 minutes.

5 Meanwhile, pour juices and brown bits from roasting pan into a small glass measure. Skim off and discard fat, reserving pan juices (1 to 2 tablespoons total). In a screw-top jar combine chicken broth and flour; cover and shake well. Pour flour mixture into a small saucepan. Add pan juices. Cook and stir over medium heat until slightly thickened and bubbly. Stir in lemon juice. Season to taste with salt and pepper. Transfer chicken to a serving platter. Pour sauce into a bowl; top with shredded sorrel.

Nutrition Facts per serving: 285 cal., 19 g total fat (4 g sat. fat), 79 mg chol., 136 mg sodium, 3 g carbo., 1 g fiber, 25 g pro.

Herbs and a splash of balsamic vinegar flavor these moist, fork-tender chicken breasts.

3 g net carb

THYME & GARLIC CHICKEN BREASTS

PREP:

15 minutes

COOK:

5 hours (low) or 2¹⁄₂ hours (high); plus 10 minutes

MAKES:

6 to 8 servings

6	cloves garlic, minced
1¹⁄₂	teaspoons dried thyme, crushed
3	to 4 pounds whole chicken breast halves (with bone), skinned
¹⁄₄	cup orange juice
1	tablespoon balsamic vinegar

1 Sprinkle garlic and thyme over chicken. Place chicken pieces in a 3¹⁄₂- or 4-quart slow cooker. Pour orange juice and vinegar over chicken.

2 Cover and cook on low-heat setting for 5 to 6 hours or on high-heat setting for 2¹⁄₂ to 3 hours.

3 Remove chicken from cooker; cover and keep warm. Skim off fat from cooking juices. Strain juices into a saucepan. Bring to boiling; reduce heat. Boil gently, uncovered, for 10 minutes or until reduced to 1 cup. Pass juices to spoon over chicken.

Nutrition Facts per serving: 178 cal., 2 g total fat (0 g sat. fat), 85 mg chol., 78 mg sodium, 3 g carbo., 0 g fiber, 34 g pro.

Five-spice powder, used in this intriguing marinade, is an aromatic combination of cinnamon, cloves, fennel, anise, and peppercorns.

4g net carb

FIVE-SPICE CHICKEN

4	skinless, boneless chicken breast halves (about 1¼ pounds total)
¼	cup bottled salsa
2	tablespoons soy sauce
2	tablespoons bottled oyster sauce
1	teaspoon five-spice powder
¼	teaspoon cayenne pepper

1 Place chicken breast halves in a self-sealing plastic bag set in a shallow dish. For marinade, in a small bowl stir together salsa, soy sauce, oyster sauce, five-spice powder, and cayenne pepper. Pour over chicken; seal bag. Turn to coat chicken. Marinate in refrigerator for 2 hours, turning occasionally.

2 Drain chicken, reserving marinade. For a charcoal grill, grill chicken on the rack of an uncovered grill directly over medium coals for 12 to 15 minutes or until chicken is no longer pink (170°F). Turn once and brush with marinade halfway through grilling. (For a gas grill, preheat grill. Reduce heat to medium. Place chicken on grill rack over heat. Cover and grill as above.) Discard any remaining marinade.

Nutrition Facts per serving: 184 cal., 2 g total fat (1 g sat. fat), 82 mg chol., 922 mg sodium, 4 g carbo., 0 g fiber, 34 g pro.

PREP:
15 minutes
MARINATE:
2 hours
GRILL:
12 minutes
MAKES:
4 servings

Herbes de Provence is a blend of dried herbs favored by cooks in southern France. Most brands contain basil, marjoram, rosemary, sage, summer savory, thyme, fennel seed, and lavender.

LEMON-&-HERB-ROASTED CHICKEN

PREP:

15 minutes

ROAST:

1³/₄ hours

STAND:

10 minutes

OVEN:

325°F

MAKES:

8 to 12 servings

1   5- to 6-pound whole roasting chicken

1   medium lemon

1   tablespoon olive oil

2   cloves garlic, finely chopped

2½   teaspoons herbes de Provence or Greek seasoning

1 Rinse inside of chicken; pat dry with paper towels. Halve the lemon; squeeze 2 tablespoons lemon juice. Reserve lemon halves. Stir together oil and lemon juice. Brush chicken with oil mixture. In a small bowl combine garlic and herb; rub onto chicken. Place the squeezed lemon halves in body cavity of chicken. Skewer neck skin to back. Tie legs to tail. Twist wing tips under back.

2 Place chicken breast side up on a rack in a shallow roasting pan. Insert a meat thermometer into the center of an inside thigh muscle. Do not allow thermometer tip to touch bone.

3 Roast, uncovered, in a 325° oven for 1¾ to 2½ hours or until drumsticks move easily in their sockets, meat is no longer pink, and thermometer registers 180°F. Remove chicken from oven. Cover chicken loosely with foil; let stand 10 minutes before carving.

Nutrition Facts per serving: 447 cal., 33 g total fat (9 g sat. fat), 148 mg chol., 111 mg sodium, 1 g carbo., 0 g fiber, 35 g pro.

The garlic in this dish mellows in flavor as it bakes. For ease, you can leave the skins on the garlic cloves. Or to enjoy buttery soft garlic, cut the skin and remove the clove with the tip of a knife.

GARLIC CLOVE CHICKEN

	Nonstick cooking spray
1½	to 2 pounds meaty chicken pieces (breasts, thighs, and drumsticks), skinned
25	cloves garlic (about ½ cup or 2 to 3 bulbs)
¼	cup dry white wine
¼	cup reduced-sodium chicken broth
	Salt
	Cayenne pepper

PREP:
15 minutes

BAKE:
45 minutes

OVEN:
325°F

MAKES:
4 servings

1 Lightly coat a large skillet with cooking spray. Heat over medium heat. Add chicken and cook for 10 minutes, turning to brown evenly.

2 Place chicken in a 2-quart square baking dish. Add unpeeled garlic cloves. In a small bowl combine wine and broth; pour over chicken. Lightly sprinkle chicken with salt and cayenne pepper.

3 Bake, covered, in a 325° oven for 45 to 50 minutes or until chicken is no longer pink (170°F for breasts; 180°F for thighs and drumsticks).

Nutrition Facts per serving: 184 cal., 6 g total fat (2 g sat. fat), 69 mg chol., 140 mg sodium, 6 g carbo., 0 g fiber, 23 g pro.

You certainly can use a broiler-fryer chicken instead of a roasting chicken in this recipe, but a roasting chicken has better flavor and won't fall apart on the grill. Leftover smoked chicken meat is also great in salads.

5g net carb

SMOKED SPICY CHICKEN

PREP:

25 minutes

SOAK:

1 hour

MARINATE:

1 hour

CHILL:

20 minutes

GRILL:

1¼ hours

STAND:

10 minutes

MAKES:

4 servings

2   cups hickory or apple wood chips
1   3- to 3½-pound whole roasting chicken
1   12-ounce can amber or dark beer
½   teaspoon garlic salt
½   teaspoon black pepper
2   small limes
1   tablespoon ground chili powder

1 At least 1 hour before grilling, soak wood chips in enough water to cover.

2 Rinse inside of chicken; pat dry with paper towels. Place chicken in a large plastic bag set in a deep bowl. Pour beer over the chicken and into the chicken cavity; seal bag. Marinate in the refrigerator for 1 hour.

3 Drain chicken, discarding marinade. Sprinkle chicken body cavity with garlic salt and black pepper. Cut limes in half. Squeeze juice from 2 of the lime halves. In a small bowl combine lime juice and the chili powder; set aside. Squeeze juice from remaining lime halves into chicken body cavity; place squeezed lime halves inside chicken cavity. Skewer the neck skin to the back. Tie legs to tail. Twist wing tips under back.

4 Brush chili powder mixture over chicken; cover and chill 20 minutes.

5 Drain wood chips. Place them in the center of a 12-inch square of foil. Bring up 2 opposite edges of foil and seal with a double fold. Fold ends to completely enclose the chips. Use a knife to carefully make several small slits in the top of the foil packet.

6 For a charcoal grill, arrange medium-hot coals around a drip pan. Pour 1 inch of water into the drip pan. Place packet of wood chips on the grill rack over coals. Cover and heat about 10 minutes or until chips begin to smoke. Test for medium heat above the pan. Place chicken breast side up on grill rack over drip pan. Cover and grill for 1¼ to 1½ hours or until an instant-read thermometer inserted in an inside thigh muscle registers 180°F. (For a gas grill, preheat grill. Reduce heat to medium. Adjust for indirect cooking. Place packet of wood chips on grill rack over heat. Cover and heat about 10 minutes or until chips begin to smoke. Place chicken breast side up on grill rack over unlit burner. Grill as above.)

7 Remove chicken from grill. Cover chicken loosely with foil; let stand for 10 minutes before carving. Remove and discard lime halves.

Nutrition Facts per serving: 374 cal., 19 g total fat (5 g sat. fat), 118 mg chol., 252 mg sodium, 6 g carbo., 1 g fiber, 37 g pro.

Jamaican jerk seasoning is a dry blend of chiles, thyme, and spices (such as cinnamon, ginger, cloves, and allspice). You can use it as a rub or mix it with a liquid for a marinade, as it is here.

GRILLED JERK CHICKEN

4   medium skinless, boneless chicken breast halves (about 1 pound total)

1   large onion, quartered

1   to 2 jalapeño peppers, seeded and cut up*

1   tablespoon snipped fresh thyme or 1 teaspoon dried thyme, crushed

½   teaspoon ground allspice

¼   teaspoon salt

¼   teaspoon ground nutmeg

    Dash ground cloves

¼   cup orange juice

    Torn mixed greens (optional)

PREP:
15 minutes

MARINATE:
4 hours

GRILL:
12 minutes

MAKES:
4 servings

1 Place chicken in a self-sealing plastic bag set in a shallow dish. For marinade, in a blender or food processor combine onion, jalapeño peppers, thyme, allspice, salt, nutmeg, and cloves. Cover and blend or process until almost smooth. With blender or food processor running, add the orange juice. Process or blend until almost smooth. Pour over chicken; seal bag. Turn to coat chicken. Marinate in the refrigerator for 4 to 24 hours, turning occasionally.

2 Drain chicken, discarding marinade. For a charcoal grill, grill chicken on the rack of an uncovered grill directly over medium coals for 12 to 15 minutes or until chicken is no longer pink (170°F), turning once. (For a gas grill, preheat grill. Reduce heat to medium. Place chicken on grill rack over heat. Cover and grill as above.) If desired, serve chicken on greens.

***NOTE:** Hot chile peppers, such as jalapeños, contain oils that can burn your eyes, lips, and skin. Wear plastic or rubber gloves while preparing hot chile peppers and be sure to thoroughly wash your hands and nails in hot, soapy water afterward.

Nutrition Facts per serving: 144 cal., 3 g total fat (1 g sat. fat), 59 mg chol., 189 mg sodium, 5 g carbo., 1 g fiber, 22 g pro.

Sesame seeds make a flavorful and crunchy coating for this easy oven-fried chicken.

6 g net carb

SESAME CHICKEN

PREP:

15 minutes

BAKE:

45 minutes

OVEN:

400°F

MAKES:

4 servings

Nonstick cooking spray

3 tablespoons sesame seeds

3 tablespoons unbleached all-purpose flour

¼ teaspoon salt

¼ teaspoon cayenne pepper

3 tablespoons reduced-sodium teriyaki sauce

4 chicken breast halves (with bones), skinned (about 2 pounds total)

1 tablespoon butter, melted

1 Lightly coat a large baking sheet with cooking spray; set aside. In a large plastic bag combine sesame seeds, flour, salt, and cayenne pepper. Put teriyaki sauce in small bowl. Dip chicken in teriyaki sauce. Add chicken to the mixture in the plastic bag; close bag. Shake bag to coat chicken.

2 Place chicken bone side down on prepared baking sheet. Drizzle melted butter over chicken.

3 Bake in a 400°F oven about 45 minutes or until chicken is no longer pink (170°F).

Nutrition Facts per serving: 275 cal., 11 g total fat (2 g sat. fat), 89 mg chol., 490 mg sodium, 7 g carbo., 1 g fiber, 35 g pro.

Mild chicken shows a more aggressive side when it's bathed in a whirled-together mint marinade. Soy sauce, chili powder, and garlic add extra zing.

2 g net carb

GARLIC & MINT CHICKEN BREASTS

½ cup fresh mint leaves

1 tablespoon lemon juice

1 tablespoon olive oil

1 tablespoon reduced-sodium soy sauce

1 teaspoon chili powder

¼ teaspoon black pepper

4 cloves garlic

4 skinless, boneless chicken breast halves
(1¼ to 1½ pounds total)

Grilled whole green onions (optional)

Fresh mint sprigs (optional)

PREP:
15 minutes
MARINATE:
4 hours
GRILL:
12 minutes
MAKES:
4 servings

1 For marinade, in a blender combine mint leaves, lemon juice, oil, soy sauce, chili powder, pepper, and garlic. Cover and blend until smooth.

2 Place chicken in a self-sealing plastic bag set in a shallow dish. Pour marinade over chicken; seal bag. Turn to coat chicken. Marinate chicken in refrigerator for 4 to 24 hours, turning bag occasionally.

3 Drain chicken, discarding marinade. For a charcoal grill, grill chicken on the rack of an uncovered grill directly over medium coals for 12 to 15 minutes or until no longer pink (170°F), turning once halfway through grilling. (For a gas grill, preheat grill. Reduce heat to medium. Place chicken on grill rack over heat. Cover and grill as above.) If desired, serve with grilled green onions and garnish with mint sprigs.

Nutrition Facts per serving: 202 cal., 6 g total fat (1 g sat. fat), 82 mg chol., 228 mg sodium, 2 g carbo., 0 g fiber, 34 g pro.

You need only five ingredients for this simply delicious roasted chicken.

1 g net carb

ROSEMARY-LEMON ROAST CHICKEN

PREP:

15 minutes

ROAST:

1 1/4 hours

OVEN:

375°F

STAND:

10 minutes

MAKES:

4 to 6 servings

1   3-pound whole broiler-fryer chicken

2   tablespoons snipped fresh rosemary or 2 teaspoons dried rosemary, crushed

2   cloves garlic, minced

1   medium lemon

    Salt

1 Rinse inside of chicken; pat dry with paper towels. In a small bowl combine rosemary and garlic. Rub chicken inside and out with garlic mixture. Halve the lemon; squeeze 2 tablespoons juice from lemon. Sprinkle the lemon juice over chicken. Sprinkle chicken with salt.

2 Place the squeezed lemon halves in body cavity of chicken. Skewer neck skin to back. Tie legs to tail. Twist wing tips under back. Place chicken breast side up on a rack in a shallow roasting pan. Insert a meat thermometer into center of an inside thigh muscle. Do not allow thermometer tip to touch bone.

3 Roast, uncovered, in a 375° oven for 1 1/4 to 1 1/2 hours or until drumsticks move easily in their sockets, meat is no longer pink, and thermometer registers 180°F, brushing occasionally with pan drippings. Remove chicken from oven. Cover chicken loosely with foil; let stand for 10 minutes before carving.

Nutrition Facts per serving: 346 cal., 14 g total fat (4 g sat. fat), 207 mg chol., 361 mg sodium, 1 g carbo., 0 g fiber, 53 g pro.

Tarragon, an assertive herb, blends pleasantly with the mild flavor of chicken.
Just a little perks up the light apple glaze.

8 g net carb

TARRAGON CHICKEN & APPLES

½ cup apple juice

¾ teaspoon snipped fresh tarragon or ¼ teaspoon dried tarragon, crushed

½ teaspoon instant chicken bouillon granules

1 clove garlic, minced

Dash black pepper

4 small skinless, boneless chicken breast halves (about 12 ounces total)

1 medium apple, cored and sliced

¼ cup sliced green onions (2)

1 tablespoon cold water

1 tablespoon unbleached all-purpose flour

Green onions (optional)

PREP:
15 minutes
COOK:
15 minutes
MAKES:
4 servings

1 In a large skillet combine the apple juice, tarragon, bouillon granules, garlic, and pepper. Bring to boiling. Add chicken breasts; reduce heat. Simmer, covered, for 7 minutes.

2 Turn chicken over; add apple slices and sliced green onions. Simmer, covered, for 4 to 5 minutes more or until chicken is tender and no longer pink.

3 With a slotted spoon, remove chicken and apples; keep warm. Reserve cooking liquid.

4 In a screw-top jar combine the cold water and flour; cover and shake well. Stir into cooking liquid in skillet. Cook and stir until thickened and bubbly. Cook and stir for 1 minute more. Spoon over chicken and apples. If desired, garnish with additional green onions.

Nutrition Facts per serving: 128 cal., 3 g total fat (1 g sat. fat), 45 mg chol., 150 mg sodium, 9 g carbo., 1 g fiber, 16 g pro.

Smoking is a wonderful way to impart extra flavor into grilled meats without adding any additional carbs. You can use either your gas or charcoal grill. If you have a smoker, follow the manufacturer's directions.

SMOKED PINEAPPLE-SOY CHICKEN

PREP:

15 minutes

MARINATE:

4 hours

SOAK:

1 hour

GRILL:

50 minutes

MAKES:

4 servings

1	3-pound whole broiler-fryer chicken, quartered
½	cup unsweetened pineapple juice
¼	cup vinegar
2	tablespoons cooking oil
1	tablespoon soy sauce
2	cups apple or hickory chips
¾	teaspoon salt
¾	teaspoon paprika
¾	teaspoon dried ground sage
¼	to ½ teaspoon black pepper
¼	teaspoon chili powder
⅛	teaspoon onion powder

1 Place chicken in a self-sealing plastic bag set in a shallow dish. For marinade, combine pineapple juice, vinegar, oil, and soy sauce. Pour over chicken; seal bag. Turn to coat chicken. Marinate in the refrigerator for 4 hours, turning bag occasionally.

2 At least 1 hour before grilling, soak wood chips in enough water to cover.

3 For rub, stir together salt, paprika, sage, pepper, chili powder, and onion powder; set aside. Drain chicken, discarding marinade. Pat dry. Sprinkle rub evenly over chicken; pat in with your fingers.

4 Drain wood chips. For a charcoal grill, arrange medium-hot coals around a drip pan. Sprinkle half of the wood chips over coals. Test for medium heat above the pan. Place chicken pieces bone sides down on grill rack over drip pan. Cover and grill 50 to 60 minutes or until chicken is tender and juices run clear (170°F for breast portions; 180°F for thigh and drumstick portions). (For a gas grill, preheat grill. Reduce heat to medium. Adjust for indirect cooking. Add drained wood chips according to manufacturer's directions. Place chicken bone sides down on grill rack over unlit burner. Grill as above.)

Nutrition Facts per serving: 349 cal., 20 g total fat (5 g sat. fat), 118 mg chol., 590 mg sodium, 3 g carbo., 0 g fiber, 37 g pro.

For a company-pleasing presentation, spoon the sauce onto dinner plates, slice the chicken breasts, fan the slices on the sauce, and garnish with sprigs of fresh tarragon or dill.

CHICKEN WITH TARRAGON MUSTARD SAUCE

4   skinless, boneless chicken breast halves (about 1¼ pounds total)

Salt

Black pepper

2   tablespoons olive oil or cooking oil

¼   cup dry white wine

2   tablespoons crème fraîche

2   tablespoons tarragon mustard or dill mustard

START TO FINISH:

25 minutes

MAKES:

4 servings

1 Place each chicken breast half between 2 pieces of plastic wrap. Pound lightly with the flat side of a meat mallet to ½-inch thickness. Remove plastic wrap. Sprinkle chicken with salt and pepper.

2 In a 12-inch skillet cook chicken breasts, 2 at a time, in hot oil over medium-high heat for 2 to 3 minutes or until golden, turning once. Transfer chicken to a serving platter; keep warm.

3 For sauce, carefully add wine to hot skillet. Cook and stir until bubbly to loosen any brown bits in bottom of skillet. Add crème fraîche and mustard to skillet; stir with a wire whisk until combined. Spoon sauce over chicken.

Nutrition Facts per serving: 255 cal., 11 g total fat (3 g sat. fat), 92 mg chol., 306 mg sodium, 1 g carbo., 0 g fiber, 33 g pro.

Chicken drumsticks or thighs are great for the slow cooker. They stay moist and tender during the long cooking times. If you like, thicken the sauce with unbleached flour.

ZESTY GINGER-TOMATO CHICKEN

PREP:

20 minutes

COOK:

6 to 7 hours (low) or 3 to 3¹/₂ hours (high)

MAKES:

6 servings

12	chicken drumsticks and/or thighs, skinned (2¹/₂ to 3 pounds total)
2	14¹/₂-ounce cans tomatoes, undrained
1	tablespoon grated fresh ginger
1	tablespoon snipped fresh cilantro or parsley
4	cloves garlic, minced
¹/₂	teaspoon crushed red pepper
¹/₂	teaspoon salt

1 Place chicken pieces in a 3¹/₂- or 4-quart slow cooker.

2 Drain 1 can of tomatoes; chop tomatoes from both cans. For sauce, in a medium bowl combine chopped tomatoes and the juice from 1 can, ginger, cilantro, garlic, crushed red pepper, and salt. Pour sauce over chicken.

3 Cover and cook on low-heat setting for 6 to 7 hours or on high-heat setting for 3 to 3¹/₂ hours. Skim fat from sauce. Serve chicken with sauce in bowls.

Nutrition Facts per serving: 168 cal., 4 g total fat (1 g sat. fat), 81 mg chol., 472 mg sodium, 10 g carbo., 1 g fiber, 23 g pro.

Make a main dish of this all-time favorite appetizer! A creamy blue cheese dressing cools down these hot-sauced wings.

BUFFALO CHICKEN WINGS

12	chicken wings (about 2½ pounds total)
2	tablespoons butter
2	tablespoons to ¼ cup bottled hot pepper sauce (½ to one 2-ounce jar)
½	cup bottled blue cheese salad dressing
	Celery sticks

1 Cut off and discard wing tips. Cut each wing into 2 sections.

2 In a foil-lined 15×10×1-inch baking pan arrange wing pieces in a single layer. Bake in a 375° oven for 20 minutes.

3 Meanwhile, in a small saucepan melt butter. Stir in hot pepper sauce. Drain off fat from wings. Brush wings with pepper sauce mixture. Bake for 10 minutes more. Turn wings over and brush with mixture again. Bake for 5 to 10 minutes more or until no longer pink. Serve wings with blue cheese dressing for dipping and celery sticks.

Nutrition Facts per main-dish serving: 542 cal., 46 g total fat (13 g sat. fat), 135 mg chol., 584 mg sodium, 4 g carbo., 1 g fiber, 29 g pro.

PREP:
15 minutes
BAKE:
35 minutes
OVEN:
375°F
MAKES:
4 main-dish servings or 24 appetizers

Roast chicken and vegetables may sound like Sunday dinner fare, but this lovely herb-infused version calls for cut-up chicken (rather than the whole bird) to save roasting time. It's too good— and quick—to save for weekends only!

6 g net carb

HERBED CHICKEN & ROASTED VEGETABLES

PREP:

15 minutes

ROAST:

35 minutes

OVEN:

425°F

MAKES:

6 servings

3	tablespoons olive oil or cooking oil
2	teaspoons dried basil, crushed
2	teaspoons dried marjoram, crushed
1	teaspoon dried rosemary, crushed
2	cloves garlic, minced
½	teaspoon salt
¼	teaspoon black pepper
4	medium carrots, peeled and cut into 1½-inch pieces
1	large onion, cut into wedges
1	3- to 3½-pound broiler-fryer chicken, cut up

1 In a small bowl combine oil, basil, marjoram, rosemary, garlic, salt, and pepper. In a shallow roasting pan combine carrots and onion. Drizzle half of the oil mixture over the vegetables; toss to combine and push to edges of pan. Brush the remaining oil mixture on the chicken pieces. Place chicken in the prepared pan.

2 Roast, uncovered, in a 425° oven for 35 to 45 minutes or until chicken is no longer pink (170°F for breasts; 180°F for thighs and drumsticks) and vegetables are tender.

Nutrition Facts per serving: 308 cal., 19 g total fat (4 g sat. fat), 79 mg chol., 283 mg sodium, 8 g carbo., 2 g fiber, 25 g pro.

Make the pesto butter up to 24 hours ahead of time and chill until needed. It's also delicious spread over grilled fish or tossed with steamed zucchini or yellow summer squash.

6 g
net
carb

PESTO CHICKEN WITH GRILLED TOMATOES

1	tablespoon olive oil
4	cloves garlic, minced
6	Roma tomatoes, halved lengthwise
1½	to 2 pounds meaty chicken pieces (breasts, thighs, and drumsticks)
3	tablespoons butter, softened
3	tablespoons purchased pesto
2	tablespoons chopped toasted walnuts
2	tablespoons finely chopped kalamata olives (optional)

PREP:

10 minutes

GRILL:

50 minutes

MAKES:

4 servings

1 Combine oil and garlic. Lightly brush tomato halves and chicken pieces with oil mixture.

2 For a charcoal grill, arrange medium-hot coals around a drip pan. Test for medium heat above the pan. Place chicken pieces bone sides down on grill rack over pan. Cover and grill for 50 to 60 minutes or until chicken is no longer pink (170°F for breasts; 180°F for thighs and drumsticks). During the last 6 to 8 minutes of grilling, place the tomatoes cut sides down directly over coals; turn once during grilling. (For a gas grill, preheat grill. Reduce heat to medium. Adjust for indirect cooking. Place chicken pieces bone sides down on grill rack over unlit burner. Grill as above.)

3 Meanwhile, combine butter, pesto, walnuts, and, if desired, olives. Cover and chill until serving time.

4 To serve, remove chicken from grill. Immediately spread pesto butter over chicken pieces and cut sides of tomatoes.

Nutrition Facts per serving: 407 cal., 30 g total fat (10 g sat. fat), 104 mg chol., 252 mg sodium, 7 g carbo., 1 g fiber, 28 g pro.

This technique of spreading the seasoning mixture between the meat and the skin allows the garlic and herbs to permeate the meat while the skin keeps the chicken moist and succulent.

2 g net carb

ROASTED ITALIAN CHICKEN

PREP:

15 minutes

ROAST:

1¼ hours

STAND:

10 minutes

OVEN:

375°F

MAKES:

6 servings

2	tablespoons balsamic vinegar
2	tablespoons olive oil
1	tablespoon lemon juice
3	cloves garlic, minced
½	teaspoon salt
½	teaspoon coarsely ground black pepper
1	tablespoon snipped fresh oregano or 1 teaspoon dried oregano, crushed
1	tablespoon snipped fresh basil or 1 teaspoon dried basil, crushed
1½	teaspoons snipped fresh thyme or ½ teaspoon dried thyme, crushed
1	3- to 3½-pound whole broiler-fryer chicken

1 In a small bowl whisk together vinegar, oil, lemon juice, garlic, salt, pepper, oregano, basil, and thyme. Set aside.

2 Place chicken breast side up on a rack in a shallow roasting pan. Slip your fingers between the skin and the breast and leg meat of the chicken, forming a pocket. Spoon herb mixture into pocket. Skewer neck skin to back. Tie legs to tail. Twist wing tips under back. Insert a meat thermometer into center of an inside thigh muscle. Do not allow thermometer tip to touch bone.

3 Roast, uncovered, in a 375° oven for 1¼ to 1½ hours or until drumsticks move easily in their sockets, meat is no longer pink, and thermometer registers 180°F. Remove chicken from oven. Cover chicken loosely with foil; let stand for 10 minutes before carving.

Nutrition Facts per serving: 266 cal., 17 g total fat (4 g sat. fat), 79 mg chol., 268 mg sodium, 2 g carbo., 0 g fiber, 25 g pro.

Widely used in Chinese cooking, hoisin sauce is thick, dark, and spicy-sweet.
Stir it into marinades or pass it as a table condiment.

EASY MARINATED CHICKEN BREASTS

8   skinless, boneless chicken breast halves
     (about 2½ pounds total)

½   cup bottled oil and vinegar salad dressing

3   tablespoons soy sauce

2   tablespoons bottled hoisin sauce

½   teaspoon ground ginger

     Bottled hoisin sauce

1 Place chicken breast halves in a self-sealing plastic bag set in a shallow dish. For marinade, in a small bowl stir together salad dressing, soy sauce, the 2 tablespoons hoisin sauce, and the ginger. Pour marinade over chicken; seal bag. Turn to coat chicken. Marinate in the refrigerator for 2 to 24 hours, turning bag occasionally.

2 Drain chicken, discarding marinade. For a charcoal grill, grill chicken on the rack of an uncovered grill directly over medium coals for 12 to 15 minutes or until chicken is no longer pink (170°F), turning once halfway through grilling. (For a gas grill, preheat grill. Reduce heat to medium. Place chicken on the grill rack over heat. Cover and grill as directed.) Pass additional hoisin sauce for dipping.

Nutrition Facts per serving: 189 cal., 5 g total fat (1 g sat. fat), 82 mg chol., 286 mg sodium, 1 g carbo., 0 g fiber, 33 g pro.

PREP:
10 minutes
MARINATE:
2 hours
GRILL:
12 minutes
MAKES:
8 servings

1 g net carb

A jar of roasted red sweet peppers helps this colorful salsa come together quickly. Chunks of fresh orange, bits of green onion, and fresh basil add extra pizzazz.

TURKEY WITH SWEET-PEPPER SALSA

PREP:

15 minutes

MARINATE:

2 hours

GRILL:

12 minutes

MAKES:

6 servings

6	turkey breast tenderloin steaks, cut ½ inch thick (about 1½ pounds total)
⅓	cup olive oil
¼	cup lemon juice
1	teaspoon finely shredded orange peel
¼	cup orange juice
4	cloves garlic, minced
¼	teaspoon salt
¼	teaspoon black pepper
1	recipe Sweet Pepper-Citrus Salsa (see below)

1 Place turkey in a self-sealing plastic bag set in a shallow dish. For marinade, in a small bowl combine oil, lemon juice, orange peel, orange juice, garlic, salt, and pepper. Pour over turkey; seal bag. Turn to coat turkey. Marinate in the refrigerator for 2 to 4 hours, turning occasionally.

2 Drain turkey, reserving marinade. For a charcoal grill, grill turkey on the rack of an uncovered grill directly over medium coals for 12 to 15 minutes or until turkey is tender and no longer pink (170°F). Turn once halfway through grilling, and brush with marinade during the first 6 minutes of grilling. (For a gas grill, preheat grill. Reduce heat to medium. Place turkey on grill rack over heat. Cover and grill as above.) Serve with Sweet Pepper-Citrus Salsa.

SWEET PEPPER-CITRUS SALSA: In a small bowl combine one 7-ounce jar roasted red sweet peppers, drained and chopped; 1 orange, peeled, seeded, and cut up; 2 green onions, sliced; 2 tablespoons balsamic vinegar; and 1 tablespoon snipped fresh basil or 1 teaspoon dried basil, crushed. Cover and refrigerate the salsa until serving time. Makes 1½ cups salsa.

Nutrition Facts per serving: 206 cal., 10 g total fat (2 g sat. fat), 50 mg chol., 107 mg sodium, 6 g carbo., 1 g fiber, 22 g pro.

Chipotle peppers, commonly used in Southwestern cooking, have a unique, smoky taste, enhancing the flavor of the meat.

0 g net carb

CHIPOTLE-RUBBED SMOKED TURKEY

1	2- to 2½-pound fresh or frozen turkey breast half with bone
3	cups hickory or mesquite wood chips
1	teaspoon ground coriander
½	teaspoon paprika
¼	to ½ teaspoon black pepper
1	small dried chipotle pepper, seeded and crushed, or ⅛ to ¼ teaspoon cayenne pepper
2	teaspoons cooking oil
	Fresh cilantro (optional)
	Fresh chile peppers (optional)

PREP:
1 hour

SOAK:
1 hour

GRILL:
1½ hours

STAND:
10 minutes

MAKES:
8 to 10 servings

1 Thaw turkey, if frozen. At least 1 hour before grilling, soak wood chips in enough water to cover. Meanwhile, in a small bowl combine coriander, paprika, black pepper, and chipotle pepper.

2 Remove skin and excess fat from turkey breast. Brush turkey with the oil. Rub with the spice mixture. Insert a meat thermometer into the thickest part of the turkey. Do not allow the thermometer tip to touch the bone.

3 Drain wood chips. For a charcoal grill, arrange medium-hot coals around a drip pan. Sprinkle half of the wood chips over coals. Test for medium heat above the pan. Place turkey bone side down in a roasting pan on the grill rack over drip pan. Cover and grill for 45 minutes. Sprinkle coals with remaining chips. Cover and grill for 45 minutes to 1¼ hours more or until thermometer registers 170°F. Add more coals as needed. (For a gas grill, preheat grill. Reduce heat to medium. Adjust for indirect cooking. Add drained wood chips according to manufacturer's directions. Place turkey in roasting pan on grill rack over unlit burner. Grill as above.)

4 Remove turkey from grill. Cover turkey loosely with foil; let stand for 10 minutes before slicing. If desired, garnish with cilantro and fresh chile peppers.

Nutrition Facts per serving: 105 cal., 3 g total fat (1 g sat. fat), 41 mg chol., 38 mg sodium, 0 g carbo., 0 g fiber, 18 g pro.

There's more than one way to stuff a turkey. Fresh spinach and tangy goat cheese make a melt-in-your-mouth filling for these turkey tenderloins. When sliced, the rosy-red, spicy crust on the meat yields to a juicy, tender interior.

0 g net carb

STUFFED TURKEY TENDERLOINS

PREP:

15 minutes

GRILL:

16 minutes

MAKES:

4 servings

2   8-ounce turkey breast tenderloins

2   cups chopped fresh spinach leaves

3   ounces semisoft goat cheese (chèvre) or feta cheese, crumbled (about ¾ cup)

½   teaspoon black pepper

1   tablespoon olive oil

1   teaspoon paprika

½   teaspoon salt

⅛   to ¼ teaspoon cayenne pepper

1 Make a pocket in each turkey tenderloin by cutting lengthwise from one side almost to, but not through, the opposite side; set aside. In a bowl combine the spinach, cheese, and black pepper. Spoon spinach mixture into pockets. Tie 100-percent-cotton kitchen string around each tenderloin in 3 or 4 places to hold in stuffing.

2 In a small bowl combine oil, paprika, salt, and cayenne pepper; brush evenly over tenderloins.

3 For a charcoal grill, grill turkey on the lightly greased rack of an uncovered grill directly over medium coals for 16 to 20 minutes or until turkey is tender and no longer pink in center of the thickest part (170°F); turn once halfway through grilling. (For a gas grill, preheat grill. Reduce heat to medium. Place turkey on lightly greased grill rack over heat. Cover and grill as above.) Remove and discard strings; slice tenderloins crosswise.

Nutrition Facts per serving: 220 cal., 12 g total fat (4 g sat. fat), 68 mg chol., 458 mg sodium, 1 g carbo., 1 g fiber, 26 g pro.

Tandoori-style dishes typically use yogurt as the marinade base and are seasoned with cumin, coriander, and turmeric, all spices common to Indian cuisine.

TANDOORI TURKEY

½	cup chopped onion
2	tablespoons lime juice
1	tablespoon cooking oil
1	teaspoon ground cumin
1	teaspoon coriander seed
½	teaspoon salt
½	teaspoon ground ginger
½	teaspoon ground turmeric
¼	teaspoon crushed red pepper
½	cup plain yogurt
4	4-ounce turkey breast tenderloin steaks

PREP:
15 minutes
MARINATE:
8 hours
GRILL:
15 minutes
MAKES:
4 servings

1 For marinade, in a food processor or blender combine onion, lime juice, oil, cumin, coriander seed, salt, ginger, turmeric, and crushed red pepper. Cover and process or blend until mixture is nearly smooth. Pour mixture into a shallow nonmetal dish or pan; stir in yogurt.

2 Cut small slits in both sides of the tenderloin steaks. Place steaks in the yogurt mixture, turning to coat both sides. Cover and marinate in the refrigerator for 8 to 24 hours, turning steaks occasionally. Remove the steaks from marinade; discard marinade.

3 For a charcoal grill, grill turkey on the lightly greased rack of an uncovered grill directly over medium coals for 15 to 18 minutes or until turkey is no longer pink (170°F). Turn once halfway through grilling. (For a gas grill, preheat grill. Reduce heat to medium. Place turkey on lightly greased grill rack over heat. Cover and grill as above.)

BROILING DIRECTIONS: Lightly grease the unheated rack of a broiler pan. Place turkey on prepared rack; broil 4 to 5 inches from the heat for 8 to 10 minutes or until tender and no longer pink (170°F), turning once halfway through broiling.

Nutrition Facts per serving: 143 cal., 4 g total fat (1 g sat. fat), 50 mg chol., 192 mg sodium, 3 g carbo., 0 g fiber, 22 g pro.

FISH & SEAFOOD

From delicate sea bass sauced with orange and dill to firm-fleshed halibut topped with a lively strawberry salsa, this variety of fish and seafood entrées is plentiful. You'll find the perfect low-carb recipe—whether grilled, oven roasted, pan fried, or lightly poached—to heighten the naturally fresh flavors of these tastes from the sea.

For a sumptuous low-carb supper, team this citrus-scented fish with a spinach salad and steamed asparagus.

4 g net carb

CITRUS BAKED HALIBUT

PREP:

15 minutes

BAKE:

15 minutes

OVEN:

400°F

MAKES:

4 servings

1   pound fresh or frozen halibut steaks, ³⁄₄ inch thick

¹⁄₃   cup finely chopped onion (1 small)

1   clove garlic, minced

1   tablespoon butter

2   tablespoons snipped fresh parsley

¹⁄₂   teaspoon finely shredded orange peel

¹⁄₄   teaspoon salt

¹⁄₈   teaspoon black pepper

¹⁄₄   cup orange juice

1   tablespoon lemon juice

1 Thaw fish, if frozen. Rinse fish and pat dry with paper towels. Cut fish into 4 serving-size pieces, if necessary. Arrange in a 2-quart square baking dish.

2 In a small saucepan cook onion and garlic in hot butter over medium heat until tender; remove from heat. Stir in parsley, orange peel, salt, and pepper; spoon over fish. Drizzle orange and lemon juice over fish. Bake, covered, in a 400° oven for 15 to 20 minutes or until fish flakes easily with a fork. Spoon pan juices over fish.

Nutrition Facts per serving: 166 cal., 6 g total fat (2 g sat. fat), 44 mg chol., 239 mg sodium, 4 g carbo., 0 g fiber, 24 g pro.

Sake and fresh ginger lend an unmistakable Japanese flavor to this piquant marinade. Steamed pea pods make a pleasing accompaniment.

2 g net carb

TERIYAKI FISH STEAKS

1   pound fresh or frozen tuna, shark, or halibut steaks, 1 inch thick

½   cup soy sauce

2   tablespoons orange or pineapple juice

1   tablespoon cooking oil

1   tablespoon sake or dry sherry

1   teaspoon grated fresh ginger or ¼ teaspoon ground ginger

1   clove garlic, minced

PREP:
15 minutes
MARINATE:
30 minutes
BROIL:
8 minutes
MAKES:
4 servings

1 Thaw fish, if frozen. Rinse fish; pat dry with paper towels. Cut steak into 4 serving-size pieces, if necessary. Place fish in a shallow dish. For marinade, stir together the soy sauce, orange juice, oil, sake, ginger, and garlic. Pour over fish. Turn fish to coat with marinade. Cover and marinate at room temperature for 30 minutes (or in the refrigerator for 2 hours), turning the steaks occasionally.

2 Drain fish, reserving marinade. Place fish on the greased unheated rack of a broiler pan. Brush fish with some of the marinade. Broil 4 inches from the heat for 5 minutes. Using a wide spatula, carefully turn over fish. Brush with marinade. Broil for 3 to 7 minutes more or until fish flakes easily with a fork. Discard any remaining marinade.

Nutrition Facts per serving: 201 cal., 7 g total fat (2 g sat. fat), 47 mg chol., 649 mg sodium, 2 g carbo., 0 g fiber, 29 g pro.

This saucy baked fish will be a hit with the whole family. Sprinkle with additional sliced green onion for an easy garnish.

3g net carb

FISH FILLETS WITH YOGURT DRESSING

PREP:

15 minutes

MARINATE:

20 minutes

BAKE:

4 to 6 minutes per ¹/₂-inch thickness

OVEN:

450°F

MAKES:

4 servings

1	pound fresh or frozen skinless cod, orange roughy, or other fish fillets, ¹/₂ to 1 inch thick
²/₃	cup bottled poppy seed salad dressing
3	tablespoons thinly sliced green onion
1	teaspoon snipped fresh thyme or ¹/₄ teaspoon dried thyme, crushed
¹/₂	cup plain yogurt

1 Thaw fish, if frozen. Rinse fish and pat dry with paper towels. Cut fish into 4 serving-size pieces. For marinade, in a large bowl combine ¹/₂ cup of the salad dressing, 2 tablespoons of the green onion, and ¹/₂ teaspoon of the fresh thyme (or ¹/₈ teaspoon dried thyme). Add fish fillets to marinade. Turn to coat. Cover and marinate in the refrigerator for 20 to 30 minutes.

2 Drain fillets, discarding the marinade. Measure the thickness of the fish. Place fish in a greased 2-quart rectangular baking dish, tucking under any thin edges. Bake fish, uncovered, in a 450° oven until fish flakes easily with a fork (allow 4 to 6 minutes per ¹/₂-inch thickness of fish). Transfer fish to a serving platter.

3 Meanwhile, for sauce, in a small serving bowl combine yogurt, remaining 3 tablespoons salad dressing, remaining 1 tablespoon green onion, and the remaining ¹/₂ teaspoon fresh thyme (or ¹/₈ teaspoon dried thyme). Serve sauce with fish.

Nutrition Facts per serving: 182 cal., 9 g total fat (2 g sat. fat), 55 mg chol., 201 mg sodium, 3 g carbo., 0 g fiber, 22 g pro.

In this fisherman's delight, salmon fillets are seasoned with a mint, soy sauce, and lime marinade.

0 g net carb

GLAZED SALMON

4	6-ounce fresh or frozen skinless salmon fillets
3	tablespoons snipped fresh mint
2	tablespoons soy sauce
2	teaspoons finely shredded lime peel
2	tablespoons lime juice
1	teaspoon olive oil
$\frac{1}{2}$	teaspoon freshly ground black pepper
	Lime wedges

1 Thaw fish, if frozen. Rinse fish and pat dry with paper towels. For marinade, in a small bowl combine mint, soy sauce, lime peel, lime juice, oil, and pepper. Place fish in a self-sealing plastic bag set in a shallow dish. Pour marinade over fish; seal bag. Turn bag to coat fish. Marinate in the refrigerator for 1 hour, turning bag occasionally.

2 Drain fish, discarding marinade. Measure thickness of fish. Place fish skin side down on unheated rack of broiler pan; tuck under any thin edges. Broil 4 inches from heat until fish flakes easily with a fork. (Allow 4 to 6 minutes per $\frac{1}{2}$-inch thickness. If fish is 1 inch or more thick, turn it over halfway through broiling.) Serve with lime wedges.

Nutrition Facts per serving: 316 cal., 19 g total fat (4 g sat. fat), 99 mg chol., 255 mg sodium, 0 g carbo., 0 g fiber, 34 g pro.

PREP:

15 minutes

MARINATE:

1 hour

BROIL:

4 to 6 minutes per $\frac{1}{2}$-inch thickness

MAKES:

4 servings

A firm texture and a low to moderate fat content make sea bass steaks perfect for marinating. The Asian-style marinade deliciously accents the mild-tasting fish.

1 g net carb

GINGER-MARINATED SEA BASS

PREP:

15 minutes

MARINATE:

1 hour

BROIL:

8 minutes

MAKES:

4 servings

4   fresh or frozen sea bass or halibut steaks, 1 inch thick (1½ to 1¾ pounds)

¼   cup teriyaki sauce

2   tablespoons lemon juice

1   tablespoon grated fresh ginger

2   cloves garlic, minced

⅛   teaspoon cayenne pepper

   Snipped fresh cilantro (optional)

1 Thaw fish, if frozen. Rinse fish and pat dry with paper towels. For marinade, in a shallow dish combine teriyaki sauce, lemon juice, ginger, garlic, and cayenne pepper. Add fish; turn to coat with marinade. Cover and marinate in the refrigerator for 1 to 2 hours, turning the fish occasionally.

2 Drain fish, reserving marinade. Place fish on the greased unheated rack of a broiler pan. Broil 4 inches from heat for 5 minutes. Using a wide spatula, carefully turn over fish. Brush with marinade. Broil 3 to 7 minutes more or until fish flakes easily with a fork. Discard any remaining marinade. If desired, sprinkle with cilantro.

Nutrition Facts per serving: 169 cal., 3 g total fat (1 g sat. fat), 69 mg chol., 268 mg sodium, 1 g carbo., 0 g fiber, 32 g pro.

Nut butters (not the peanut butter variety, but toasted nuts in melted butter) are wonderful, simple accompaniments to grilled fish. If you prefer, try this recipe with pistachios in place of hazelnuts.

1 g net carb

HALIBUT IN HAZELNUT BUTTER

2	cups wood chips (apple, pecan, or oak)
4	6-ounce fresh or frozen halibut steaks, cut 1 inch thick
1/3	cup butter
1/3	cup blanched hazelnuts (filberts)
1	tablespoon dry white wine
1	tablespoon snipped fresh parsley (optional)

PREP:
20 minutes

SOAK:
1 hour

GRILL:
30 minutes

MAKES:
4 servings

1 At least 1 hour before grilling, soak wood chips in enough water to cover.

2 Thaw fish, if frozen. Rinse fish; pat dry with paper towels. For a charcoal grill, arrange medium-hot coals around a drip pan. Test for medium heat above pan. Drain wood chips; then sprinkle them over the coals. Place fish on greased grill rack over drip pan. Cover and grill for 30 to 36 minutes or until fish flakes easily with a fork. (For a gas grill, preheat grill. Adjust for indirect cooking. Add soaked wood chips according to manufacturer's directions. Place fish on the greased grill rack over unlit burner. Cover and grill as above.) Remove fish from grill; keep warm.

3 For sauce, in a small skillet melt butter over medium heat. Add hazelnuts and cook, stirring occasionally, until nuts are toasted and butter is brown but not burned. Remove from heat. Stir in wine. Serve immediately over grilled fish. If desired, garnish with parsley.

Nutrition Facts per serving: 402 cal., 27 g total fat (11 g sat. fat), 98 mg chol., 257 mg sodium, 2 g carbo., 1 g fiber, 37 g pro.

To check for doneness of fish, stick the tines of a fork into the thickest portion of the fish at a 45-degree angle. Then gently twist the fork and pull up some of the flesh. If the fish flakes easily, it's done.

SPICY BROILED SHARK STEAKS

PREP:

15 minutes

MARINATE:

20 minutes

BROIL:

10 minutes

MAKES:

4 servings

1 pound fresh or frozen shark or swordfish steaks, cut ¾ inch thick

2 green onions, thinly sliced

2 tablespoons orange juice

2 tablespoons chile sauce

1 tablespoon snipped fresh basil or 1 teaspoon dried basil, crushed

1 tablespoon finely chopped fresh ginger

1 tablespoon reduced-sodium soy sauce

Several dashes hot chile oil

Nonstick cooking spray

Fresh chives (optional)

1 Thaw fish, if frozen. Rinse fish; pat dry with paper towels. Cut into 4 serving-size pieces. For marinade, in a shallow dish combine the green onions, orange juice, chile sauce, basil, ginger, soy sauce, and chile oil. Add the fish, turning to coat with marinade. Cover and marinate at room temperature for 20 minutes.

2 Coat the unheated rack of a broiler pan with cooking spray. Drain fish, reserving marinade. Place fish on prepared rack. Broil 4 inches from the heat for 5 minutes. Using a wide spatula, carefully turn fish over. Brush with the reserved marinade. Broil for 5 to 7 minutes more or until fish flakes easily with a fork. If desired, garnish with fresh chives.

Nutrition Facts per serving: 160 cal., 5 g total fat (1 g sat. fat), 45 mg chol., 342 mg sodium, 3 g carbo., 0 g fiber, 23 g pro.

Roasting brings out the rich, full flavor of the salmon and the tomatoes. While the main course cooks in the oven, steam some fresh asparagus or broccoli spears to complete the meal.

ROASTED SALMON & TOMATOES

1	1¼-pound fresh salmon fillet, about 1 inch thick
	Nonstick cooking spray
⅛	teaspoon salt
6	Roma tomatoes, seeded and chopped (about 1 pound)
1	tablespoon white wine Worcestershire sauce
¼	teaspoon coarsely ground black pepper
⅛	teaspoon salt
1	tablespoon Dijon-style mustard
1	tablespoon snipped fresh marjoram or oregano
	Fresh oregano sprigs (optional)

PREP:
15 minutes
ROAST:
12 minutes
OVEN:
450°F
MAKES:
4 servings

1 Thaw fish, if frozen. Coat a 13×9×2-inch baking pan with cooking spray. Rinse fish; pat dry with paper towels. Cut fish into 4 serving-size pieces. Sprinkle with ⅛ teaspoon salt. Place fish pieces skin side up in prepared pan, tucking under any thin edges. Arrange tomatoes around salmon. Sprinkle tomatoes with Worcestershire sauce, pepper, and ⅛ teaspoon salt.

2 Bake, uncovered, in a 450° oven for 12 to 16 minutes or until fish flakes easily with a fork. Remove skin from fish; discard skin. Transfer fish to dinner plates. Stir mustard and marjoram into tomatoes. Serve tomato mixture with fish. If desired, garnish with oregano sprigs.

Nutrition Facts per serving: 231 cal., 10 g total fat (2 g sat. fat), 75 mg chol., 370 mg sodium, 6 g carbo., 1 g fiber, 30 g pro.

Whole brown or white mushrooms work great for these kabobs. However, if you like, you can cut meaty portobello mushrooms into 1-inch pieces to thread onto the skewers.

3 g net carb

FISH KABOBS

PREP:
10 minutes

MARINATE:
30 minutes

GRILL:
8 minutes

MAKES:
6 servings

2　pounds fresh or frozen halibut, salmon, or swordfish steaks, cut 1 inch thick

½　cup lemon juice

⅓　cup olive oil

1　bay leaf

1　tablespoon snipped fresh dill

¼　teaspoon coarsely ground black pepper
　　Several drops bottled hot pepper sauce

1　large cucumber or zucchini, halved lengthwise and cut into ¾-inch slices

12　small to medium mushrooms

½　of a 12-ounce jar roasted red sweet peppers, drained and cut into 1-inch pieces

12　pimiento-stuffed green olives

1 Thaw fish, if frozen. Rinse fish and pat dry with paper towels. If necessary, remove and discard bones and skin. Cut fish into 1-inch cubes. Place fish in a self-sealing plastic bag set in a shallow dish.

2 For marinade, in a small bowl combine lemon juice, oil, bay leaf, dill, black pepper, and hot pepper sauce. Pour over fish; seal bag. Turn bag to coat fish. Marinate at room temperature for 30 minutes, turning bag occasionally.

3 Drain fish, reserving marinade. Onto six long metal skewers, alternately thread fish, cucumber, mushrooms, red pepper, and olives. Brush with some of the marinade.

4 For a charcoal grill, grill kabobs on the greased rack of an uncovered grill directly over medium coals for 8 to 12 minutes or until fish flakes easily with a fork. Turn and brush with reserved marinade halfway through grilling time. (For a gas grill, preheat grill. Reduce heat to medium. Place kabobs on greased grill rack over heat. Cover and grill as above.) Discard any remaining marinade.

Nutrition Facts per serving: 230 cal., 9 g total fat (1 g sat. fat), 48 mg chol., 241 mg sodium, 4 g carbo., 1 g fiber, 33 g pro.

When it's time to give the fish-and-lemon combo a vacation, explore other citrus possibilities. Here, sea bass is scented with orange by grilling it on a bed of orange slices.

ORANGE & DILL SEA BASS

4	5- to 6-ounce fresh or frozen sea bass or orange roughy fillets, ¾ inch thick
2	tablespoons snipped fresh dill
2	tablespoons olive oil
¼	teaspoon salt
¼	teaspoon white pepper
4	large oranges, cut into ¼-inch slices
1	orange, cut into wedges
	Fresh dill sprigs (optional)

PREP:
15 minutes

GRILL:
6 minutes

MAKES:
4 servings

1 Thaw fish, if frozen. Rinse fish; pat dry with paper towels. In a small bowl stir together snipped dill, oil, salt, and pepper. Brush both sides of fish with dill mixture.

2 For a charcoal grill, arrange a bed of orange slices on the greased grill rack directly over medium coals. Place fish on orange slices. Cover and grill for 6 to 9 minutes or until fish flakes easily with a fork (do not turn fish). (For a gas grill, preheat grill. Reduce heat to medium. As above, arrange orange slices and fish on greased grill rack over heat. Grill as above.)

3 To serve, use a spatula to transfer fish and grilled orange slices to a serving platter or plates. Squeeze the juice from orange wedges over fish. If desired, garnish with dill sprigs.

Nutrition Facts per serving: 207 cal., 10 g total fat (2 g sat. fat), 59 mg chol., 230 mg sodium, 2 g carbo., 0 g fiber, 26 g pro.

Whether you buy your trout at a fish market or catch them from a stream, this fresh-tasting grilled fish makes a special springtime treat.

1 g net carb

GRILLED TROUT WITH CILANTRO & LIME

PREP:

10 minutes

GRILL:

8 minutes

MAKES:

4 servings

4   8- to 10-ounce fresh or frozen dressed trout, heads removed

3   tablespoons lime juice

2   tablespoons olive oil

2   tablespoons snipped fresh cilantro or parsley

½   teaspoon kosher salt

¼   teaspoon cracked black pepper

Lime wedges

1 Thaw fish, if frozen. Rinse fish; pat dry with paper towels. In a small bowl combine lime juice and oil; brush inside and outside of each fish with the lime juice mixture. Sprinkle insides of each fish cavity evenly with cilantro, salt, and pepper.

2 Place fish in a well-greased grill basket. For a charcoal grill, grill trout on the rack of an uncovered grill directly over medium coals for 8 to 12 minutes or until fish flakes easily with a fork, turning basket once halfway through grilling. (For a gas grill, preheat grill. Reduce heat to medium. Place grill basket on grill rack over heat. Cover and grill as above.) Serve trout with lime wedges.

Nutrition Facts per serving: 376 cal., 19 g total fat (4 g sat. fat), 133 mg chol., 372 mg sodium, 1 g carbo., 0 g fiber, 47 g pro.

Strain the flavor-rich cooking liquid and use it in recipes calling for fish stock. Store the stock in a covered container in the refrigerator for up to 3 days or freeze for up to 1 month.

2 g net carb

TARRAGON-CHARDONNAY SALMON

4	5- to 6-ounce fresh or frozen salmon steaks, 1 inch thick
1	cup Chardonnay or other dry white wine
1	medium red onion, cut into thin wedges
2	stalks celery, sliced
1	teaspoon dried tarragon, crushed
¼	teaspoon salt
¼	teaspoon coarsely ground black pepper

PREP:
15 minutes
COOK:
8 minutes
MAKES:
4 servings

1 Thaw fish, if frozen. Rinse fish; pat dry with paper towels. In a large skillet combine wine, onion, celery, tarragon, salt, and pepper. Bring to boiling; add fish steaks. Simmer, covered, for 8 to 12 minutes or until fish flakes easily when tested with a fork. Use a slotted spatula to transfer fish and vegetables from cooking liquid to a serving platter.

Nutrition Facts per serving: 421 cal., 23 g total fat (5 g sat. fat), 111 mg chol., 255 mg sodium, 3 g carbo., 1 g fiber, 39 g pro.

Jalapeño pepper gives the strawberry salsa extra zip but doesn't overpower its fruity flavor.

HALIBUT WITH STRAWBERRY SALSA

PREP:

15 minutes

BROIL:

6 minutes

MAKES:

4 servings

4   fresh or frozen halibut steaks, cut ¾ inch thick (about 1 pound)

3   tablespoons plum sauce

3   tablespoons lime juice

½   teaspoon grated fresh ginger

¼   teaspoon salt

⅛   teaspoon black pepper

1   cup coarsely chopped strawberries

½   cup chopped, seeded cucumber

2   tablespoons thinly sliced green onion

2   tablespoons snipped fresh cilantro

½   of a small jalapeño pepper, seeded and finely chopped*

     Nonstick cooking spray

1   teaspoon sesame seeds

1 Thaw fish, if frozen. Rinse fish; pat dry with paper towels. For strawberry salsa, in a small bowl combine plum sauce, lime juice, and ginger. Remove 3 tablespoons of this mixture and combine with the salt and black pepper; set aside. To the remaining mixture add strawberries, cucumber, green onion, cilantro, and jalapeño pepper; cover and chill while preparing fish.

2 Coat the unheated rack of a broiler pan with cooking spray. Place halibut steaks on the prepared rack. Brush steaks with the reserved 3 tablespoons plum sauce mixture. Sprinkle with sesame seeds. Broil 4 inches from the heat for 6 to 9 minutes or until fish flakes easily with a fork. Serve with strawberry salsa.

*NOTE: Hot chile peppers such as jalapeños contain oils that can burn your eyes, lips, and skin. Wear plastic or rubber gloves while preparing hot peppers and be sure to thoroughly wash your hands and nails in hot, soapy water afterward.

Nutrition Facts per serving: 164 cal., 4 g total fat (0 g sat. fat), 36 mg chol., 204 mg sodium, 9 g carbo., 1 g fiber, 25 g pro.

The fascinating flavor combination of cilantro, cumin, garlic, and cayenne pepper hails from Morocco.

GRILLED SHRIMP CHARMOULA

2½	to 3 pounds fresh or frozen jumbo shrimp in shells (36 to 42)
½	cup olive oil or cooking oil
½	cup lemon juice
½	cup snipped fresh parsley
½	cup snipped fresh cilantro
6	cloves garlic
1	tablespoon paprika
2	teaspoons ground cumin
½	teaspoon cayenne pepper
½	teaspoon salt
¼	teaspoon black pepper

PREP:

10 minutes

MARINATE:

20 minutes

GRILL:

7 minutes

MAKES:

4 to 6 servings

1 Thaw shrimp, if frozen. Shell and devein shrimp. Set aside.

2 For marinade, in a blender or food processor combine oil, lemon juice, parsley, cilantro, garlic, paprika, cumin, cayenne pepper, salt, and black pepper. Cover and blend or process until finely pureed.

3 In a large bowl stir together shrimp and marinade. Cover and marinate in refrigerator for 20 to 30 minutes. Drain shrimp, reserving marinade. Thread shrimp onto skewers.

4 For a charcoal grill, grill shrimp on an uncovered grill directly over medium coals for 7 to 9 minutes or until opaque, turning often and brushing with marinade. (For a gas grill, preheat grill. Reduce heat to medium. Place shrimp on grill rack over heat. Cover and grill as above.) Discard any remaining marinade.

Nutrition Facts per serving: 205 cal., 7 g total fat (1 g sat. fat), 230 mg chol., 274 mg sodium, 2 g carbo., 0 g fiber, 31 g pro.

Toasting sesame seeds is easy. Place them in a small, heavy skillet over low heat and cook about 5 to 7 minutes, stirring frequently, until they're golden brown and fragrant.

 1 g net carb

SESAME-GINGER GRILLED SALMON

PREP:

15 minutes

MARINATE:

30 minutes

GRILL:

22 minutes

MAKES:

4 servings

4 5-ounce fresh or frozen skinless salmon fillets, ¾ to 1 inch thick

¼ cup reduced-sodium soy sauce

2 tablespoons lime juice

1 tablespoon grated fresh ginger

½ teaspoon toasted sesame oil

2 tablespoons toasted sesame seeds

1 Thaw fish, if frozen. Rinse fish; pat dry with paper towels. For marinade, in a shallow dish combine soy sauce, lime juice, ginger, and sesame oil. Add fish, turning to coat. Cover and marinate at room temperature for 30 minutes or in the refrigerator for 2 hours, turning fish occasionally. Drain fish, discarding marinade.

2 For a charcoal grill, arrange medium-hot coals around a drip pan. Test for medium heat above the pan. Place fish on lightly greased grill rack directly over the drip pan, tucking under any thin edges. Sprinkle fish with sesame seeds. Cover and grill until fish flakes easily with a fork. (Allow 15 to 18 minutes per ½-inch thickness of fish.) Do not turn. (For a gas grill, preheat grill. Reduce heat to medium. Adjust for indirect cooking. Grill as above.)

Nutrition Facts per serving: 287 cal., 18 g total fat (3 g sat. fat), 83 mg chol., 229 mg sodium, 1 g carbo., 0 g fiber, 30 g pro.

Garnish this refreshing salmon dish as you please—with a sprightly squeeze of lemon or a rich dab of the lemon-thyme mayonnaise.

SMOKED SALMON WITH LEMON-THYME MAYONNAISE

⅓	cup mayonnaise or salad dressing
2	tablespoons dairy sour cream
½	teaspoon finely shredded lemon peel
1	teaspoon lemon juice
2	teaspoons snipped fresh thyme
1	8-ounce piece smoked salmon
1	tablespoon finely chopped red onion
1	tablespoon capers, rinsed and drained
1	lemon, cut into wedges

PREP:

10 minutes

CHILL:

1 hour

MAKES:

2 to 3 servings

1 For lemon-thyme mayonnaise, in a small bowl stir together mayonnaise, sour cream, lemon peel, lemon juice, and thyme. Cover and chill for 1 to 6 hours.

2 To serve, place salmon on platter; sprinkle with onion and capers. Serve with lemon-thyme mayonnaise and lemon wedges.

Nutrition Facts per serving: 516 cal., 44 g total fat (8 g sat. fat), 96 mg chol., 824 mg sodium, 4 g carbo., 0 g fiber, 28 g pro.

Cilantro has a freshness that goes beautifully with fish.

4 g net carb

SNAPPER WITH CILANTRO PESTO

PREP:

15 minutes

GRILL:

4 to 6 minutes per ¹/₂-inch thickness

MAKES:

4 servings

4 4- to 5-ounce fresh or frozen red snapper or halibut fillets, ¹/₂ to ³/₄ inch thick

1 cup loosely packed fresh parsley leaves

¹/₂ cup loosely packed fresh cilantro leaves

3 tablespoons grated Parmesan cheese

2 tablespoons pine nuts or slivered almonds

3 cloves garlic, minced

2 teaspoons lemon juice

¹/₈ teaspoon salt

2 tablespoons olive oil

1 tablespoon lemon juice

2 teaspoons olive oil

Salt

Black pepper

1 Roma tomato, seeded and chopped

1 Thaw fish, if frozen. Rinse fish; pat dry with paper towels. Set fish aside.

2 For pesto, in a blender or food processor combine the parsley, cilantro, cheese, nuts, garlic, the 2 teaspoons lemon juice, and the ¹/₈ teaspoon salt. Cover and blend or process with several on-off turns until nearly smooth, stopping the machine and scraping down sides as necessary. With the machine running slowly, gradually add the 2 tablespoons oil; blend or process until the consistency of softened butter, scraping sides as necessary. Transfer to a small bowl. Set aside.

3 In a small bowl stir together the 1 tablespoon lemon juice and the 2 teaspoons oil. Brush fish with lemon mixture. Sprinkle fish with salt and pepper.

4 Place fish in a greased grill basket, tucking under any thin edges. For a charcoal grill, grill fish on the rack of an uncovered grill directly over medium coals until fish flakes easily with a fork (allow 4 to 6 minutes per ¹/₂-inch thickness of fish). Turn basket once halfway through grilling. (For a gas grill, preheat grill. Reduce heat to medium. Place fish on grill rack over heat. Cover and grill as above.) To serve, spoon pesto over fish and top with tomato.

Nutrition Facts per serving: 254 cal., 15 g total fat (3 g sat. fat), 45 mg chol., 281 mg sodium, 4 g carbo., 0 g fiber, 27 g pro.

Pan-searing is a nifty technique to cook rich-tasting, firm-textured fish such as tuna. It takes only minutes and seals in the flavorful juices.

ASIAN SEARED TUNA

4	6-ounce fresh or frozen tuna fillets, about ¾ inch thick
1	tablespoon olive oil
⅓	cup hoisin sauce
3	tablespoons orange juice
1	tablespoon toasted sesame seeds

PREP:

10 minutes

COOK:

8 minutes

MAKES:

4 servings

1 Thaw fish, if frozen. Rinse fish and pat dry with paper towels. In a large skillet cook fish in hot oil over medium-high heat about 4 minutes on each side or until fish flakes easily with a fork (tuna can be slightly pink in the center).

2 Meanwhile, for sauce, in a small saucepan stir together the hoisin sauce and orange juice; heat through. Transfer fish to serving plates; drizzle each with sauce and sprinkle with sesame seeds.

Nutrition Facts per serving: 271 cal., 7 g total fat (1 g sat. fat), 76 mg chol., 297 mg sodium, 9 g carbo., 0 g fiber, 41 g pro.

Cooked cucumbers provide a pleasant change of pace on these kabobs. Though their characteristic crispness disappears with cooking, their delicacy does not, making them a perfect companion for light and elegant fish dishes.

5 g net carb

SALMON WITH CUCUMBER KABOBS

PREP:

15 minutes

MARINATE:

10 minutes

GRILL:

8 minutes

MAKES:

4 servings

4   6- to 8-ounce fresh or frozen skinless salmon fillets,
     ½ to 1 inch thick

⅓   cup lemon juice

1   tablespoon olive oil or cooking oil

2   teaspoons snipped fresh tarragon

1   medium cucumber, halved lengthwise and
     cut into 1-inch slices

1   medium red onion, cut into wedges

8   cherry tomatoes

1 Thaw fish, if frozen. Rinse fish; pat dry with paper towels. Place fish in a self-sealing plastic bag set in a shallow dish. For marinade, combine lemon juice, oil, and tarragon. Reserve half for basting sauce. Pour remaining marinade over fish; seal bag. Turn bag to coat fish. Marinate at room temperature for 10 to 20 minutes.

2 Meanwhile, onto four 10-inch skewers, alternately thread cucumber and onion.

3 Drain fish, discarding marinade. Place fish in a well-greased grill basket. For a charcoal grill, grill the fish and vegetables on the rack of an uncovered grill directly over medium coals until fish flakes easily with a fork and vegetables are tender. Turn basket and vegetables once and brush occasionally with basting sauce. (Allow 4 to 6 minutes per ½-inch thickness of fish and 8 to 12 minutes for vegetables.) Add tomatoes to ends of kabobs the last 2 minutes of grilling. (For a gas grill, preheat grill. Reduce heat to medium. Place fish and vegetables on grill rack over heat. Cover and grill as above.)

Nutrition Facts per serving: 201 cal., 8 g total fat (2 g sat. fat), 31 mg chol., 106 mg sodium, 6 g carbo., 1 g fiber, 25 g pro.

Shrimp seasoned with soy sauce and garlic is served with a tropical dipping sauce.

SHRIMP WITH COCONUT SAUCE

¹/₃   cup purchased unsweetened coconut milk

2   teaspoons unbleached all-purpose flour

2   to 4 teaspoons wasabi paste

2   teaspoons grated fresh ginger

2   tablespoons lime juice

1   pound fresh or frozen jumbo shrimp in shells (15 to 18)

2   teaspoons cooking oil

1   tablespoon soy sauce

1   tablespoon minced garlic

¹/₄   to 1 teaspoon crushed red pepper (optional)

START TO FINISH:

25 minutes

MAKES:

4 servings

1 For dipping sauce, in a small saucepan stir together the coconut milk and flour. Cook and stir, uncovered, over low heat for 3 to 5 minutes or until thickened and bubbly. Set mixture aside to cool. Meanwhile, in a small bowl combine the wasabi paste, the ginger, and ¹/₂ teaspoon of the lime juice. Stir in thickened coconut milk mixture. Cover and chill in refrigerator.

2 Peel and devein shrimp, leaving tails on, if desired. In a large skillet or wok heat oil over medium-high heat for 30 seconds. Add shrimp and cook for 2 minutes, turning once. Add soy sauce, garlic, and, if desired, crushed red pepper. Cook for 30 to 60 seconds more or until shrimp are opaque.

3 Remove skillet from heat. Sprinkle remaining lime juice over shrimp mixture. Serve with dipping sauce.

Nutrition Facts per serving: 137 cal., 7 g total fat (4 g sat. fat), 131 mg chol., 428 mg sodium, 4 g carbo., 0 g fiber, 15 g pro.

For a refreshing summer meal, serve these poached fish steaks on a bed of shredded lettuce.

SALMON WITH LEMON-DILL DRESSING

PREP:

15 minutes

COOK:

8 minutes

CHILL:

2 hours

MAKES:

6 servings

6	fresh or frozen salmon or halibut steaks, 1 to 1¼ inches thick (about 2 pounds)
1½	cups water
¼	cup lemon juice
1	medium onion, sliced
10	whole black peppercorns
3	sprigs parsley
2	bay leaves
½	teaspoon salt
1	recipe Lemon-Dill Dressing (see below)

1 Thaw fish, if frozen. Rinse fish and pat dry with paper towels; set aside.

2 In a 12-inch skillet combine water, lemon juice, onion, peppercorns, parsley, bay leaves, and salt. Bring to boiling; add fish steaks. Simmer, covered, for 8 to 12 minutes or until fish flakes easily with a fork.

3 Remove fish from skillet; discard poaching liquid. Cover and chill fish in refrigerator for 2 to 24 hours. Serve fish with Lemon-Dill Dressing.

LEMON-DILL DRESSING: In a small bowl stir together ¾ cup mayonnaise or salad dressing, 3 tablespoons buttermilk, 2 tablespoons snipped fresh dill or 2 teaspoons dried dill, 1 tablespoon snipped fresh chives, ½ teaspoon finely shredded lemon peel, and 2 teaspoons lemon juice. Cover and chill 1 to 24 hours.

Nutrition Facts per serving: 339 cal., 27 g total fat (4 g sat. fat), 43 mg chol., 433 mg sodium, 1 g carbo., 0 g fiber, 22 g pro.

Though its presence in this recipe is subtle, fans of fiery wasabi, the bright-green Japanese horseradish condiment, will notice its head-clearing heat. Wasabi is found in powdered or paste form in Japanese markets or in large supermarkets.

5 g net carb

WASABI-GLAZED WHITEFISH WITH SLAW

4	4-ounce fresh or frozen white-fleshed skinless fish fillets, about ¾ inch thick*
2	tablespoons reduced-sodium soy sauce
1	teaspoon toasted sesame oil
¼	teaspoon wasabi powder or 1 tablespoon prepared horseradish
1	medium zucchini, coarsely shredded (about 1⅓ cups)
1	cup sliced radishes
1	cup fresh pea pods
3	tablespoons snipped fresh chives
3	tablespoons rice vinegar

PREP:
15 minutes

GRILL:
6 minutes

MAKES:
4 servings

1 Thaw fish, if frozen. Rinse fish; pat dry with paper towels. In a small bowl combine soy sauce, ½ teaspoon of the sesame oil, and the wasabi powder. Brush soy mixture over fish.

2 For a charcoal grill, grill fish on the lightly greased rack of an uncovered grill directly over medium coals for 6 to 9 minutes or until fish flakes easily with a fork. Turn after 4 minutes. (For a gas grill, preheat grill. Reduce heat to medium. Place fish on the greased grill rack over heat. Cover and grill as above.)

3 Meanwhile, for vegetable slaw, in a medium bowl combine the zucchini, radishes, pea pods, and 2 tablespoons of the chives. Stir together vinegar and the remaining ½ teaspoon sesame oil. Drizzle over the zucchini mixture; toss to combine. Sprinkle remaining 1 tablespoon chives over fish. Serve fish with vegetable slaw.

*NOTE: Use whitefish, sea bass, orange roughy, or any other similar fish fillets.

Nutrition Facts per serving: 141 cal., 3 g total fat (1 g sat. fat), 60 mg chol., 363 mg sodium, 6 g carbo., 1 g fiber, 24 g pro.

A quick, dill-infused, Dijon-flavored mayonnaise caps off these Scandinavian-style salmon fillets.
For a built-in salad and extra freshness, serve them on a bed of shredded cucumber.

DILLY SALMON FILLETS

PREP:

15 minutes

MARINATE:

10 minutes

GRILL:

5 minutes

MAKES:

4 servings

4   6-ounce fresh or frozen skinless salmon fillets,
    ½ to ¾ inch thick

3   tablespoons lemon juice

2   tablespoons snipped fresh dill

2   tablespoons mayonnaise or salad dressing

2   teaspoons Dijon-style mustard
    Dash freshly ground black pepper

1 Thaw fish, if frozen. Rinse fish; pat dry with paper towels. Place fish in a shallow dish. In a small bowl combine the lemon juice and 1 tablespoon of the dill; pour over fish and marinate at room temperature for 10 minutes. Meanwhile, in a small bowl stir together the remaining 1 tablespoon dill, the mayonnaise, mustard, and pepper; set aside.

2 For a charcoal grill, arrange medium-hot coals around drip pan. Test for medium heat above the pan. Place the fish on the lightly greased grill rack over the drip pan. Cover and grill for 3 minutes. Turn fish; spread the mayonnaise mixture over fish. Cover and grill for 2 to 6 minutes more or until fish flakes easily with a fork. (For a gas grill, preheat grill. Reduce heat to medium. Adjust for indirect cooking. Grill as above.)

Nutrition Facts per serving: 211 cal., 11 g total fat (2 g sat. fat), 35 mg chol., 204 mg sodium, 1 g carbo., 0 g fiber, 25 g pro.

Flavored with fresh basil and mint and served with grilled summer squash, this delicious halibut is ready from start to finish in about 25 minutes!

MINTY HALIBUT WITH SQUASH

1¼ to 1½ pounds fresh or frozen halibut or salmon steaks, 1 inch thick

¼ cup lemon juice

2 tablespoons olive oil

3 cloves garlic, minced

2 medium yellow summer squash or zucchini, halved lengthwise

   Salt

   Black pepper

2 tablespoons snipped fresh basil

1 tablespoon snipped fresh mint

PREP:
15 minutes
GRILL:
8 minutes
MAKES:
4 servings

1 Thaw fish, if frozen. Rinse fish; pat dry with paper towels. In a small bowl whisk together the lemon juice, oil, and garlic. Reserve 3 tablespoons of the mixture. Brush remaining lemon juice mixture on fish and the cut sides of the squash. Lightly sprinkle fish and squash with salt and pepper.

2 For a charcoal grill, grill fish on the lightly greased rack of an uncovered grill directly over medium coals for 8 to 12 minutes or until fish flakes easily with a fork, turning once. During the last 5 to 6 minutes of grilling, grill the squash just until tender, turning once. (For a gas grill, preheat grill. Reduce heat to medium. Place fish on the greased grill rack over heat. Cover and grill as above.)

3 Meanwhile, stir basil and mint into the reserved lemon juice mixture.

4 Transfer the squash to a cutting board; cool slightly and cut into ¼-inch slices. Place squash on a serving platter; drizzle with some of the basil mixture. Top with fish; drizzle with the remaining basil mixture.

Nutrition Facts per serving: 233 cal., 10 g total fat (1 g sat. fat), 46 mg chol., 112 mg sodium, 5 g carbo., 1 g fiber, 30 g pro.

Some say Cajun dishes change with every bite—and the last bite is as good as the first. A savory mix of fresh herbs and spices ensures this shrimp lives up to its name.

3 g net carb

CAJUN SHRIMP

PREP:

15 minutes

COOK:

25 minutes

MAKES:

8 servings

⅓	cup butter
⅓	cup olive oil
8	cloves garlic, minced
2	tablespoons snipped fresh basil
1	tablespoon snipped fresh rosemary
1	cup seafood stock or chicken broth
2	tablespoons lemon juice
4	teaspoons Worcestershire sauce
½	teaspoon salt
1	teaspoon paprika
1½	teaspoons crushed red pepper
2	pounds medium unshelled shrimp*

1 In a 12-inch cast-iron or heavy skillet, melt butter. Add oil and garlic. Stir over medium heat for 1 minute. Add basil, rosemary, stock, lemon juice, Worcestershire sauce, salt, paprika, and pepper. Bring to boiling; reduce heat. Simmer, uncovered, for 15 minutes. Add shrimp; cook and stir over medium heat about 5 minutes or until shrimp are opaque. Transfer shrimp and juices to a deep serving platter. Serve with slotted spoon.

*NOTE: If possible, purchase deveined shrimp in shells. Cooking the shrimp in the shells intensifies the flavor. Although a little messy to eat, this dish is fun and delicious.

Nutrition Facts per serving: 255 cal., 18 g total fat (6 g sat. fat), 151 mg chol., 432 mg sodium, 3 g carbo., 0 g fiber, 18 g pro.

Combine the marinade ingredients ahead of time, but marinate the fish for only 1 hour before grilling. Longer marinating will result in tough and chewy fish. An hour is plenty of time for the lime juice to infuse the fish with a tangy citrus flavor.

3 g net carb

LIME-MARINATED SWORDFISH

6	4-ounce fresh or frozen swordfish or tuna steaks, cut ¾ inch thick
½	teaspoon finely shredded lime peel
¼	cup lime juice
2	teaspoons cooking oil
2	cloves garlic, minced
1	tablespoon snipped fresh cilantro
1	teaspoon coarsely ground black pepper
¼	teaspoon salt
1	recipe Southwestern Pesto (see below)

PREP:
15 minutes

MARINATE:
1 hour

GRILL:
6 minutes

MAKES:
6 servings

1 Thaw fish, if frozen. Rinse fish and pat dry with paper towels. For marinade, in a small bowl combine lime peel, lime juice, oil, garlic, cilantro, pepper, and salt. Place fish in a self-sealing plastic bag set into a shallow dish. Pour marinade over fish; seal bag. Turn to coat fish. Marinate in the refrigerator for 1 hour, turning bag occasionally.

2 Remove fish from marinade; discard marinade. For a charcoal grill, grill fish on the greased rack of an uncovered grill directly over medium coals for 6 to 8 minutes or until fish flakes easily with a fork. Turn once halfway through grilling time. (For a gas grill, preheat grill. Reduce heat to medium. Place fish on the greased grill rack over heat. Cover and grill as above.) Serve fish with Southwestern Pesto.

SOUTHWESTERN PESTO: Bring 2 ounces Mexican grating cheese such as Asadero or Cotija to room temperature. Cut up cheese. In a blender or food processor combine the cheese; 2 garlic cloves, peeled; and 1 jalapeño pepper, seeded and cut into quarters.* Cover and blend or process until finely grated. Add two 4-ounce cans diced green chile peppers, drained; ¼ cup pine nuts or slivered almonds; ¼ cup lightly packed fresh parsley sprigs; and ¼ cup lightly packed fresh cilantro leaves. With machine running, gradually add 2 tablespoons olive oil, blending or processing until nearly smooth. Store any leftover pesto in the refrigerator up to 3 days or freeze up to 1 month. Makes 1⅓ cups.

*NOTE: Hot chile peppers such as jalapeños contain oils that can burn your eyes, lips, and skin. Wear plastic or rubber gloves while preparing hot peppers and be sure to thoroughly wash your hands and nails in hot, soapy water afterward.

Nutrition Facts per serving: 212 cal., 11 g total fat (3 g sat. fat), 49 mg chol., 306 mg sodium, 3 g carbo., 0 g fiber, 25 g pro.

Cinnamon and almonds are used generously in Spanish cooking, even in savory foods, such as this satisfying dish. This makes a lovely first course, or serve it with a leafy green salad for a light main dish.

6 g net carb

SHRIMP & MUSHROOMS IN ALMOND SAUCE

START TO FINISH:

1 hour

MAKES:

*4 main-dish or
12 appetizer servings*

12	ounces fresh or frozen medium shrimp in shells
½	cup dry white wine
1	tablespoon unbleached all-purpose flour
1	teaspoon olive oil
1½	cups sliced assorted mushrooms
½	teaspoon olive oil
1	small onion, thinly sliced (⅓ cup)
2	large cloves garlic, minced
1	medium tomato, seeded and chopped (½ cup)
1	cup clam juice (8 ounces)
½	teaspoon dried thyme, crushed
¼	teaspoon ground cinnamon
1	bay leaf
2	to 3 tablespoons ground blanched almonds
	Salt
	Black pepper

1 Thaw shrimp, if frozen. Rinse shrimp; pat dry with paper towels. Peel and devein shrimp, leaving tails intact. Marinate shrimp in wine for 30 minutes. Drain the shrimp, reserving the wine. Toss shrimp with flour; set aside.

2 Lightly coat a nonstick skillet with the 1 teaspoon olive oil. Add the mushrooms; cook and stir over medium heat for 3 to 5 minutes or until the mushrooms are just tender. Transfer mushrooms to a medium bowl.

3 Add shrimp to skillet; cook and stir over medium heat for 2 to 3 minutes or until the shrimp turn opaque. Transfer shrimp to the bowl with mushrooms.

4 Add the remaining ½ teaspoon oil to skillet. Add the onion and garlic; cook and stir just until tender. Stir in tomato and reserved wine, scraping any brown bits of vegetables from bottom of pan with a wooden spoon. Bring wine mixture to boiling. Add the clam juice, thyme, cinnamon, and bay leaf; bring to boiling. Reduce heat and boil gently, uncovered, for 10 minutes, stirring occasionally.

5 Return shrimp and mushrooms to skillet. Add almonds to the sauce. Heat over low heat just until shrimp and mushrooms are warm. Remove bay leaf. Add salt and pepper to taste. Serve immediately.

Nutrition Facts per main-dish serving: 143 cal., 5 g total fat (1 g sat. fat), 280 mg sodium, 7 g carbo., 1 g fiber, 13 g pro.

These tongue-tingling seafood brochettes—soaked in a simple marinade of sherry, mustard, and soy sauce—can be made with scallops, shrimp, or a combination of both.

SCALLOP BROCHETTES

1 pound fresh or frozen sea scallops and/or peeled and deveined large shrimp

2 tablespoons cooking oil

2 tablespoons dry sherry

2 tablespoons stone-ground mustard

1½ teaspoons soy sauce

PREP:
15 minutes
MARINATE:
30 minutes
GRILL:
5 minutes
MAKES:
4 servings

① Thaw scallops, if frozen. Rinse scallops; pat dry with paper towels. Halve large scallops (you should have about 20 pieces). Place scallops in a self-sealing plastic bag set in a shallow dish. For marinade, in a small bowl combine oil, sherry, mustard, and soy sauce. Pour over scallops; seal bag. Marinate in the refrigerator for 30 minutes, turning bag occasionally.

② Drain scallops, discarding marinade. Onto 6-inch skewers, thread scallops. (If using both scallops and shrimp, thread a scallop in the "curl" of each shrimp.)

③ For a charcoal grill, grill kabobs on the greased rack of an uncovered grill directly over medium coals for 5 to 8 minutes or until scallops turn opaque, turning occasionally. (For a gas grill, preheat grill. Reduce heat to medium. Place kabobs on grill rack over heat. Cover and grill as above.)

Nutrition Facts per serving: 120 cal., 3 g total fat (0 g sat. fat), 37 mg chol., 242 mg sodium, 3 g carbo., 0 g fiber, 19 g pro.

Fresh ginger and jalapeño pepper team up to give a peppy kick to this colorful medley of zucchini, asparagus, and shrimp.

7 g net carb

ZUCCHINI WITH SHRIMP

PREP:
25 minutes

COOK:
7 minutes

MAKES:
4 servings

8 ounces fresh or frozen peeled, deveined medium shrimp (12 ounces in shells)

5 zucchini (about 1¼ pounds)

8 ounces fresh asparagus spears

1 fresh jalapeño pepper, seeded and finely chopped*

1 tablespoon grated fresh ginger

2 cloves garlic, minced

2 tablespoons cooking oil

2 tablespoons snipped fresh cilantro

1 tablespoon toasted sesame seeds

2 teaspoons toasted sesame oil

¼ teaspoon salt

¼ teaspoon black pepper

1 Thaw shrimp, if frozen. Halve each zucchini lengthwise. Place each half, cut side down, on a board and cut into long, thin strips. Set aside. Snap off and discard woody bases from asparagus. Cut asparagus diagonally into 1-inch pieces.

2 Place asparagus in a steamer basket over gently boiling water. Cover and steam for 2 minutes; add zucchini and steam for 2 to 3 minutes more or until vegetables are just crisp-tender (don't overcook). Drain well; keep warm.

3 Meanwhile, in a large skillet cook jalapeño pepper, ginger, and garlic in hot cooking oil over medium-high heat for 30 seconds. Add shrimp. Cook over medium-high heat for 2 to 3 minutes or until shrimp turn opaque, stirring often. Stir in cilantro, sesame seeds, sesame oil, salt, and pepper. Add zucchini and asparagus to skillet; toss gently to coat. Transfer to a serving platter.

*NOTE: Hot chile peppers such as jalapeños contain oils that can burn your eyes, lips, and skin. Wear plastic or rubber gloves while preparing hot peppers and be sure to thoroughly wash your hands and nails in hot, soapy water afterward.

Nutrition Facts per serving: 197 cal., 12 g total fat (2 g sat. fat), 86 mg chol., 239 mg sodium, 8 g carbo., 1 g fiber, 17 g pro.

Oven-baked and flavorful, these fish fillets are easy alternatives to deep frying. For a special presentation, serve the fillets over a bed of colorful coleslaw.

1 g net carb

CAJUN CATFISH

1 tablespoon black pepper

1 tablespoon dried oregano, crushed

2 to 3 teaspoons seasoned salt

2 teaspoons onion powder

1 teaspoon crushed red pepper

¾ teaspoon chili powder

½ teaspoon ground cumin

4 skinned catfish fillets, about ½ inch thick

1 For seasoning mix, in a small bowl stir together black pepper, oregano, salt, onion powder, crushed red pepper, chili powder, and cumin. Use about 1 tablespoon seasoning mixture to coat both sides of catfish. Arrange fish in a lightly greased shallow baking pan.

2 Bake in a 350° oven for 10 minutes. Turn over fish and bake for 5 to 8 minutes more or until fish flakes easily with a fork. Store remaining seasoning mix in an airtight container at room temperature up to 1 month. Use for fish or pork.

Nutrition Facts per serving: 233 cal., 13 g total fat (3 g sat. fat), 79 mg chol., 283 mg sodium, 1 g carbo., 0 g fiber, 27 g pro.

PREP:
10 minutes
BAKE:
15 minutes
OVEN:
350°F
MAKES:
4 servings

SIDE DISHES

Looking for a change from your usual side dish? Then you've come to the right place. These side dishes are not only low in carbs but also packed with flavor and attractive enough to serve for guests. Try crunchy and sweet Broccoli and Pineapple Slaw as a side for grilled chicken or Tangy Green Beans with broiled steak. Or, make your own combinations with any one of these versatile dishes.

9

Use any color sweet pepper in this Mediterranean-style side dish.

4g net carb

SUMMER SQUASH WITH PEPPERS

PREP:
15 minutes

ROAST:
15 minutes

OVEN:
425°F

MAKES:
6 servings

2   pounds zucchini and/or yellow summer squash, cut into bite-size chunks

1   sweet pepper, cut into strips

2   tablespoons olive oil

1½ teaspoons Greek-style or Mediterranean-style seasoning blend

¼   teaspoon black pepper

1 Place the squash pieces and sweet pepper strips in a large shallow roasting pan. Drizzle with oil and sprinkle with seasoning and pepper, tossing to coat. Roast, uncovered, in a 425° oven for 15 minutes or just until tender, stirring once.

Nutrition Facts per serving: 66 cal., 5 g total fat (1 g sat. fat), 0 mg chol., 25 mg sodium, 6 g carbo., 2 g fiber, 2 g pro.

You probably don't think of broccoli when you consider vegetables for the grill. But grilling gives it a great smoky flavor worth trying.

3g net carb

BROCCOLI & OLIVES

3½	cups broccoli florets
½	cup pitted ripe olives
½	of a 2-ounce can anchovy fillets, drained and finely chopped (optional)
2	tablespoons snipped fresh oregano or Italian flat-leaf parsley
2	tablespoons olive oil
2	tablespoons red wine vinegar
5	cloves garlic, minced
¼	teaspoon crushed red pepper
	Dash salt

1 In a large saucepan bring a small amount of water to boiling; add broccoli. Simmer, covered, for 2 minutes; drain. In a medium bowl combine broccoli and olives. For marinade, in a small bowl whisk together anchovies (if using), oregano, oil, vinegar, garlic, red pepper, and salt. Pour over broccoli and olives; toss to coat. Marinate at room temperature for 10 minutes, stirring occasionally. Drain broccoli and olives; discard marinade.

2 Onto long metal skewers alternately thread broccoli florets and olives. For a charcoal grill, grill kabobs on the rack of an uncovered grill directly over medium coals for 6 to 8 minutes or until broccoli is light brown and tender, turning occasionally. (For a gas grill, preheat grill. Reduce heat to medium. Place kabobs on grill rack over heat. Cover and grill as above.) Remove broccoli and olives from skewers.

Nutrition Facts per serving : 91 cal., 8 g total fat (1 g sat. fat), 0 mg chol., 125 mg sodium, 6 g carbo., 3 g fiber, 3 g pro.

PREP:
15 minutes

MARINATE:
10 minutes

GRILL:
6 minutes

MAKES:
4 servings

A popular adage says there are two things money can't buy: love and homegrown tomatoes.
If you don't have the latter, search out a farmer's market for the makings of this summer dish.
It will garner you love from all who are lucky enough to taste it.

4 g net carb

GRILLED TOMATOES WITH PESTO

PREP:

15 minutes

GRILL:

15 minutes

MAKES:

6 servings

3   to 5 small to medium red, orange, and/or yellow tomatoes, cored and halved crosswise

2   tablespoons purchased pesto

6   very thin onion slices

½   cup shredded Monterey Jack cheese (2 ounces)

⅓   cup smoky-flavored whole almonds, chopped

2   tablespoons snipped fresh parsley

Salt

Black pepper

1 Using a spoon, hollow out the top ¼ inch of tomato halves. Top with pesto, then onion slices. Place tomatoes in a foil pie plate.

2 For a charcoal grill, arrange medium-hot coals around a drip pan. Test for medium heat above the pan. Place the tomatoes in pie plate over drip pan. Cover and grill for 10 to 15 minutes or until tomatoes are heated through. (For a gas grill, preheat grill. Reduce heat to medium. Adjust for indirect cooking. Place tomatoes in pie plate on grill rack over unlit burner. Grill as above.)

3 Meanwhile, in a small bowl stir together cheese, almonds, and parsley. Sprinkle over tomatoes. Cover and grill about 5 minutes more or until cheese is melted. Sprinkle lightly with salt and pepper.

Nutrition Facts per serving: 132 cal., 10 g total fat (2 g sat. fat), 9 mg chol., 119 mg sodium, 6 g carbo., 2 g fiber, 5 g pro.

The cooked flesh of this creamy-yellow squash separates into spaghetti-like strands. Topped with grilled tomatoes and fresh basil, this dish is a great way to get acquainted.

SPAGHETTI SQUASH WITH GRILLED TOMATOES

1   2½-pound spaghetti squash, halved lengthwise and seeded

2   tablespoons water

4   teaspoons olive oil

1   teaspoon dried Italian seasoning

½   teaspoon salt

¼   teaspoon black pepper

½   cup finely shredded Parmesan cheese

4   medium red and/or yellow Roma tomatoes, quartered

2   tablespoons snipped fresh basil

PREP:
15 minutes
COOK:
10 minutes
GRILL:
10 minutes
MAKES:
4 to 6 servings

1 Place squash cut sides down in a microwave-safe 2-quart rectangular baking dish; add the water. Prick skin all over with a fork. Cover with vented plastic wrap. Microwave on 100% power (high) about 10 minutes or until squash is tender. Let squash stand for 5 minutes.

2 Combine oil, Italian seasoning, salt, and pepper. Using fork, remove pulp from squash shells, separating it into strands. Transfer to bowl; toss with 2 teaspoons of the oil mixture and the Parmesan cheese. Fold a 36×18-inch piece of heavy foil in half to make a double thickness of foil that measures 18×18 inches. Place squash mixture in center of foil. Bring up opposite edges of foil and seal with double fold. Fold remaining edges to completely enclose the squash mixture, leaving space for steam to build.

3 For a charcoal grill, grill squash packet on the rack of an uncovered grill directly over medium coals for 10 minutes, turning once. Toss tomatoes with remaining oil mixture. For last 5 minutes of grilling, place tomatoes on grill rack beside packet. Grill tomatoes just until tender, turning once. (For a gas grill, preheat grill. Reduce heat to medium. Place squash packet on grill rack over heat. Cover and grill as above.) Transfer tomatoes to cutting board; cool slightly and chop. Spoon over squash; sprinkle with basil.

Nutrition Facts per serving: 133 cal., 8 g total fat (1 g sat. fat), 10 mg chol., 447 mg sodium, 9 g carbo., 2 g fiber, 6 g pro.

Thanks to soy sauce and the nutty intrigue that sesame oil imparts, this dish brings a pleasant, Asian-inspired counterpoint to the menu.

SOY-SAUCED BROCCOLI & PEPPERS

PREP:

10 minutes

COOK:

7 minutes

MAKES:

12 servings

3 tablespoons soy sauce

1 tablespoon lemon juice

1 teaspoon toasted sesame oil

8 cups broccoli florets (about 1 pound florets or about 2 pounds with stalks)

2 medium red and/or yellow sweet peppers, cut into strips (about 1½ cups)

1 For sauce, stir together soy sauce, lemon juice, and oil; set aside.

2 Place steamer basket in a very large skillet. Add water to just below the steamer basket. Bring to boiling. Add broccoli; cover. Reduce heat, and steam for 4 minutes. Add the sweet peppers; cover and steam for 3 to 4 minutes more or until vegetables are crisp-tender. Drain vegetables; transfer vegetables to a serving bowl. Drizzle sauce over vegetables, tossing gently to coat.

Nutrition Facts per serving: 30 cal., 1 g total fat (0 g sat. fat), 0 mg chol., 246 mg sodium, 5 g carbo., 2 g fiber, 0 g pro.

Feta cheese adds flavor and walnuts add a toasty crunch to this irresistible green bean side dish.

4g net carb

TANGY GREEN BEANS

PREP:

10 minutes

COOK:

14 minutes

MAKES:

4 servings

12	ounces fresh green beans, cut into 1-inch pieces (about 2¼ cups)
2	tablespoons water
⅓	cup chopped walnuts
2	tablespoons butter
½	cup crumbled feta cheese or ½ cup mozzarella cheese cut into ½-inch cubes (2 ounces)

1 In a microwave-safe casserole combine green beans and water. Cover and microwave on 100% power (high) for 12 to 14 minutes or just until tender, stirring once after 6 minutes. Drain. Cover; keep warm.

2 In a microwave-safe baking dish combine walnuts and butter. Cover with vented clear plastic wrap. Microwave on high for 1½ to 2½ minutes or until butter is bubbly and just beginning to brown, stirring after 1 minute.

3 Add walnut mixture and cheese to beans in casserole; toss to combine. Serve warm.

Nutrition Facts per serving: 194 cal., 17 g total fat (7 g sat. fat), 33 mg chol., 277 mg sodium, 8 g carbo., 4 g fiber, 6 g pro.

This versatile side dish fits a variety of menus. For brunch or breakfast, serve the savory tomato halves with scrambled eggs, or serve them with grilled pork or fish for a dinner accompaniment.

HERBED-YOGURT BAKED TOMATOES

PREP:

10 minutes

BAKE:

20 minutes

OVEN:

375°F

MAKES:

4 servings

2　large tomatoes

½　cup plain yogurt

2　teaspoons unbleached all-purpose flour

½　teaspoon dried marjoram, crushed

⅛　to ¼ teaspoon black pepper

3　tablespoons grated Romano or Parmesan cheese

1 Remove cores from tomatoes; halve tomatoes crosswise. Place tomato halves, cut sides up, in an ungreased 2-quart square baking dish.

2 In a small bowl combine yogurt, flour, marjoram, and pepper. Spoon about 2 tablespoons of the yogurt mixture onto each tomato half. Sprinkle cheese over the yogurt mixture.

3 Bake in a 375° oven for 20 to 25 minutes or until tomatoes are heated through.

Nutrition Facts per serving: 51 cal., 1 g total fat (1 g sat. fat), 4 mg chol., 75 mg sodium, 7 g carbo., 1 g fiber, 4 g pro.

Scrumptious squash, carrots, red pepper, and broccoli combine to create a festival of colors in this mustard-seasoned medley.

 5g net carb

VEGETABLE PRIMAVERA

2   tablespoons reduced-sodium chicken broth or water

2   teaspoons Dijon-style mustard

2   teaspoons olive oil

2   teaspoons white wine vinegar
    Nonstick cooking spray

1   cup sliced yellow summer squash

⅔   cup packaged peeled baby carrots

⅔   cup chopped red sweet pepper

2   cups broccoli florets

4   teaspoons snipped fresh parsley

1 In a small bowl combine 1 tablespoon of the broth, the mustard, oil, and vinegar. Set aside.

2 Lightly coat a medium nonstick skillet with cooking spray. Heat over medium heat. Add squash, carrots, and sweet pepper to skillet. Cook and stir about 5 minutes or until vegetables are nearly tender. Add broccoli and remaining 1 tablespoon broth. Cook, covered, about 3 minutes or until broccoli is crisp-tender.

3 Stir in the mustard mixture; heat through. Sprinkle with parsley.

Nutrition Facts per serving: 58 cal., 3 g total fat (0 g sat. fat), 0 mg chol., 54 mg sodium, 8 g carbo., 3 g fiber, 2 g pro.

START TO FINISH:
20 minutes
MAKES:
4 servings

The next time your garden overflows with zucchini, try these tasty patties.

2 g net carb

ZUCCHINI LATKES

PREP:

10 minutes

COOK:

35 minutes

STAND:

30 minutes

MAKES:

about 30 latkes

4	cups shredded zucchini
¼	teaspoon salt
1	cup snipped fresh parsley
2	slightly beaten eggs
⅓	cup matzo meal
1	teaspoon lemon-pepper seasoning
	Cooking oil
	Dairy sour cream (optional)

1 In a large bowl combine zucchini and salt; let stand for 30 minutes. Strain excess liquid from zucchini.

2 Return zucchini to bowl and add parsley, eggs, matzo meal, and lemon-pepper seasoning; mix until combined.

3 In a large skillet heat a little cooking oil. Drop zucchini mixture by tablespoons into hot oil to form 3-inch latkes. Cook over medium heat for 2 to 3 minutes per side or until golden brown, turning once. Remove and keep warm.

4 Repeat with remaining mixture, adding more oil, if needed. If desired, serve warm latkes with sour cream.

MAKE-AHEAD DIRECTIONS: Prepare the latkes as directed; cool. Place on a baking sheet in a single layer and freeze until firm. Place frozen latkes in a freezer bag or freezer container; seal. Freeze up to 4 weeks. To serve, place on baking sheet. Heat in a 450°F oven for 7 to 10 minutes.

Nutrition Facts per latke: 18 cal., 1 g total fat (0 g sat. fat), 14 mg chol., 63 mg sodium, 2 g carbo., 0 g fiber, 1 g pro.

Brussels sprouts and carrots celebrate togetherness in a delicate orange sauce. These colorful vegetables complement roasted meat or poultry.

CITRUS BRUSSELS SPROUTS

8 g net carb

2	cups fresh Brussels sprouts or a 10-ounce package frozen Brussels sprouts, thawed
4	small carrots, quartered lengthwise and cut into 1-inch pieces
⅓	cup orange juice
1	teaspoon unbleached all-purpose flour
¼	teaspoon salt
¼	teaspoon ground nutmeg (optional)

PREP:
15 minutes
COOK:
10 minutes
MAKES:
4 servings

1 Halve Brussels sprouts. In a covered medium saucepan cook Brussels sprouts and carrots in a small amount of boiling water for 10 to 12 minutes or until vegetables are crisp-tender. Drain in colander.

2 In the same saucepan combine orange juice, flour, salt, and, if desired, nutmeg. Return Brussels sprouts and carrots to saucepan. Cook and stir until thickened and bubbly. Cook and stir for 2 minutes more.

Nutrition Facts per serving: 52 cal., 0 g total fat (0 g sat. fat), 0 mg chol., 171 mg sodium, 11 g carbo., 3 g fiber, 2 g pro.

Marinated in a mixture of bottled dressing and celery seeds, these thinly sliced cucumbers and onions can pull double duty as a relish or side salad.

MARINATED CUCUMBERS

PREP:

10 minutes

CHILL:

4 hours

MAKES:

6 servings

⅓ cup bottled oil and vinegar salad dressing

¼ teaspoon salt

¼ teaspoon celery seeds

¼ teaspoon dried dill

⅛ teaspoon freshly ground black pepper

1 large cucumber, very thinly sliced (3½ cups)

½ of a sweet onion, very thinly sliced and separated into rings (1 cup)

1 In a large bowl combine salad dressing, salt, celery seeds, dill, and pepper. Gently stir in cucumber and onion. Cover and chill for 4 to 24 hours.

Nutrition Facts per serving: 85 cal., 7 g total fat (1 g sat. fat), 0 mg chol., 165 mg sodium, 5 g carbo., 1 g fiber, 1 g pro.

This recipe makes plenty of orange-marinated olives, so you'll have extras on hand for snacks.

2 g net carb

HERB-BAKED OLIVES

3½	cups mixed imported Greek and/or Italian olives
4	4-inch sprigs fresh rosemary
1	cup dry white wine
¼	cup olive oil
4	teaspoons finely shredded orange peel
⅓	cup orange juice
⅓	cup olive oil
2	tablespoons snipped fresh rosemary
2	tablespoons snipped fresh parsley
1	tablespoon minced garlic (6 cloves)
¼	teaspoon black pepper

PREP:
10 minutes

BAKE:
45 minutes

OVEN:
375°F

MARINATE:
2 hours

MAKES:
14 servings (3½ cups)
(¼ cup or 12 olives per serving)

1 Arrange olives in a single layer in a 15×10×1-inch baking pan. Add the rosemary sprigs. Stir together wine and the ¼ cup olive oil; drizzle over olives and rosemary. Bake in a 375° oven for 45 to 60 minutes or until most of the liquid has been absorbed, stirring occasionally.

2 Meanwhile, for the dressing, combine orange peel, orange juice, the ⅓ cup olive oil, the snipped rosemary, parsley, garlic, and pepper.

3 Transfer the olive mixture to a medium bowl. Discard the rosemary sprigs. Stir in dressing. Cover and marinate in the refrigerator for 2 hours or up to 1 week.

Nutrition Facts per serving: 148 cal., 14 g total fat (2 g sat. fat), 0 mg chol., 376 mg sodium, 4 g carbo., 2 g fiber, 0 g pro.

These golden dinnertime treats, flavored with Parmesan cheese and onion, will reign as a favorite pancake recipe.

7 g net carb

BUMPER-CROP ZUCCHINI PANCAKES

PREP:

30 minutes

COOK:

20 minutes

MAKES:

12 side-dish servings (24 pancakes)

4	to 5 medium zucchini (about 1½ pounds)
2	eggs
¾	cup unbleached all-purpose flour
¼	cup grated Parmesan cheese
1	tablespoon finely chopped onion
½	teaspoon salt
¼	teaspoon black pepper
¼	teaspoon garlic powder (optional)

1 Trim and shred zucchini. Place in a colander or sieve and let drain for 15 minutes, gently pressing zucchini occasionally to extract moisture. Spread zucchini on paper towels; blot to remove moisture. Measure 5 cups shredded zucchini.

2 In a large bowl beat eggs with a rotary beater or fork. Stir in flour, Parmesan cheese, onion, salt, black pepper, and, if desired, garlic powder just until moistened (batter should be lumpy). Stir in shredded zucchini just until combined.

3 For each pancake, spoon a generous 1 tablespoon of batter onto a hot, lightly greased griddle or heavy skillet, spreading to form a 4-inch circle. Cook over medium-low heat for 1½ to 2 minutes on each side or until the pancake is golden brown. If desired, season the pancakes with some additional salt and black pepper to taste.

Nutrition Facts per serving (2 pancakes): 57 cal., 2 g total fat (1 g sat. fat), 37 mg chol., 140 mg sodium, 8 g carbo., 1 g fiber, 3 g pro.

If you don't have fresh spinach on hand, substitute one 10-ounce package of frozen chopped spinach, cooked and well drained. Simply add it to the cooked raisin mixture and serve.

9 g net carb

ROMA-STYLE SPINACH

¼	cup golden raisins
2	tablespoons pine nuts or chopped walnuts
2	small cloves garlic, minced
¼	teaspoon salt
	Dash cayenne pepper
4	teaspoons olive oil
12	cups (1 lb.) torn spinach (8 ounces)
4	teaspoons finely shredded Parmesan cheese

START TO FINISH:

15 minutes

MAKES:

2 servings

1 In a large saucepan cook and stir raisins, nuts, garlic, salt, and cayenne pepper in hot oil over medium heat about 1 minute or until garlic is light brown.

2 Add spinach; toss to coat. Cook and stir for 1 to 2 minutes or just until spinach is wilted and heated through. Before serving, sprinkle with Parmesan cheese.

Nutrition Facts per serving: 128 cal., 8 g total fat (1 g sat. fat), 2 mg chol., 244 mg sodium, 12 g carbo., 3 g fiber, 5 g pro.

This humble squash gets a French accent with deeply flavored walnut oil—a Gallic favorite. Walnut oil is delicate and should be refrigerated. If the oil becomes cloudy and solid, let it stand several minutes at room temperature before using.

6 g net carb

SUMMER SQUASH COMBO

PREP:

15 minutes

GRILL:

5 minutes

MAKES:

4 to 6 servings

2	tablespoons walnut oil or olive oil
1	tablespoon olive oil
2	teaspoons snipped fresh rosemary or ½ teaspoon dried rosemary, crushed
½	teaspoon salt
½	to 1 teaspoon crushed red pepper
1	clove garlic, minced
2	medium red onions, cut crosswise into ¾-inch slices
2	medium zucchini, cut lengthwise into quarters
2	medium yellow summer squash, cut lengthwise into quarters

1 In a small bowl stir together walnut oil, olive oil, rosemary, salt, red pepper, and garlic. Brush the onions, zucchini, and yellow squash with some of the oil mixture.

2 For a charcoal grill, grill vegetables on the rack of an uncovered grill directly over medium to medium-hot coals for 5 to 6 minutes or until crisp-tender and light brown. Turn and brush once with remaining oil mixture. (For a gas grill, preheat grill. Reduce heat to medium. Place vegetables on grill rack over heat. Cover and grill as above.)

Nutrition Facts per serving: 126 cal., 10 g total fat (1 g sat. fat), 0 mg chol., 272 mg sodium, 8 g carbo., 2 g fiber, 1 g pro.

Whole cloves of garlic, briefly cooked and then discarded, flavor the oil in which the zucchini cooks. The garlic imparts its flavor and aroma without overwhelming the mild taste of the squash.

ZUCCHINI A LA ROMANO

2	cloves garlic
2	teaspoons olive oil
4	cups sliced zucchini (4 to 5 small)
1	tablespoon snipped fresh mint or basil, or 1 teaspoon dried mint or basil, crushed
¼	teaspoon salt
	Dash black pepper
2	tablespoons finely shredded Romano or Parmesan cheese

START TO FINISH:

15 minutes

MAKES:

6 servings

1 In a large skillet cook the whole garlic cloves in hot oil until light brown; discard garlic. Add the zucchini, dried mint (if using), salt, and pepper to the oil in the skillet.

2 Cook, uncovered, over medium heat about 5 minutes or until the zucchini is crisp-tender, stirring occasionally. To serve, sprinkle with the cheese and fresh mint (if using).

Nutrition Facts per serving: 35 cal., 2 g total fat (1 g sat. fat), 2 mg chol., 125 mg sodium, 3 g carbo., 1 g fiber, 2 g pro.

Ceci beans are the Italian version of garbanzo beans or chickpeas. This marinated salad is great for picnics or cookouts. If you like, serve it on a bed of mixed salad greens.

10g net carb

MARINATED CECI BEANS

PREP:

10 minutes

CHILL:

8 hours

STAND:

30 minutes

MAKES:

8 servings (about 2 cups)

1   15-ounce can garbanzo beans, rinsed and drained

4   teaspoons olive oil or salad oil

1   tablespoon white wine vinegar

1   clove garlic, minced

1   teaspoon snipped fresh rosemary or $^1/_2$ teaspoon dried rosemary, crushed

$^1/_8$ teaspoon salt
    Dash black pepper

1 Place garbanzo beans in a large bowl. In a screw-top jar combine oil, vinegar, garlic, rosemary, salt, and pepper. Cover and shake well. Pour over beans; toss to coat. Cover and chill for 8 to 24 hours, stirring occasionally.

2 Let stand at room temperature about 30 minutes before serving. Drain beans or serve with slotted spoon.

Nutrition Facts per serving: 110 cal., 6 g total fat (0 g sat. fat), 0 mg chol., 370 mg sodium, 14 g carbo., 4 g fiber, 8 g pro.

An herb-spiked ricotta-and cream-cheese mixture fills these colorful vegetable snacks.

3 g net carb

CHEESE-STUFFED BABY VEGETABLES

⅓ cup ricotta cheese

2 tablespoons cream cheese (tub style)

2 tablespoons finely shredded radish

1 tablespoon snipped fresh chives

2 teaspoons snipped fresh thyme, basil, dill, or marjoram or ½ teaspoon dried thyme, basil, dill, or marjoram, crushed

⅛ teaspoon onion salt

20 to 24 cherry tomatoes and/or 10 to 12 baby summer squash (such as zucchini or pattypan)

Fresh thyme, basil, dill, or marjoram (optional)

START TO FINISH:

30 minutes

MAKES:

5 servings

1 For filling, in a small bowl stir together the ricotta cheese, cream cheese, radish, chives, herbs, and onion salt. Mix well. Set aside.

2 Slice a thin layer off the top of each tomato. Using a small spoon, carefully scoop out and discard pulp. Invert tomatoes onto paper towels to drain. If using squash, cut in half lengthwise for zucchini or horizontally for pattypan; scoop out pulp and invert as for the cherry tomatoes.

3 Stuff the tomatoes and/or squash with filling. Serve immediately or cover and chill up to 2 hours. If desired, garnish with additional fresh herbs.

Nutrition Facts per serving: 64 cal., 4 g total fat (2 g sat. fat), 14 mg chol., 80 mg sodium, 4 g carbo., 1 g fiber, 2 g pro.

This quick-to-fix melange of tomatoes, shallots, thyme, and mozzarella is terrific over wilted greens.

EASY TOMATO SAUTÉ

PREP:

12 minutes

COOK:

3 minutes

MAKES:

4 servings

2½   cups whole red grape or yellow teardrop tomatoes and/or cherry tomatoes

     Nonstick olive oil cooking spray

¼   cup finely chopped shallots

1   clove garlic, minced

1   teaspoon snipped fresh lemon-thyme or thyme

¼   teaspoon salt

¼   teaspoon black pepper

1   cup fresh mozzarella cut in ½-inch cubes (4 ounces)

1 Halve about 1½ cups of the tomatoes; set aside. Lightly coat a 10-inch nonstick skillet with cooking spray. Add shallots, garlic, and lemon-thyme. Cook and stir over medium heat for 2 to 3 minutes or until shallots are tender. Add all of the tomatoes, the salt, and pepper. Cook and stir for 1 to 2 minutes more or until tomatoes are just warmed.

2 Remove from heat. Stir in mozzarella cubes.

Nutrition Facts per serving: 107 cal., 5 g total fat (3 g sat. fat), 16 mg chol., 289 mg sodium, 9 g carbo., 1 g fiber, 6 g pro.

Napa cabbage (also called Chinese cabbage) is long and pale yellow-green with a tightly packed head. The leaves are crisp and wrinkly, and the flavor is mild and faintly sweet.

ORIENTAL CABBAGE SLAW

1	medium cucumber, halved lengthwise and thinly sliced
1	cup fresh pea pods, halved
¼	cup rice vinegar
1	tablespoon salad oil
2	teaspoons toasted sesame oil
⅛	teaspoon salt
½	teaspoon red chile paste (optional)
4	cups shredded napa cabbage
½	cup coarsely chopped honey-roasted peanuts

1 In a large bowl combine cucumber and pea pods. For dressing, in a small bowl stir together vinegar, salad oil, sesame oil, salt, and, if desired, chile paste. Pour over cucumber and pea pods, stirring to coat.

2 Cover and chill for 4 to 24 hours. Just before serving, stir in cabbage and peanuts.

Nutrition Facts per serving: 85 cal., 6 g total fat (1 g sat. fat), 0 mg chol., 61 mg sodium, 6 g carbo., 2 g fiber, 3 g pro.

PREP:

20 minutes

CHILL:

4 hours

MAKES:

8 servings

Grilling adds a new flavor twist to vegetables. If you'd rather cook indoors, bake the vegetable packet in a 350°F oven about 25 minutes or until vegetables are tender.

GRILLED HERBED VEGETABLES

PREP:

10 minutes

GRILL:

20 minutes

MAKES:

4 servings

1 tablespoon olive oil

1 clove garlic, minced

2 teaspoons snipped fresh rosemary or 2 tablespoons snipped fresh basil; or ¼ teaspoon dried rosemary or 1 teaspoon dried basil, crushed

¼ teaspoon salt

4 cups assorted vegetables cut into bite-size pieces (eggplant; summer squash or zucchini; green beans; red onion; and red, green, or yellow sweet pepper)

Freshly ground black pepper

1 In a medium bowl combine olive oil, garlic, rosemary, and salt.

2 Add the vegetables to oil mixture, tossing to coat. Spoon vegetable mixture onto a 24×12-inch piece of heavy foil. Bring opposite edges of foil together; seal tightly with a double fold. Fold in remaining ends to completely enclose vegetables, leaving a little space for steam to build.

3 For a charcoal grill, grill the vegetable packet on the rack of an uncovered grill directly over medium-hot coals about 20 minutes or until vegetables are tender, turning the packet over halfway through grilling. (For a gas grill, preheat grill. Reduce heat to medium. Place vegetable packet on grill rack over heat. Cover and grill as above.) Season vegetables to taste with black pepper.

Nutrition Facts per servings: 63 cal., 4 g total fat (1 g sat. fat), 0 mg chol., 149 mg sodium, 8 g carbo., 3 g fiber, 1 g pro.

You can prepare the salad and dressing up to 2 hours ahead of time. Just be sure to add the dressing minutes before serving.

9 g net carb GREEN BEAN & BLUE CHEESE SALAD

2   16-ounce packages frozen cut green beans
1   cup crumbled blue cheese (4 ounces)
1   cup halved and thinly sliced red onion
¼   cup olive oil
3   tablespoons white wine vinegar or white balsamic vinegar
2   teaspoons Dijon-style mustard
¼   teaspoon salt
¼   teaspoon black pepper

PREP:
10 minutes
COOK:
10 minutes
MAKES:
8 servings

1 Cook beans according to package directions. Place cooked beans in a colander; rinse with cold water until cool. Drain well. In a large salad bowl combine beans, blue cheese, and onion. (If desired, cover and chill for up to 2 hours.)

2 For dressing, in a screw-top jar combine oil, vinegar, mustard, salt, and pepper. Cover and shake well. (If desired, chill, covered, for up 2 hours; shake before serving.) To serve, drizzle dressing over bean mixture; toss to coat.

Nutrition Facts per serving: 157 cal., 12 g total fat (4 g sat. fat), 13 mg chol., 349 mg sodium, 9 g carbo., 0 g fiber, 5 g pro.

When "keep it simple" is your mealtime motto, reach for this fresh and easy salad recipe. Ripe tomatoes and garden zucchini star, with a drizzle of oil-and-vinegar dressing.

MARINATED TOMATO PLATTER

PREP:

20 minutes

CHILL:

30 minutes

MAKES:

6 servings

3 tablespoons olive oil

3 tablespoons white wine vinegar

1 tablespoon thinly sliced green onion or snipped chives

2 teaspoons honey mustard

$\frac{1}{8}$ teaspoon black pepper

2 medium zucchini or cucumbers

6 fresh lettuce leaves (optional)

3 large red and/or yellow tomatoes, sliced

$\frac{1}{4}$ cup crumbled feta cheese with tomato and basil or plain feta cheese (1 ounce)

1 For dressing, in a screw-top jar combine oil, vinegar, green onion, mustard, and pepper. Cover and shake well; chill until needed.

2 Cut zucchini or cucumbers in half lengthwise. Seed cucumbers, if using. With a vegetable peeler, cut zucchini or cucumber halves into thin, lengthwise strips (about $\frac{1}{2}$ to 1 inch wide). Line a serving platter with lettuce, if desired, and top with sliced tomatoes. Arrange zucchini or cucumber strips among the tomatoes, tucking and folding the strips as desired. Shake dressing and drizzle over vegetables. Cover and chill at least 30 minutes. Sprinkle with feta cheese before serving.

Nutrition Facts per serving: 117 cal., 9 g total fat (3 g sat. fat), 9 mg chol., 138 mg sodium, 7 g carbo., 2 g fiber, 3 g pro.

*Look for fresh peeled and cored pineapple in the produce section of your supermarket.
You may even find fresh pineapple cut into chunks.*

BROCCOLI & PINEAPPLE SLAW

1	16-ounce package shredded broccoli (broccoli slaw mix)
2	cups fresh pineapple chunks or one 20-ounce can pineapple chunks (juice-pack), drained
2	cups broccoli florets
1/2	cup mayonnaise or salad dressing
1	to 2 tablespoons adobo sauce from canned chipotle peppers in adobo sauce
1/4	teaspoon salt

1 Rinse and drain shredded broccoli; dry thoroughly. In a bowl combine shredded broccoli, pineapple, and broccoli florets. In a small bowl stir together mayonnaise, adobo sauce, and salt. Add mayonnaise mixture to broccoli mixture. Toss to coat. Cover and chill for 1 to 4 hours. Toss gently before serving.

Nutrition Facts per serving: 141 cal., 11 g total fat (2 g sat. fat), 8 mg chol., 181 mg sodium, 9 g carbo., 3 g fiber, 3 g pro.

PREP:

10 minutes

CHILL:

1 hours

MAKES:

10 servings

Serve this versatile salsa with seafood, fish, or chicken or as a dip with low-carb tortillas that have been cut into wedges and toasted.

FRUIT SALSA

PREP:

30 minutes

CHILL:

8 hours

MAKES:

8 servings (about 2¼ cups)

1	cup chopped papaya or mango
1	cup finely chopped fresh pineapple
¼	cup finely slivered red onion
¼	cup slivered yellow, orange, and/or green sweet pepper
3	tablespoons snipped fresh cilantro
1	teaspoon finely shredded lime or lemon peel
2	tablespoons lime or lemon juice
2	teaspoons finely chopped fresh jalapeño pepper*
1	teaspoon grated fresh ginger

1 In a medium bowl stir together the papaya, pineapple, red onion, sweet pepper, cilantro, lime peel, lime juice, jalapeño pepper, and ginger. Cover and chill for 8 to 24 hours.

*NOTE: Hot chile peppers such as jalapeños contain oils that can burn your eyes, lips, and skin. Wear plastic or rubber gloves while preparing hot peppers and be sure to thoroughly wash your hands and nails in hot, soapy water afterward.

Nutrition Facts per serving: 26 cal., 0 g total fat (0 g sat. fat), 0 mg chol., 3 mg sodium, 6 g carbo., 1 g fiber, 0 g pro.

Inexpensive and full of good, crisp vegetables, enjoy these Oriental-flavored pancakes are delicious any time.

7 g
net
carb

VEGETABLE & RICE PANCAKES

1	cup finely shredded cabbage
1	cup cooked brown rice
¼	cup unbleached all-purpose flour
¼	cup finely chopped onion
¼	cup finely chopped red or green sweet pepper
½	teaspoon celery seed
4	slightly beaten eggs
1	tablespoon reduced-sodium soy sauce
¼	teaspoon black pepper
1	cup reduced-sodium chicken broth
2	tablespoons unbleached all-purpose flour
1½	teaspoons reduced-sodium soy sauce
½	teaspoon grated fresh ginger or ⅛ teaspoon ground ginger

PREP:

25 minutes

COOK:

4 minutes

MAKES:

12 pancakes

1 In a bowl combine cabbage, rice, the ¼ cup flour, onion, sweet pepper, and celery seed. In another bowl combine eggs, soy sauce, and pepper. Add to cabbage mixture. Stir just until combined but still slightly lumpy.

2 For each pancake, pour about ¼ cup batter onto a hot, lightly greased griddle or heavy skillet. Spread batter into a circle about 4 inches in diameter. Cook over medium heat until pancakes are golden brown, turning to cook second sides when pancake surfaces are bubbly and edges are slightly dry (about 2 to 3 minutes per side). Serve immediately or keep warm in a loosely covered ovenproof dish in a 300°F oven.

3 Meanwhile, for the Chinese sauce, in a screw-top jar combine broth and the 2 tablespoons flour; cover and shake well. Pour flour mixture into a small saucepan. Cook and stir over medium heat until thickened and bubbly. Cook and stir for 1 minute more. Stir in soy sauce and ginger; heat through. Serve warm with pancakes.

Nutrition Facts per pancake with 1 tablespoon sauce: 63 cal., 2 g total fat (1 g sat. fat), 71 mg chol., 143 mg sodium, 8 g carbo., 1 g fiber, 3 g pro.

SNACKS

These low-carb selections fit any occasion perfectly, from party snacks to between-meal munchies. Try Queso Fondue for game time or Crab & Vegetable Roll-Ups for cocktail time. Create both sweet and savory treats for yourself or your guests with these enticing flavor combinations.

10

Toss popcorn with a blend of spices to create this zippy nibble.

4g net carb

BBQ POPCORN

PREP:
10 minutes
BAKE:
12 minutes
OVEN:
300°F
MAKES:
12 servings (8 cups)

10	cups popped popcorn
2	tablespoons butter
1	tablespoon low-carbohydrate catsup
1	teaspoon chili powder
½	teaspoon onion salt
¼	teaspoon paprika
⅛	teaspoon garlic powder
⅛	teaspoon dry mustard
	Dash liquid smoke (optional)

1 In a large roasting pan place the popcorn. In a small saucepan combine butter, catsup, chili powder, onion salt, paprika, garlic powder, dry mustard, and, if desired, liquid smoke. Heat and stir over low heat until butter is melted. Drizzle over popcorn; toss to coat.

2 Bake the popcorn mixture in a 300° oven for 12 minutes, stirring once; cool. Store at room temperature in a tightly covered container up to 3 days.

Nutrition Facts per serving: 45 cal., 2 g total fat (1 g sat. fat), 5 mg chol., 100 mg sodium, 5 g carbo., 1 g fiber, 1 g pro.

Take some of these peppy pistachios along as a party thank you.

6 g
net
carb

PISTACHIOS WITH A KICK

2 tablespoons butter, melted

1 teaspoon ground coriander

½ teaspoon salt

¼ teaspoon ground cloves

¼ teaspoon cayenne pepper

1½ cups shelled pistachio nuts

1 In a 9×9×2-inch baking pan combine melted butter, coriander, salt, cloves, and cayenne pepper. Add nuts; toss to coat.

2 Bake, uncovered, in a 350° oven for 20 to 25 minutes or until nuts are toasted, stirring occasionally. Spread on foil; cool. Store in an airtight container.

Nutrition Facts per ¼ cup: 216 cal., 18 g total fat (4 g sat. fat), 11 mg chol., 236 mg sodium, 9 g carbo., 3 g fiber, 7 g pro.

PREP:
5 minutes

BAKE:
20 minutes

OVEN:
350°F

MAKES:
1½ cups nuts

Popcorn provides the crunch while the peanuts and cashews add protein. The spicy butter coating boosts flavor to a satisfying max.

SPICY POPCORN SNACK MIX

PREP:

10 minutes

BAKE:

20 minutes

OVEN:

300°F

COOL:

1 hour

MAKES:

12 (¹/₂-cup) servings

1   cup cashews

1   cup peanuts

2   tablespoons butter

1   teaspoon Worcestershire sauce

¹/₂   teaspoon dry mustard

¹/₄   teaspoon garlic powder

¹/₈   teaspoon cayenne pepper

4   cups plain popped popcorn

1 In a foil-lined 13×9×2-inch baking pan place cashews and peanuts; set aside. In a small saucepan melt butter. Remove saucepan from heat; stir in Worcestershire sauce, mustard, garlic powder, and cayenne pepper until combined. Drizzle over nuts in pan, tossing gently to coat.

2 Bake, uncovered, in a 300° oven for 20 minutes, stirring after 10 minutes. Remove pan from oven. Stir in popcorn. Use foil to remove baked mixture from pan; cool completely.

Nutrition Facts per serving: 164 cal., 13 g total fat (3 g sat. fat), 5 mg chol., 80 mg sodium, 8 g carbo., 2 g fiber, 5 g pro.

Of course you can use cubes of bread for dipping, but veggie dippers are just as tasty with this delicious fondue. Try jicama or sweet pepper strips and cauliflower or broccoli florets.

1 g net carb

QUESO FONDUE

3	cups shredded Monterey Jack cheese (12 ounces)
2	tablespoons unbleached all-purpose flour
1/3	cup finely chopped onion
1	tablespoon butter
3/4	cup half-and-half or light cream
2	4-ounce cans diced green chile peppers, drained
1/3	cup chopped roasted red sweet peppers
1/3	cup finely chopped, peeled jicama
	Low-carb bread slices, cut into cubes

1 For fondue, toss together cheese and flour; set aside. In a medium saucepan cook onion in hot butter until tender; stir in half-and-half. Gradually add small amounts of the cheese mixture, stirring constantly over low heat until cheese is melted. Stir in chile peppers, roasted sweet peppers, and jicama; heat through. Transfer to a fondue pot; keep warm over a fondue burner.

TO TOTE: Cover fondue tightly. Transport in an insulated carrier. Transfer to a fondue pot or crockery cooker to serve. Transport dippers in an airtight container.

Nutrition Facts per 2 teaspoons fondue: 37 cal., 3 g total fat (2 g sat. fat), 8 mg chol., 55 mg sodium, 1 g carbo., 0 g fiber, 2 g pro.

PREP:

45 minutes

MAKES:

2 cups

The long, white, carrot-shaped daikon is a Japanese radish with a mild spicy flavor. If you can't find daikons in your supermarket, substitute shredded radishes or zucchini.

7 g net carb

VEGETABLE SPRING ROLLS

PREP:

30 minutes

CHILL:

2 hours

MAKES:

12 servings

½	cup shredded daikon (Oriental white radish) or radishes
2	green onions, thinly sliced
2	tablespoons rice vinegar
1	small fresh jalapeño or serrano chile pepper, seeded and finely chopped*
½	teaspoon toasted sesame oil
½	cup shredded carrot
½	cup short thin strips cucumber
2	tablespoons snipped fresh cilantro
1	tablespoon reduced-sodium soy sauce
6	8½-inch-diameter rice papers
1½	cups shredded Boston or curly leaf lettuce

1 In a medium bowl combine daikon, green onions, vinegar, chile pepper, and sesame oil. In another bowl combine carrot, cucumber, cilantro, and soy sauce. Cover both mixtures; chill for 2 to 24 hours. Stir once. Drain both mixtures.

2 Pour 1 cup warm water into a pie plate. Carefully dip rice papers into water, 1 at a time. Place papers, not touching, on clean dry kitchen towels. Let soften for a few minutes until pliable.

3 Place ¼ cup shredded lettuce on each rice paper near one edge. Place about 1 rounded tablespoon of each vegetable mixture on the lettuce. Fold in the ends. Beginning at the filled edge, tightly roll the rice paper. Place seam side down on a plate. Cover with a damp towel. Repeat with remaining filling and papers. Cover and refrigerate for up to 2 hours. Cut each roll in half crosswise on a diagonal to make 12 pieces.

***NOTE:** Hot chile peppers contain oils that can burn your eyes, lips, and skin. Wear plastic or rubber gloves while preparing hot peppers and be sure to thoroughly wash your hands and nails in hot, soapy water afterward.

Nutrition Facts per serving: 31 cal., 0 g total fat (0 g sat. fat), 0 mg chol., 48 mg sodium, 7 g carbo., 0 g fiber, 0 g pro.

Look for low-carb tortillas in your supermarket. They are available in both plain and whole wheat varieties.

WRAP-&-ROLL PINWHEELS

3	7- to 8-inch low-carb flour tortillas
1	5.2-ounce carton boursin cheese or one 5-ounce container semisoft cheese with garlic and herb
12	large fresh basil leaves
½	of a 7-ounce jar roasted red sweet peppers, cut into ¼-inch-wide strips
4	ounces thinly sliced cooked roast beef, ham, or turkey
1	tablespoon mayonnaise or salad dressing
	Fresh basil leaves (optional)

PREP:
20 minutes

CHILL:
2 hours

MAKES:
about 24 pinwheels

1 Spread each tortilla with one-third of the cheese. Add a layer of the large basil leaves to cover cheese. Divide roasted pepper strips among the tortillas, arranging pepper strips over the basil leaves 1 to 2 inches apart. Top with meat slices. Spread 1 teaspoon mayonnaise over the meat on each tortilla. Roll up the tortillas tightly into a spiral, enclosing the filling. Wrap each roll in plastic wrap. Chill the tortilla rolls in the refrigerator for 2 to 4 hours to blend flavors.

2 To serve, remove the plastic wrap from the tortilla rolls. Cut each roll into 1-inch slices, making diagonal slices, if desired. Garnish with the remaining basil leaves, if desired.

Nutrition Facts per pinwheel: 46 cal., 3 g total fat (2 g sat. fat), 9 mg chol., 47 mg sodium, 3 g carbo., 1 g fiber, 2 g pro.

What's great about this dip—other than its flavor—is how quickly it goes together. When you have an after-work party to attend, blend the ingredients together the night before, cover and refrigerate the dip, then pick it up on your way to the party.

EASY VEGETABLE DIP

PREP:

15 minutes

CHILL:

2 hours

MAKES:

2¹/₂ cups

1 cup mayonnaise or salad dressing

1 8-ounce carton dairy sour cream

6 green onions, cut into 3-inch pieces

6 sprigs fresh parsley, stems removed

¹/₄ teaspoon garlic powder

Assorted vegetable dippers (such as sweet red pepper, broccoli or cauliflower florets, or carrot sticks)

1 In a blender or food processor combine mayonnaise, sour cream, green onions, parsley, and garlic powder. Cover and blend or process until smooth. Cover and chill for 2 to 48 hours. Serve with vegetable dippers.

Nutrition Facts per 2 tablespoons dip and ¹/₂ **cup vegetables:** 137 cal., 13 g total fat (3 g sat. fat), 13 mg chol., 94 mg sodium, 6 g carbo., 2 g fiber, 2 g pro.

Lime juice adds the zing to this version of guacamole—a party favorite any time of year.

CHUNKY GUACAMOLE

1	medium Roma tomato, seeded and cut up
2	tablespoons coarsely chopped red onion
1	tablespoon lime juice
1½	teaspoons olive oil
⅛	teaspoon salt
	Dash black pepper
1	clove garlic, halved
1	ripe avocado, halved, seeded, peeled, and cut up
	Low-carb tortillas, cut into wedges and toasted

1 In a food processor bowl combine tomatoes, red onion, lime juice, oil, salt, pepper, and garlic. Cover and process until mixture is coarsely chopped. Add avocados. Cover and process just until mixture is chopped. Transfer to a serving bowl. Serve immediately or cover surface with plastic wrap and chill for up to 1 hour. Serve with chips.

Nutrition Facts per tablespoon: 37 cal., 3 g total fat (2 g sat. fat), 8 mg chol., 55 mg sodium, 1 g carbo., 0 g fiber, 2 g pro.

PREP:
20 minutes
CHILL:
1 hour
MAKES:
1 cup (eight 2-tablespoon servings)

Similar to sushi (without the rice and seaweed), this fresh-tasting snack uses zucchini ribbons to wrap up a crab-filled package of flavor. Creating an assembly line with the ingredients lets you wrap and roll with ease.

CRAB & VEGETABLE ROLL-UPS

START TO FINISH:

40 minutes

MAKES:

16 roll-ups

2   medium zucchini or yellow summer squash

½   cup cooked lump crabmeat

1   tablespoon mayonnaise or salad dressing

1   teaspoon wasabi paste

⅛   teaspoon salt

½   of a medium avocado

2   tablespoons coarsely shredded carrot

16   small fresh basil leaves

1 Trim ends of zucchini. Using a sharp vegetable peeler, slice zucchini lengthwise into wide, flat ribbons. Discard first and last slices, and the seedy portions in the middle. (You will need 32 ribbons.) Set ribbons aside.

2 Carefully clean crabmeat, removing any shell or cartilage pieces. Drain crabmeat well in a colander, pressing with the back of a spoon to remove most of the liquid. Pat dry with paper towels. In a small bowl combine crabmeat, mayonnaise, wasabi paste, and salt. Seed and peel the avocado; cut into thin strips.

3 On a clean work surface, place one zucchini ribbon on top of another. For each roll-up, place 1 slightly rounded teaspoon of crab mixture at one end of a doubled zucchini ribbon. Top with avocado strips, a few shreds of carrot, and a basil leaf. Roll up; secure with toothpicks. If desired, cover and chill up to 30 minutes.

Nutrition Facts per roll-up: 23 cal., 2 g total fat (0 g sat. fat), 4 mg chol., 37 mg sodium, 1 g carbo., 1 g fiber, 1 g pro.

Vegetable dippers make this a winning low-carb appetizer or snack.

ROASTED RED PEPPER DIP

2   red sweet peppers or one 7-ounce jar roasted red sweet peppers, drained

1   fresh red chile pepper or 1 to 2 teaspoons bottled chopped red jalapeño pepper

8   ounces soft goat cheese or cream cheese, cut up

2   tablespoons olive oil or cooking oil

1   clove garlic, quartered

2   tablespoons snipped fresh rosemary, basil, or oregano, or 1 teaspoon dried rosemary, basil, or oregano (crushed)

     Assorted vegetables (such as broccoli florets, jicama strips, and zucchini slices)

1 Roast fresh sweet peppers and fresh chile pepper according to the directions below.

2 In a food processor or blender combine roasted sweet peppers, roasted or bottled chile pepper, goat cheese, oil, and garlic.

3 Cover and process or blend until smooth. Add rosemary; pulse until combined. Transfer dip to a serving bowl.

4 Serve immediately or cover and chill for up to 2 days. Serve with assorted vegetables.

TO ROAST PEPPERS: Cut peppers in half lengthwise; remove stems, seeds, and membranes. (When working with the chile pepper, wear plastic or rubber gloves so the oils in the pepper don't burn your skin.) Place cut sides down on a large foil-lined baking sheet. Bake in a 450° oven for 15 to 20 minutes or until skins are blistered and bubbly. Fold up foil on baking sheet around peppers to form a packet, sealing edges. Let stand for 20 minutes to loosen skins. Peel peppers; cut into pieces.

Nutrition Facts per tablespoon dip: 41 cal., 3 g total fat (2 g sat. fat), 4 mg chol., 35 mg sodium, 1 g carbo., 0 g fiber, 2 g pro.

PREP:
10 minutes

BAKE:
15 minutes

OVEN:
450°F

STAND:
20 minutes

MAKES:
1¹/₂ cups

Carrots add more than color and sweetness to this spicy hummus. Their abundance of beta-carotene, combined with the health attributes of garbanzo beans, makes this dip a hearty choice.

CARROT HUMMUS

PREP:

15 minutes

CHILL:

1 hour

MAKES:

2 cups

1   cup chopped carrots

1   15-ounce can garbanzo beans (chickpeas), rinsed and drained

¼   cup tahini (sesame seed paste)

2   tablespoons lemon juice

2   cloves garlic, quartered

½   teaspoon ground cumin

¼   teaspoon salt

2   tablespoons snipped fresh parsley

     Assorted dippers (such as sweet pepper strips, celery sticks, and/or low-carb crackers)

1 In a small covered saucepan cook carrots in a small amount of boiling water for 6 to 8 minutes or until tender; drain. In a food processor combine cooked carrots, garbanzo beans, tahini, lemon juice, garlic, cumin, and salt. Cover and process until smooth. Transfer to a small serving bowl. Stir in parsley.

2 Cover and chill for at least 1 hour or up to 3 days. If necessary, stir in enough water, 1 tablespoon at a time, to make of dipping consistency. Serve with assorted dippers.

Nutrition Facts per tablespoon: 30 cal., 1 g total fat (0 g sat. fat), 0 mg chol., 62 mg sodium, 4 g carbo., 1 g fiber, 1 g pro.

This dip was inspired by a trip to an upscale deli that serves a stacked ham, apple, and melted Swiss cheese sandwich on rye bread. The flavors prove phenomenal, even without the bread and adapt well to a dip.

2g net carb

HAM-SWISS DIP

8	ounces cooked ham, finely chopped
4	ounces process Swiss cheese slices, torn into small pieces
1	3-ounce package cream cheese, cubed
½	cup chopped onion
¼	cup hard apple cider
1	tablespoon Dijon-style mustard
¼	teaspoon caraway seeds
	Apple wedges or low-carb bread

PREP:
15 minutes

COOK:
2 hours

MAKES:
2 cups

1 In a 1½-quart slow cooker combine ham, Swiss cheese, cream cheese, onion, apple cider, mustard, and caraway seeds. Cover and cook for 2 to 3 hours.

2 Stir before serving. Serve dip with apple wedges or low-carb bread.

Nutrition Facts per ¼ cup dip: 143 cal., 10 g total fat (6 g sat. fat), 40 mg chol., 621 mg sodium, 2 g carbo., 0 g fiber, 9 g pro.

Hungry fans still reach for this golden oldie, a party-scene hit since Grandma's day. Blue cheese adds even more flavor.

CREAMY ONION DIP

PREP:

10 minutes

CHILL:

4 hours

MAKES:

1³/₄ cups

1½   cups dairy sour cream

2   tablespoons dry onion soup mix

½   cup crumbled blue cheese

Snipped fresh parsley (optional)

Assorted vegetable dippers (carrot sticks, zucchini slices, cauliflower florets, and/or jicama or red sweet pepper strips)

1 In a medium bowl stir together the sour cream and onion soup mix. Stir in blue cheese. Cover and chill in the refrigerator for 4 to 48 hours. If desired, sprinkle with snipped parsley. Serve with vegetable dippers.

Nutrition Facts per 2 tablespoons dip: 68 cal., 6 g total fat (4 g sat. fat), 12 mg chol., 158 mg sodium, 4 g carbo., 0 g fiber, 2 g pro.

A little bit nutty, a little bit spicy, this intriguing Indian-inspired recipe journeys off the well-beaten dip path. Choose a chutney to suit your taste—some are mild, others are hot.

4 g net carb

CURRY-CHUTNEY DIP

¼ cup mango chutney

½ of an 8-ounce package cream cheese, softened

⅔ cup dairy sour cream

1 teaspoon curry powder

¼ cup chopped dry-roasted cashews

Assorted vegetable dippers (carrot sticks, zucchini slices, cauliflower florets, and/or jicama strips)

1 Snip any large pieces in chutney; set aside. In a small bowl stir together cream cheese, sour cream, and curry powder. Stir in chutney. Cover and chill for 2 to 48 hours.

2 Before serving, sprinkle the dip with cashews. Serve with vegetable dippers.

Nutrition Facts per tablespoon dip: 54 cal., 4 g total fat (2 g sat. fat), 9 mg chol., 24 mg sodium, 4 g carbo., 0 g fiber, 1 g pro.

PREP:
10 minutes
CHILL:
2 hours
MAKES:
1¼ cups

This ever-so-easy snack stars brick cheese. Brick, known as the poor man's Limburger, is mild and earthy when young and gets stronger as it ages.

1 g net carb

CREAMY CHEESE SPREAD

PREP:

15 minutes

STAND:

30 minutes

MAKES:

1¹/₂ cups

2   cups shredded brick cheese (8 ounces)

1   8-ounce tub cream cheese with chives and onion

¹/₂   teaspoon bottled hot pepper sauce

Toasted low-carb bread slices, cut into quarters, or low-carb crackers

1 Let brick cheese and cream cheese stand at room temperature for 30 minutes.

2 In a medium mixing bowl beat brick cheese, cream cheese, and hot pepper sauce with an electric mixer on medium speed until mixture is nearly smooth.

3 Serve as a spread with bread or crackers.

NOTE: For a warm, fonduelike dip, microwave the spread in a microwave-safe bowl on 100% power (high) for 1¹/₂ to 2¹/₂ minutes or until warm, stirring once. Serve as a dip or fondue.

Nutrition Facts per tablespoon dip: 68 cal., 6 g total fat (4 g sat. fat), 18 mg chol., 94 mg sodium, 1 g carbo., 0 g fiber, 2 g pro.

Aromatic basil and lemon complement the hearty flavor of ground garbanzo beans and walnuts in this simple spread. To finish the remaining garbanzo beans, sprinkle them over salads or add them to soups and stews.

1 g net carb

MEDITERRANEAN WALNUT SPREAD

1	cup canned garbanzo beans (about ½ of a 15-ounce can)
½	cup chopped walnuts
½	cup lightly packed fresh basil
2	tablespoons olive oil
2	to 3 teaspoons lemon juice
⅛	teaspoon salt
⅛	teaspoon black pepper
	Low-carb bread or toasted low-carb tortilla wedges

START TO FINISH:
15 minutes
MAKES:
1¼ cups

1 Drain garbanzo beans, reserving the liquid. In a blender or food processor combine beans and 2 tablespoons of the reserved liquid. Add walnuts, basil, oil, lemon juice, salt, and pepper. Cover and blend or process until nearly smooth. (Scrape down sides and add additional reserved liquid if mixture appears stiff.)

2 Serve the spread on bread or tortilla wedges. To store, place in a covered airtight container in the refrigerator up to 5 days.

Nutrition Facts per tablespoon spread: 34 cal., 3 g total fat (0 g sat. fat), 0 mg chol., 25 mg sodium, 1 g carbo., 0 g fiber, 1 g pro.

Fresh apple gives this snack a refreshing juiciness. Curry powder tints the mixture gold.

CURRIED APPLE SPREAD

START TO FINISH:

10 minutes

MAKES:

³/₄ cup

½ of an 8-ounce package cream cheese, softened

1 teaspoon finely shredded orange peel

1 tablespoon orange juice

½ teaspoon curry powder

¼ of a medium apple (such as Delicious, Gala, or Braeburn),
    finely chopped

Toasted low-carb bread slices, cut into quarters

1 In a small bowl combine cream cheese, orange peel, orange juice, and curry powder. Gently stir in apple.

2 Serve the spread with toasted low-carb bread.

Nutrition Facts per tablespoon spread: 36 cal., 3 g total fat (2 g sat. fat), 10 mg chol., 28 mg sodium, 1 g carbo., 0 g fiber, 1 g pro.

To keep berries fresh, don't wash them until you are ready to eat them.

STRAWBERRIES WITH LIME DIPPING SAUCE

1   8-ounce carton dairy sour cream

2   teaspoons finely shredded lime peel

1   tablespoon lime juice

     No-calorie, heat-stable granular sugar substitute (Splenda)

3   cups small strawberries

1 For lime dipping sauce, in a small bowl stir together sour cream, lime peel, and lime juice. Sweeten to taste with sugar substitute. Set aside.

2 Wash strawberries, but do not remove stems. Drain on several layers of paper towels. Serve the strawberries with the lime dipping sauce.

Nutrition Facts per serving: 78 cal., 6 g total fat (4 g sat. fat), 12 mg chol., 16 mg sodium, 5 g carbo., 1 g fiber, 1 g pro.

PREP:

10 minutes

MAKES:

8 servings

For a tempting snack, try this fresh-tasting citrus dish. The aromatic rosemary and piquant pepper add new dimensions to grapefruit.

7 g net carb

RUBY & GOLD GRAPEFRUIT COCKTAIL

START TO FINISH:

15 minutes

MAKES:

4 servings

2   cups red and/or white peeled grapefruit sections

2   teaspoons rosemary-flavored oil or olive oil

½   teaspoon cracked black pepper

    Snipped fresh rosemary

1 In a medium bowl combine grapefruit sections, oil, and pepper; toss gently to coat.

2 Spoon the grapefruit mixture into small serving bowls. Sprinkle with fresh rosemary.

Nutrition Facts per serving: 55 cal., 2 g total fat (0 g sat. fat), 0 mg chol., 0 mg sodium, 9 g carbo., 2 g fiber, 1 g pro.

These exotic tropical-flavored pops are as good as a cool breeze on a hot day.

 9 g net carb

PASSION FRUIT FROZEN POPS

½   cup unsweetened pineapple juice

½   cup passion fruit juice blend

2   teaspoons lime juice (optional)

¼   teaspoon vanilla

1 In a glass measuring cup combine pineapple juice, passion fruit juice blend, lime juice (if desired), and vanilla. Pour into four 3- to 4-ounce disposable paper or plastic drink cups.

2 Cover the cups with foil. Using a sharp knife, make a slit in the foil covering each cup. Insert wooden sticks or plastic spoons for handles. Freeze pops for 3 to 4 hours or until firm.

Nutrition Facts per serving: 37 cal., 0 g total fat (0 g sat. fat), 0 mg chol., 2 mg sodium, 9 g carbo., 0 g fiber, 0 g pro.

PREP:

10 minutes

FREEZE:

3 hours

MAKES:

4 servings

Pick your favorite nuts and seeds for this snack recipe. Orange juice spiked with piquant spices gives the mixture a burst of flavor.

4 g net carb

SPICED CHILI NUTS & SEEDS

PREP:

10 minutes

BAKE:

15 minutes

OVEN:

300°F

MAKES:

4 cups

2	tablespoons frozen orange juice concentrate, thawed
2	teaspoons Worcestershire sauce
1	teaspoon garlic powder
1	teaspoon ground cumin
1	teaspoon chili powder
½	teaspoon cayenne pepper
¼	teaspoon salt
¼	teaspoon ground allspice
¼	teaspoon black pepper
⅛	teaspoon onion salt
2	cups unsalted peanuts, hazelnuts, and/or brazil nuts
1	cup pecan halves
6	tablespoons unsalted shelled sunflower seeds
2	tablespoons sesame seeds
	Nonstick cooking spray

1 In a large bowl combine orange juice concentrate, Worcestershire sauce, garlic powder, cumin, chili powder, cayenne pepper, salt, allspice, black pepper, and onion salt. Stir in nuts and seeds; toss to coat.

2 Line a 15×10×1-inch baking pan with foil; coat with cooking spray. Spread nuts and seeds on foil. Bake in 300° oven for 15 to 20 minutes or until toasted, stirring once. Cool. Store in an airtight container at room temperature for up to 1 week.

Nutrition Facts per ¼ cup: 183 cal., 16 g total fat (2 g sat. fat), 0 mg chol., 59 mg sodium, 7 g carbo., 3 g fiber, 6 g pro.

Each serving of these roasted soybeans is rich in protein and polyunsaturated fats.
Enjoy these soynuts alone or mix with popcorn.

1 g net carb

HERBED SOY SNACKS

8   ounces dry-roasted soybeans (2 cups)
1½   teaspoons dried thyme, crushed
¼   teaspoon garlic salt
⅛   to ¼ teaspoon cayenne pepper

1 Spread roasted soybeans in an even layer in a 15×10×1-inch baking pan. In a small bowl combine thyme, garlic salt, and cayenne pepper. Sprinkle the soybeans with the thyme mixture. Bake in 350° oven for 5 minutes or just until heated through, shaking pan once. Cool completely. Store for up to 1 week at room temperature in an airtight container.

INDIAN-SPICED SOY SNACKS: Prepare Herbed Soy Snacks as directed, except combine ½ teaspoon garam masala and ¼ teaspoon salt with cayenne pepper; sprinkle over soybeans before baking. Omit thyme and garlic salt.

SESAME-GINGER SOY SNACKS: Prepare Herbed Soy Snacks as directed, except combine 2 teaspoons toasted sesame oil, ¾ teaspoon ground ginger, and ½ teaspoon onion salt; sprinkle over soybeans before baking. Omit thyme, garlic salt, and cayenne pepper.

Nutrition Facts per serving: 75 cal., 3 g total fat (1 g sat. fat), 0 mg chol., 17 mg sodium, 4 g carbo., 3 g fiber, 7 g pro.

START TO FINISH:
10 minutes
BAKE:
5 minutes
OVEN:
350°F
MAKES:
16 servings

Plan on using the seeds from about 4 pumpkins for this recipe. If you don't have enough, ask your friends to share the seeds from their pumpkins.

6g net carb

ROASTED PUMPKIN SEEDS

PREP:

15 minutes

STAND:

24 hours

BAKE:

40 minutes

OVEN:

325°F

MAKES:

16 (^{1}/4-cup) servings

4^1/4   cups raw pumpkin seeds

2   tablespoons cooking oil

1   teaspoon salt

1 Rinse pumpkin seeds in water until pulp and strings are washed off, then drain.

2 In a medium bowl combine pumpkin seeds, cooking oil, and salt. Spread mixture onto a waxed-paper-lined 15×10×1-inch baking pan. Let stand for 24 to 48 hours or until dry, stirring occasionally.

3 Remove waxed paper from baking pan. Toast seeds in a 325° oven for 40 minutes, stirring once or twice. Drain seeds on paper towels.

Nutrition Facts per serving: 213 cal., 19 g total fat (3 g sat. fat), 0 mg chol., 152 mg sodium, 7 g carbo., 1 g fiber, 9 g pro.

Here's a dip you can share with the kids. They'll love the yummy combination of peanut butter and yogurt. Many supermarkets stock natural peanut butter, so you won't need to make a special run to the health food store.

1 g net carb

PEANUTTY DIP

½   cup natural peanut butter

½   cup plain yogurt

No-calorie, heat-stable granular sugar substitute (Splenda)

Vegetables dippers (such as apple wedges, celery sticks, cucumber sticks, and/or bias-sliced carrots)

1 In a small bowl stir together the peanut butter and yogurt until well mixed. If desired, sweeten with sugar substitute to taste. Serve with dippers. Transfer any leftover dip to a storage container and store, covered, in the refrigerator for up to 2 days.

Nutrition Facts per tablespoon dip: 55 cal., 4 g total fat (1 g sat. fat), 0 mg chol., 35 mg sodium, 2 g carbo., 1 g fiber, 2 g pro.

START TO FINISH:

10 minutes

MAKES:

about 1 cup

These buttery herbed almonds are terrific for impromptu get-togethers.

3 g net carb

SPICY TOASTED ALMONDS

PREP:

10 minutes

BAKE:

10 minutes

OVEN:

350°F

MAKES:

8 (¹/4-cup) servings

8	ounces whole almonds or pecan halves (about 2 cups)
1¹/2	teaspoons butter
1	tablespoon finely snipped fresh thyme
¹/4	to ¹/2 teaspoon salt
¹/4	teaspoon cayenne pepper

1 Spread almonds in a single layer in a shallow pan. Bake in a 350° oven for 10 to 15 minutes or until nuts are lightly toasted, stirring every 5 minutes.

2 Meanwhile, melt butter in a medium saucepan over medium heat until sizzling. Remove from heat. Stir in thyme, salt, and cayenne pepper. Add almonds to butter mixture and toss to coat. Cool before serving.

3 To store, seal cooled nuts in an airtight container and store for up to 1 month in refrigerator or up to 3 months in freezer.

Nutrition Facts per serving: 171 cal., 15 g total fat (2 g sat. fat), 2 mg chol., 81 mg sodium, 6 g carbo., 3 g fiber, 6 g pro.

Garam masala, a traditional Indian mix of cumin, cardamom, cinnamon, and other spices, is available in many supermarket spice sections and at specialty food stores.

GINGER CASHEWS

2   cups lightly salted cashews

1   tablespoon butter, melted

1   tablespoon minced or grated fresh ginger

2   teaspoons garam masala

1 Line a shallow baking pan with foil or parchment paper. In a bowl toss together the cashews, butter, ginger, and garam masala. Spread nuts in foil-lined pan.

2 Roast the nuts in a 300° oven about 20 minutes or until golden brown and very fragrant, stirring occasionally. Serve warm or at room temperature. Store nuts in a tightly covered container at room temperature for 24 hours or in the refrigerator for 2 days. If desired, rewarm nuts on a baking sheet in a 300° oven about 5 minutes.

Nutrition Facts per 2 tablespoons: 114 cal., 10 g total fat (2 g sat. fat), 2 mg chol., 42 mg sodium, 5 g carbo., 1 g fiber, 4 g pro.

PREP:

10 minutes

ROAST:

20 minutes

OVEN:

300°F

MAKES:

2 cups

DESSERTS

When you crave something sweet or want to offer guests an indulgent dessert, look through this collection of rich, fulfilling temptations. The spectacular array of fruits, custards, granitas, sauces, and mousses offers options that taste as refreshing as they look. Although one bite may make you feel like you're cheating, all of the recipes are "legal" on most low-carb diets.

11

Sugar substitute keeps this old-fashioned dessert in a low-carb meal plan.

7 g net carb

SPICED BAKED CUSTARD

PREP:
10 minutes

BAKE:
30 minutes

OVEN:
325°F

MAKES:
4 servings

3 beaten eggs

1½ cups milk

⅓ cup no-calorie, heat-stable granular sugar substitute (Splenda)

1½ teaspoons vanilla

½ teaspoon ground allspice

1 In a small bowl combine eggs, milk, sugar substitute, and vanilla. Beat until combined. Place four 6-ounce custard cups in a 2- or 3-quart rectangular baking dish. Divide egg mixture among custard cups; sprinkle with allspice. Place baking dish on oven rack. Pour boiling water into baking dish around custard cups to a depth of 1 inch.

2 Bake in a 325° oven for 30 to 45 minutes or until a knife inserted near the center of each cup comes out clean. Remove cups from water. Cool slightly on a wire rack before serving. (Or cool completely in cups; cover and chill for up to 24 hours.)

Nutrition Facts per serving: 101 cal., 4 g total fat (1 g sat. fat), 161 mg chol., 97 mg sodium, 7 g carbo., 0 g fiber, 8 g pro.

Serve this velvety smooth sauce over fresh raspberries, blackberries, or strawberries, or a combination of all three. Store any leftover sauce, covered with plastic wrap, in the refrigerator.

3 g net carb

CUSTARD SAUCE

5   beaten egg yolks

1½   cups whipping cream

¼   cup no-calorie, heat-stable granular sugar substitute (Splenda)

1½   teaspoons vanilla

1 In a heavy medium saucepan stir together egg yolks, whipping cream, and sugar substitute. Cook and stir continuously over medium heat until the mixture just coats the back of a clean metal spoon. Remove pan from heat.

2 Quickly cool custard by placing saucepan in a large bowl of ice water for 1 to 2 minutes, stirring constantly. Pour custard through a fine mesh strainer into a bowl. Stir in vanilla. Cover the surface of custard sauce with plastic wrap. Chill 2 to 12 hours. Serve the custard sauce with fresh berries.

Nutrition Facts per ¼-cup sauce: 226 cal., 23 g total fat (13 g sat. fat), 222 mg chol., 25 mg sodium, 3 g carbo., 0 g fiber, 3 g pro.

PREP:

20 minutes

CHILL:

2 hours

MAKES:

7 servings (about 1¾ cups)

To keep the pastry crisp, spoon the luscious raspberry filling into the bite-size tart shells just before serving.

RASPBERRY & CHOCOLATE TULIPS

PREP:

15 minutes

COOL:

30 minutes

MAKES:

15 tarts

1   cup fresh raspberries

¼   cup no-calorie, heat-stable granular sugar substitute (Splenda)

¼   cup whipping cream

1   tablespoon no-calorie, heat-stable granular sugar substitute (Splenda)

¼   teaspoon vanilla

1   2.1-ounce package miniature phyllo tart shells (15)

1   tablespoon grated unsweetened chocolate

1 In a small saucepan combine the raspberries and the ¼ cup sugar substitute. Cook and stir over medium heat for 3 to 5 minutes or until slightly thickened. Remove from heat. Cool completely.

2 In a chilled small mixing bowl combine whipping cream, the 1 tablespoon sugar substitute, and the vanilla. Beat with an electric mixer on medium speed until soft peaks form.

3 To serve, place the phyllo shells on a platter. Spoon about 1 teaspoon raspberry mixture into the bottom of each shell. Top with whipped cream. Sprinkle with grated chocolate.

Nutrition Facts per tart: 46 cal., 3 g total fat (1 g sat. fat), 5 mg chol., 12 mg sodium, 4 g carbo., 1 g fiber, 1 g pro.

These miniature cheesecakes can be made up to 3 days ahead. If you serve only a few, leave the fruit topping off the ones you wish to save for another time.

6g net carb

KIWI CHEESECAKE TARTS

- 1 cup finely chopped toasted walnuts
- ¼ teaspoon ground nutmeg
- 2 8-ounce packages cream cheese, softened
- ⅓ cup no-calorie, heat-stable granular sugar substitute (Splenda)
- 1½ teaspoons finely shredded lemon peel
- 1½ teaspoons vanilla
- 2 eggs
- 2 medium kiwifruits, peeled and sliced
- ⅓ cup sugar-free apricot preserves, melted

1 Line twelve 2½-inch muffin cups with paper or foil bake cups. In a small bowl combine walnuts and nutmeg. Sprinkle in the bottom of bake cups. Set aside.

2 In a large mixing bowl beat cream cheese, sugar substitute, lemon peel, and vanilla with an electric mixer on medium speed until smooth. Add eggs; beat on low speed just until combined. Carefully spoon a scant ¼ cup into each bake cup (bake cups will be nearly full).

3 Bake in a 325° oven about 20 minutes or until tops appear set. (Tops may crack slightly.) Cool in pan on a wire rack for 30 minutes. Remove tarts from pan. Cover and chill at least 1 hour or up to 3 days.

4 To serve, remove cheesecakes from bake cups. Top with kiwi slices. Spoon melted preserves over kiwi.

Nutrition Facts per tart: 227 cal., 21 g total fat (9 g sat. fat), 77 mg chol., 123 mg sodium, 7 g carbo., 1 g fiber, 6 g pro.

PREP:
30 minutes

BAKE:
20 minutes

OVEN:
325°F

COOL:
30 minutes

CHILL:
1 hour

MAKES:
12 tarts

Spiked with orange liqueur, this fluffy whipped cream makes a sublime topping for fresh fruit.

ORANGE CREAM

START TO FINISH:

15 minutes

MAKES:

8 servings (about 2 cups)

1   cup whipping cream

    Sugar substitute to equal 2 tablespoons sugar

2   tablespoons dairy sour cream

1   tablespoon orange liqueur or ½ teaspoon orange extract

½   teaspoon finely shredded orange peel

½   teaspoon vanilla

1 In a chilled medium mixing bowl beat whipping cream, sugar substitute, and sour cream with an electric mixer on medium speed until mixture starts to thicken.

2 Add orange liqueur, orange peel, and vanilla; beat on medium speed just until soft peaks form.

Nutrition Facts per ¼-cup cream: 128 cal., 12 g total fat (8 g sat. fat), 42 mg chol., 12 mg sodium, 4 g carbo., 0 g fiber, 0 g pro.

Try this coffee-flavored whipped cream with fresh orange sections.

ESPRESSO CREAM

1   cup whipping cream

     Sugar substitute to equal ¼ cup sugar

4   teaspoons instant espresso coffee powder

½   teaspoon vanilla

1 In a chilled medium mixing bowl beat whipping cream, sugar substitute, espresso coffee powder, and vanilla with an electric mixer on medium speed just until soft peaks form.

Nutrition Facts per ¼-cup cream: 109 cal., 11 g total fat (7 g sat. fat), 41 mg chol., 12 mg sodium, 2 g carbo., 0 g fiber, 1 g pro.

This baked dessert has a texture similar to bread pudding but contains ground almonds instead of bread. The batter is thick, so be sure to spread it into an even layer in the baking pan.

5 g net carb

ALMOND PUDDING

PREP:

30 minutes

BAKE:

20 minutes

OVEN:

350°F

MAKES:

8 servings

Nonstick cooking spray

6 egg yolks

½ teaspoon almond extract

⅔ cup no-calorie, heat-stable granular sugar substitute (Splenda)

¾ cup almonds, finely ground

6 egg whites

1 cup sliced fresh strawberries

½ cup whipping cream, whipped

1 Lightly coat a 9½-inch round cake pan with cooking spray; set aside.

2 In a large mixing bowl beat egg yolks with an electric mixer on high speed about 5 minutes or until thick and lemon colored. Add almond extract; beat on low speed until combined. Gradually add sugar substitute, beating on low speed until combined. Fold in almonds. Set aside.

3 Thoroughly wash and dry the beaters. In a medium mixing bowl beat egg whites on medium speed until stiff peaks form (tips stand straight). Fold about one-fourth of the egg whites into the egg yolk mixture until combined. Fold remaining egg whites into egg yolk mixture. Spoon into prepared pan, spreading evenly.

4 Bake in a 350° oven about 20 minutes or until puffed and golden and a knife inserted near the center comes out clean. Cut into wedges. Serve warm with strawberries and whipped cream.

Nutrition Facts per serving: 196 cal., 16 g total fat (5 g sat. fat), 180 mg chol., 55 mg sodium, 7 g carbo., 2 g fiber, 8 g pro.

Top this refreshing fruit ice with sliced fresh strawberries and garnish with lime slices.

6 g net carb

STRAWBERRY-LIME ICE

<table>
<tr><td>1</td><td>16-ounce package frozen unsweetened whole strawberries, thawed</td></tr>
<tr><td>½</td><td>cup water</td></tr>
<tr><td>¼</td><td>cup lime juice</td></tr>
<tr><td></td><td>Sugar substitute to equal ½ cup sugar</td></tr>
</table>

1 In a blender or food processor combine strawberries, water, lime juice, and sugar substitute. Cover and blend or process until smooth. Transfer mixture to a freezer container. Cover and freeze for 4 hours or until firm.

2 To serve, let stand at room temperature for 15 minutes. Use a large metal spoon or ice cream scoop to scrape ice into dessert dishes.

Nutrition Facts per serving: 28 cal., 0 g total fat (0 g sat. fat), 0 mg chol., 4 mg sodium, 7 g carbo., 1 g fiber, 0 g pro.

PREP:
5 minutes
FREEZE:
4 hours
STAND:
15 minutes
MAKES:
8 servings

These chocolaty custards are so rich that a small serving satisfies any dessert craving. Serve with additional unsweetened whipped cream, if you like.

6 g net carb

MOCHA POTS DE CRÈME

PREP:
15 minutes

COOK:
15 minutes

CHILL:
2 hours

MAKES:
6 servings

1 cup half-and-half or light cream

2 ounces unsweetened chocolate, coarsely chopped

½ cup no-calorie, heat-stable granular sugar substitute (Splenda)

1 teaspoon instant espresso powder

3 beaten egg yolks

1 teaspoon vanilla

1 In a heavy small saucepan combine the half-and-half, chocolate, sugar substitute, and espresso powder. Cook and stir over medium heat about 10 minutes or until mixture thickens and is bubbly.

2 Gradually stir about half of the hot mixture into the beaten egg yolks. Return all of the egg yolk mixture to the saucepan. Cook and stir over medium-low heat just until mixture comes to a boil, about 5 minutes (mixture will be very thick). Remove from heat; stir in vanilla. Pour chocolate mixture into 6 pots de crème cups or 2- to 3-ounce dessert dishes. Cover surface of each with plastic wrap. Chill for 2 to 24 hours.

Nutrition Facts per serving: 139 cal., 12 g total fat (7 g sat. fat), 121 mg chol., 22 mg sodium, 7 g carbo., 1 g fiber, 4 g pro.

This fluffy dessert goes together more quickly if you chill the gelatin mixture in an ice-water bath about 15 minutes or until partially set. Beat until light and foamy. If necessary, chill again in an ice bath until mixture mounds, stirring occasionally.

RASPBERRY WHIP

1 cup fresh or frozen raspberries

1 4-serving-size package sugar-free raspberry-flavored gelatin

1 cup boiling water

⅔ cup cold water

1 8-ounce carton plain low-fat yogurt

1 Thaw raspberries, if frozen; drain.

2 In a medium mixing bowl dissolve gelatin in the boiling water. Add the cold water and yogurt. Cover and chill 30 to 45 minutes or until partially set (the consistency of unbeaten egg whites).

3 Beat with an electric mixer on medium speed for 1 to 2 minutes or until light and foamy. If necessary, chill mixture until it mounds when dropped from a spoon.

4 Meanwhile, divide half of the raspberries among 6 dessert dishes. Spoon gelatin mixture on top of raspberries. Top with remaining raspberries. Chill about 30 minutes more or until firm. Serve or cover and chill up to 24 hours.

Nutrition Facts per serving: 40 cal., 1 g total fat (0 g sat. fat), 2 mg chol., 63 mg sodium, 5 g carbo., 1 g fiber, 3 g pro.

PREP:

20 minutes

CHILL:

1 hour

MAKES:

6 servings

Serve this light, refreshing ice in chilled glasses and savor every citrusy spoonful.

CITRUS GRANITA

PREP:

15 minutes

STAND:

5 minutes

FREEZE:

11 hours

MAKES:

8 servings

2   cups water

1   cup no-calorie, heat-stable granular sugar substitute (Splenda)

½   cup lemon juice

⅓   cup lime juice

Lime slices (optional)

1 In a medium bowl stir together water, sugar substitute, lemon juice, and lime juice. Pour into an 8×8×2-inch baking pan. Cover and freeze about 2 hours or until mixture is slushy on the edges. Stir, scraping the frozen mixture off the bottom and sides of pan. Cover and freeze for 3 to 4 hours or until all of the mixture is slushy, stirring every 30 minutes. Cover and freeze at least 6 hours or until firm.

2 Before serving chill 8 dessert dishes in the freezer for at least 1 hour. Let frozen granita stand at room temperature for 5 to 10 minutes. Using a large metal spoon, scrape the surface of the granita and spoon into the chilled dessert dishes. If desired, garnish with lime slices. Serve immediately.

Nutrition Facts per serving: 18 cal., 0 g total fat (0 g sat. fat), 0 mg chol., 4 mg sodium, 5 g carbo., 0 g fiber, 0 g pro.

You'll have enough cocoa syrup to make two batches (six servings) of this fizzy chocolate beverage.

7 g net carb

EGG CREAM

¼ cup Cocoa Syrup (see below)

1 cup half-and-half or light cream

¼ cup seltzer water or club soda, chilled

1 Prepare Cocoa Syrup. Let cool.

2 Divide half-and-half between two 8-ounce glasses. Stir 2 tablespoons seltzer water into each glass. Stir 2 tablespoons Cocoa Syrup into each glass. Serve immediately.

COCOA SYRUP: In a small saucepan stir together ½ cup no-calorie, heat-stable granular sugar substitute (Splenda), ⅓ cup unsweetened cocoa powder, and a dash salt. Gradually add ½ cup boiling water, stirring until smooth. Bring to boiling over medium heat, stirring constantly. Reduce heat. Simmer, uncovered, about 2 minutes. Remove from heat. Stir in ½ teaspoon vanilla. Cool. Store in a tightly covered container in the refrigerator for up to 3 weeks. Makes about ½ cup.

Nutrition Facts per serving: 132 cal., 10 g total fat (6 g sat. fat), 29 mg chol., 61 mg sodium, 7 g carbo., 0 g fiber, 3 g pro.

PREP:

15 minutes

COOL:

30 minutes

MAKES:

2 servings

A vibrant green color and a splash of tequila make this one fun dessert. Serve in margarita glasses and top with whipped cream, if you like.

 1 g net carb

MARGARITA WHIP

PREP:

15 minutes

CHILL:

5 hours

MAKES:

8 servings

1	4-serving-size package sugar-free lime-flavored gelatin
1	4-serving-size package sugar-free lemon-flavored gelatin
2	cups boiling water
1	cup cold water
1/3	cup dairy sour cream
1/2	of an 8-ounce package cream cheese
2	tablespoons tequila or water
1	teaspoon finely shredded lime peel

1 In a large bowl dissolve lime and lemon gelatin in the boiling water. Stir in cold water. Pour into a 2-quart square baking dish. Cover and chill for 4 hours or until firm.

2 In a blender combine sour cream, cream cheese, tequila, and lime peel. Cover and blend until fluffy. Cut gelatin mixture into squares. With the blender running, add gelatin, a few cubes at a time, through the opening in the lid, blending until frothy and smooth. Immediately pour mixture into 8 dessert dishes. Cover and chill at least 1 hour or up to 24 hours.

Nutrition Facts per serving: 85 cal., 7 g total fat (4 g sat. fat), 19 mg chol., 104 mg sodium, 1 g carbo., 0 g fiber, 2 g pro.

If you don't have eight matching molds, use an assortment of small molds or divide the creamy mixture into small teacups, demitasse cups, or small bowls.

PANNA COTTA

6 g net carb

Nonstick cooking spray

2 tablespoons cold water

2 tablespoons orange liqueur or orange juice

1 envelope unflavored gelatin

1 8-ounce carton mascarpone cheese or one 8-ounce package cream cheese, softened

1 8-ounce carton dairy sour cream

⅓ cup no-calorie, heat-stable granular sugar substitute (Splenda)

1 teaspoon vanilla

1¼ cups whipping cream

1 cup port wine (optional)

Assorted fresh berries, such as raspberries, blackberries, or sliced strawberries (optional)

PREP:

25 minutes

CHILL:

4 hours

MAKES:

8 servings

1 Lightly coat eight ½-cup molds or small cups with cooking spray; set aside.

2 In a microwave-safe glass measuring cup combine water and orange liqueur. Sprinkle gelatin over the top. Let stand 5 minutes or until gelatin is softened. Microwave on 100% power (high) for 30 to 45 seconds or until gelatin is dissolved. (Or in a small saucepan combine gelatin with water and orange liqueur; let stand 5 minutes. Heat over low heat until gelatin is dissolved, stirring constantly.)

3 In a medium mixing bowl beat mascarpone cheese with an electric mixer on medium speed until light and fluffy. Add the gelatin mixture, sour cream, sugar substitute, and vanilla, beating on low speed until smooth. Stir in whipping cream. Pour into prepared molds or cups. Cover and chill in the refrigerator until firm, at least 4 hours or up to 2 days.

4 If desired, for sauce, in a small saucepan bring the port wine to boiling. Reduce heat and simmer, uncovered, for 20 minutes or until reduced to ¼ cup.

5 To remove panna cotta from molds, wrap a warm cloth around mold just to loosen. Or, if using cups, do not unmold. Spoon sauce over panna cotta. Serve with fresh berries, if desired.

Nutrition Facts per serving: 332 cal., 33 g total fat (20 g sat. fat), 100 mg chol., 48 mg sodium, 6 g carbo., 0 g fiber, 8 g pro.

The classic combo of strawberries and cream takes a new twist when the berries are coated with sugar-free apricot preserves and the cream is scented with lemon.

LEMON BERRY PARFAITS

START TO FINISH:

15 minutes

MAKES:

4 servings

½ cup whipping cream

½ teaspoon vanilla

2 teaspoons finely shredded lemon peel

1 cup sliced fresh strawberries

2 tablespoons sugar-free apricot preserves, melted

1 In a chilled medium mixing bowl beat whipping cream and vanilla with an electric mixer on medium speed until soft peaks form; fold in lemon peel.

2 In a small bowl toss together sliced strawberries and melted preserves. Set aside about 12 of the preserve-coated berry slices. Divide the remaining berry mixture among 4 martini glasses or dessert dishes. Top each serving with whipped cream. Garnish with reserved berry slices. Serve immediately.

Nutrition Facts per serving: 121 cal., 11 g total fat (7 g sat. fat), 41 mg chol., 12 mg sodium, 6 g carbo., 1 g fiber, 1 g pro.

You can assemble these cream cheese-filled tarts just before serving or a few hours ahead.

FRUIT-TOPPED PHYLLO CUPS

2 tablespoons low-sugar apricot or strawberry preserves

½ of an 8-ounce package cream cheese, softened

1 2.1-ounce package miniature phyllo tart shells (15)

15 red and/or green seedless grape halves, strawberry halves, or small pieces of mango

START TO FINISH:

15 minutes

MAKES:

15 tarts

1 In a small saucepan heat and stir the preserves over medium-low heat until melted. Cut up any large pieces of preserves; stir into the cream cheese until smooth. Divide cream cheese mixture among tart shells.

2 Place a piece of fruit on top of each tart. Serve immediately or chill up to 4 hours before serving.

Nutrition Facts per tart: 55 cal., 4 g total fat (2 g sat. fat), 8 mg chol., 32 mg sodium, 4 g carbo., 0 g fiber, 1 g pro.

Tangy and creamy, this five-ingredient dessert is super-easy to make.

RASPBERRY MOUSSE

PREP:

15 minutes

CHILL:

3¹/₂ hours

MAKES:

4 servings

1   4-serving-size package sugar-free raspberry-flavored gelatin

³/₄   cup boiling water

³/₄   cup low-calorie cranberry juice cocktail, chilled

1   teaspoon finely shredded lemon peel

1   cup whipping cream

    Fresh raspberries (optional)

1 In a medium bowl dissolve gelatin in boiling water. Stir in cranberry juice cocktail and lemon peel. Cover and chill about 30 minutes or until partially set (the consistency of unbeaten egg whites).

2 In a chilled medium mixing bowl beat the whipping cream with an electric mixer on medium-high speed until stiff peaks form (tips stand straight). Fold whipped cream into gelatin mixture until combined. Spoon into 4 dessert dishes. Cover and chill for 3 to 4 hours or until firm. If desired, garnish with fresh raspberries.

Nutrition Facts per serving: 219 cal., 22 g total fat (14 g sat. fat), 82 mg chol., 39 mg sodium, 4 g carbo., 0 g fiber, 2 g pro.

Strawberry-kiwi-flavored gelatin and rum lend tropical touches to this layered dessert.

TROPICAL BERRY SQUARES

2	4-serving-size packages sugar-free strawberry-kiwi- or strawberry-flavored gelatin
1½	cups boiling water
1⅓	cups cold water
2	tablespoons rum or water
½	of an 8-ounce container extra-creamy frozen whipped dessert topping, thawed
1	cup fresh raspberries

PREP:
10 minutes

CHILL:
6 hours

MAKES:
9 servings

1 In a large bowl dissolve gelatin in the boiling water. Stir in the cold water and rum. Cover and chill until partially set (consistency of unbeaten egg whites), about 1 to 1½ hours.

2 Place 1½ cups of the gelatin mixture in a medium bowl; cover and set aside at room temperature. Whisk ½ of the dessert topping (¼ of an 8-ounce container) into the remaining gelatin mixture until combined. Pour into a 2-quart square baking dish. Cover and chill until almost firm, about 2 hours.

3 Stir raspberries into reserved gelatin mixture. Spoon over top of gelatin mixture in dish. Cover and chill at least 3 hours or overnight until firm. Cut into squares to serve. Top each square with some of the remaining whipped topping.

Nutrition Facts per serving: 59 cal., 3 g total fat (3 g sat. fat), 0 mg chol., 51 mg sodium, 4 g carbo., 1 g fiber, 1 g pro.

A gelatin mold makes this ruby red dessert flecked with golden peaches truly stunning.
If you don't have a mold, use a 3-quart bowl.

PEACH MELBA TEA DESSERT

3 g net carb

PREP:

10 minutes

CHILL:

3 hours

MAKES:

6 servings

2 tablespoons low-calorie artificially sweetened raspberry-flavored tea mix

1 cup cold water

1 4-serving-size package sugar-free raspberry-flavored gelatin

¾ cup boiling water

Nonstick cooking spray

1 cup frozen unsweetened peach slices, thawed and chopped

⅓ cup frozen whipped dessert topping, thawed

1 In a small bowl dissolve tea mix in the cold water. Set aside.

2 In another small bowl dissolve gelatin in the boiling water. Stir in tea mixture. Cover and chill until partially set (the consistency of unbeaten egg whites), about 1 hour.

3 Meanwhile, lightly coat a 3-cup gelatin mold with cooking spray. Fold chopped peaches into gelatin mixture. Pour into prepared mold. Cover and chill for 2 to 24 hours. Before serving, remove gelatin from mold. Garnish with dessert topping.

Nutrition Facts per serving: 32 cal., 1 g total fat (1 g sat. fat), 0 mg chol., 38 mg sodium, 4 g carbo., 1 g fiber, 1 g pro.

The trick to keeping the tangy lemon cream light and fluffy is to beat the cream and gelatin mixture in a thoroughly chilled bowl with icy cold beaters. Place the bowl and beaters in the freezer or refrigerator when you chill the gelatin in step 1.

4g net carb

CREAMY LEMON BLUEBERRY DESSERT

1	4-serving-size package sugar-free lemon-flavored gelatin
1¼	cups boiling water
1	cup whipping cream
1	cup fresh blueberries
1	teaspoon finely shredded lemon peel
	Lemon peel strips (optional)

PREP:
25 minutes
CHILL:
6³/₄ hours
MAKES:
6 servings

1 In a small bowl dissolve gelatin in the boiling water. Cover and chill until partially set (consistency of unbeaten egg whites), about 45 minutes, stirring occasionally.

2 In a chilled medium mixing bowl beat whipping cream with chilled beaters of an electric mixer on medium speed until slightly thickened. Add partially set gelatin mixture. Beat until fluffy and mixture mounds. Fold in blueberries and 1 teaspoon lemon peel. Spoon into 6 dessert dishes. If desired, garnish with lemon peel strips. Cover and chill until firm.

Nutrition Facts per serving: 158 cal., 15 g total fat (9 g sat. fat), 55 mg chol., 53 mg sodium, 5 g carbo., 1 g fiber, 2 g pro.

If ladyfingers don't fit into your low-carb plan, leave them out and top the coffee-flavored filling with fresh berries.

EASY COFFEE TRIFLE

START TO FINISH:

15 minutes

MAKES:

6 servings

3 tablespoons fat-free, sugar-free instant Swiss-style coffee powder

2 tablespoons hot water

½ of a 3-ounce package ladyfingers, split and torn into 1-inch pieces

½ of an 8-ounce tub (½ cup) light cream cheese

1 teaspoon vanilla

1 cup whipping cream

1 In a medium bowl stir together 1 tablespoon of the coffee powder and the hot water. Add ladyfinger pieces, stirring to coat; set aside.

2 In a large mixing bowl beat cream cheese and vanilla with an electric mixer on medium to high speed for 30 seconds or until creamy. Add whipping cream and the remaining 2 tablespoons coffee powder. Beat until soft peaks form.

3 Place half of the ladyfinger pieces in 6 small parfait glasses or dessert dishes. Top with half of the whipped cream mixture. Repeat layers. Serve immediately.

Nutrition Facts per serving: 211 cal., 18 g total fat (11 g sat. fat), 90 mg chol., 128 mg sodium, 8 g carbo., 0 g fiber, 3 g pro.

This decadent dessert is aptly named for the classic pie. With a soft, fluffy texture and rich chocolate flavor, you'll never miss the crust.

FRENCH SILK DESSERT

½ cup no-calorie, heat-stable granular sugar substitute (Splenda)

¼ cup butter, softened

2 ounces unsweetened chocolate, melted and cooled

½ teaspoon vanilla

¼ cup refrigerated or frozen egg product, thawed

½ cup whipping cream

1 tablespoon chopped toasted walnuts

1 In a medium mixing bowl beat sugar substitute and butter with an electric mixer on medium speed about 4 minutes or until fluffy. Stir in chocolate and vanilla. Gradually add egg product, beating on high speed and scraping sides of the bowl frequently, until light and fluffy.

2 In a chilled small mixing bowl beat whipping cream with an electric mixer on medium speed just until soft peaks form; fold into chocolate mixture.

3 Spoon into 6 dessert dishes. Cover and chill for 2 to 24 hours. Sprinkle with walnuts before serving.

Nutrition Facts per serving: 212 cal., 22 g total fat (13 g sat. fat), 49 mg chol., 112 mg sodium, 6 g carbo., 2 g fiber, 3 g pro.

PREP:
20 minutes
CHILL:
2 hours
MAKES:
6 servings

A crunchy walnut crust, a luscious cream cheese layer, and fresh strawberries add up to one scrumptious dessert.

6 g net carb

CREAM CAKE WITH STRAWBERRIES

PREP:

20 minutes

BAKE:

10 minutes

OVEN:

375°F

CHILL:

4 hours

MAKES:

8 servings

1½	cups toasted walnuts
2	tablespoons no-calorie, heat-stable granular sugar substitute (Splenda)
2	slightly beaten egg whites
12	ounces cream cheese, softened
½	cup vanilla fat-free yogurt with sweetener
⅓	cup no-calorie, heat-stable granular sugar substitute (Splenda)
4	teaspoons lemon juice
1	cup sliced strawberries

1 In a blender or food processor combine walnuts and the 2 tablespoons sugar substitute. Cover and blend or process until nuts are finely ground.

2 In a small bowl stir together nuts and egg whites. Using a spatula, press mixture onto the bottom of an 8-inch springform pan. Bake in a 375° oven for 10 to 12 minutes or until crust appears dry. Cool on a wire rack.

3 In a large mixing bowl beat cream cheese, yogurt, the ⅓ cup sugar substitute, and the lemon juice with an electric mixer on medium speed until fluffy. Carefully spread cream cheese mixture over cooled crust. Cover and chill for 4 to 24 hours. Using a spatula, loosen the crust from the sides of the pan. Remove sides of pan; cut cake into wedges. Top individual servings with the strawberries.

Nutrition Facts per serving: 319 cal., 30 g total fat (11 g sat. fat), 50 mg chol., 150 mg sodium, 8 g carbo., 2 g fiber, 8 g pro.

Swirl fresh raspberries with whipped cream to create this heavenly dessert. Whip the cream until it's very stiff so you can marble it with the raspberry filling.

RASPBERRY-CHOCOLATE CREAM

2	cups fresh raspberries
½	cup no-calorie, heat-stable granular sugar substitute (Splenda)
1½	cups whipping cream
1	tablespoon raspberry liqueur (optional)
1	teaspoon vanilla
½	ounce unsweetened chocolate, grated

1 In a small saucepan combine raspberries and sugar substitute. Cook and stir over medium heat until bubbly. Remove from heat. Transfer to a small bowl. Cover and chill at least 2 hours.

2 In a large chilled mixing bowl combine whipping cream, liqueur (if using), and vanilla. Beat with chilled beaters of an electric mixer on medium speed until stiff peaks form. Gently fold or swirl in chilled raspberry mixture, leaving some white to create a marbled appearance. Spoon into 8 martini glasses or 6-ounce dessert dishes. Sprinkle with chocolate. Serve immediately.

Nutrition Facts per serving: 188 cal., 18 g total fat (11 g sat. fat), 62 mg chol., 19 mg sodium, 7 g carbo., 2 g fiber, 1 g pro.

PREP:
20 minutes
CHILL:
2 hours
MAKES:
8 servings

5 g net carb

Swedish and Norwegian immigrants first brought these delicate fried cookies to Minnesota. From there, they became an American coffee-time tradition.

NUTMEG ROSETTES

2 g net carb

PREP:
20 minutes

COOK:
30 seconds per rosette

MAKES:
about 42 rosettes

2   beaten eggs

1   cup unbleached all-purpose flour

½   cup whipping cream

½   cup water

2   tablespoons no-calorie, heat-stable granular sugar substitute (Splenda)

1   teaspoon ground nutmeg

1   teaspoon vanilla

¼   teaspoon salt

    Cooking oil for deep-fat frying

1 In a medium bowl combine eggs, flour, whipping cream, water, sugar substitute, nutmeg, vanilla, and salt. Beat with a rotary beater until smooth.

2 Heat a rosette iron in deep, hot oil (375°F) for 30 seconds. Remove iron from oil and briefly drain on paper towels. Dip hot iron into batter (batter should extend three-fourths of the way up sides of iron.) Immediately dip iron into hot oil. Fry for 30 to 45 seconds or until rosette is golden. Lift out iron and tip slightly to drain. With a fork, push rosette off iron onto paper towels placed over wire racks.

3 Repeat with remaining batter, reheating rosette iron in oil about 10 seconds each time before dipping it into batter.

TO STORE: Place in layers separated by waxed paper into an airtight container; cover. Store at room temperature up to 3 days or freeze up to 3 months.

Nutrition Facts per rosette: 48 cal., 4 g total fat (1 g sat. fat), 14 mg chol., 18 mg sodium, 2 g carbo., 0 g fiber, 1 g pro.

To resist the temptation to eat more of these moist, tender bars than you should, store them, individually wrapped, in the freezer.

DATE-WALNUT BARS

½ cup boiling water

⅓ cup snipped pitted whole dates

   Nonstick cooking spray

½ cup unbleached all-purpose flour

½ teaspoon baking powder

½ teaspoon ground cinnamon

⅛ teaspoon baking soda

1 egg

½ cup no-calorie, heat-stable granular sugar substitute (Splenda)

⅓ cup whipping cream

¼ cup finely chopped toasted walnuts

PREP:
25 minutes
BAKE:
10 minutes
OVEN:
350°F
MAKES:
16 bars

1 In a small bowl combine boiling water and dates. Cover and let stand for 10 minutes. Drain.

2 Coat an 8×8×2-inch baking pan with cooking spray; set aside. Combine flour, baking powder, cinnamon, and baking soda; set aside.

3 In a medium mixing bowl beat egg with an electric mixer on medium speed or a rotary beater until frothy. Stir in sugar substitute, whipping cream, and drained dates.

4 Add flour mixture to egg mixture, stirring with a wooden spoon until combined. Stir in nuts. Spread batter evenly into the prepared baking pan.

5 Bake in a 350° oven about 10 minutes or until a wooden toothpick inserted near the center comes out clean. Cool in pan on a wire rack. Cut into bars.

Nutrition Facts per bar: 61 cal., 3 g total fat (1 g sat. fat), 20 mg chol., 29 mg sodium, 7 g carbo., 1 g fiber, 1 g pro.

HOLIDAYS

Holidays are a time to share good cheer with family and friends. While reminiscing about festive foods in years past, browse through this selection of low-carb recipes to create memorable feasts for today. Taste tempters such as Bell-Ringer Salsa Cheesecake and Hickory-Smoked Turkey Breast will add festivity to your holiday celebrations.

Serve this creamy three-ingredient spread with fresh fruit or toasted low-carb tortilla wedges.

ALMOND BRIE SPREAD

PREP:

10 minutes

STAND:

30 minutes

MAKES:

1¼ cups

2   4½-ounce rounds Brie cheese

2   tablespoons cream sherry

3   tablespoons toasted sliced almonds

 Fresh fruit or toasted low-carb tortilla wedges

1 Use a vegetable peeler or small paring knife to cut the thin white covering from chilled cheese. Place cheese in a mixing bowl; let stand at room temperature about 30 minutes or until softened. Beat with an electric mixer on medium speed for 1 minute. Add sherry. Beat until light and smooth. Chop 2 tablespoons of the almonds; stir into cheese mixture.

2 Serve the spread immediately or cover and chill up to 24 hours. If chilled, let the spread stand at room temperature for 30 minutes before serving. Sprinkle with remaining 1 tablespoon almonds. Serve with fresh fruit.

Nutrition Facts per tablespoon: 51 cal., 4 g total fat (2 g sat. fat), 13 mg chol., 80 mg sodium, 0 g carbo., 0 g fiber, 3 g pro.

The combination of pesto and pine nuts adds a pleasant flavor twist to this appetizer mold.

PESTO CHEESE MOLD

2   3-ounce packages cream cheese

2   tablespoons dairy sour cream

4   teaspoons finely chopped onion

1   small clove garlic

¼   cup purchased refrigerated pesto

1   tablespoon pine nuts

Pine nuts, walnuts, fresh cilantro, chopped red sweet peppers, and/or fresh basil (optional)

Assorted low-carb crackers

1 Let cream cheese stand at room temperature for 30 minutes to soften. In a mixing bowl beat cream cheese and sour cream with an electric mixer on low to medium speed until smooth. Stir in onion, garlic, pesto, and the 1 tablespoon pine nuts.

2 Line a small bowl or a 6- to 10-ounce mold or custard cup with plastic wrap. Spoon cheese mixture into prepared mold. Smooth top. Cover and chill for 4 to 24 hours.

3 To serve, unmold cheese and remove plastic wrap. Place on a platter. If desired, garnish with nuts, cilantro, chopped red peppers, and/or basil. Serve with crackers.

Nutrition Facts per serving: 90 cal., 9 g total fat (3 g sat. fat), 15 mg chol., 78 mg sodium, 2 g carbo., 0 g fiber, 2 g pro.

PREP:
15 minutes
STAND:
30 minutes
CHILL:
4 hours
MAKES:
12 servings

*Decked in green guacamole and red tomato, this savory appetizer rings in the season.
Leftovers make a tasty snack the following day.*

3 g net carb

BELL-RINGER SALSA CHEESECAKE

PREP:

15 minutes

BAKE:

35 minutes

OVEN:

350°F

COOL:

2 hours

CHILL:

4 hours

MAKES:

20 servings

2   8-ounce packages cream cheese

2   cups shredded Monterey Jack cheese or Colby-Monterey Jack cheese blend (8 ounces)

1   8-ounce carton dairy sour cream

3   eggs

1   cup bottled mild or hot salsa

1   4-ounce can diced green chile peppers, drained

1   8-ounce carton dairy sour cream

1   6-ounce container frozen avocado dip (guacamole), thawed

1   medium tomato, peeled, seeded, and chopped

      Snipped fresh cilantro or parsley (optional)

      Toasted low-carb tortilla wedges or low-carb crackers

1 For filling, let cream cheese stand at room temperature for 30 minutes to soften. In a large mixing bowl beat the cream cheese with an electric mixer on medium speed until smooth. Add the Monterey Jack cheese and 8 ounces sour cream; beat until combined. Add the eggs all at once, beating on low speed just until mixture is combined. Stir in salsa and chile peppers.

2 Pour filling into a 9-inch springform pan. Place pan in a shallow baking pan. Bake the cheesecake in a 350° oven for 35 to 40 minutes or until center of cheesecake appears nearly set when shaken. Place pan on a wire rack.

3 Dollop remaining carton of sour cream over top of hot cheesecake; let stand about 1 minute to soften, then carefully spread over top. Cool cheesecake thoroughly. Cover and chill cheesecake for 4 to 24 hours before serving.

4 To serve, remove the sides of the pan. Dollop the top outside edge of the cheesecake with avocado dip. Sprinkle cheesecake with chopped tomato. If desired, garnish with cilantro. Serve with toasted tortilla wedges.

Nutrition Facts per serving (without tortilla wedges or crackers): 203 cal., 19 g total fat (10 g sat. fat), 77 mg chol., 224 mg sodium, 3 g carbo., 0 g fiber, 7 g pro.

Toasted coconut and orange juice lend a slightly sweet hint to this creamy spread. For a holiday snack tray, arrange red sweet pepper strips and green pea pods around the cheese ball.

GINGERED ORANGE CHEESE BALL

1	8-ounce package cream cheese
½	cup butter (no substitutes)
1	tablespoon finely shredded orange peel
1	tablespoon orange juice
4	teaspoons very finely chopped crystallized ginger
3	tablespoons toasted unsweetened coconut
3	tablespoons finely chopped toasted macadamia nuts
	Red sweet pepper strips, fresh pea pods, or low-carb crackers

PREP:
25 minutes
STAND:
30 minutes
CHILL:
4 hours
MAKES:
1½ cups

1 Let cream cheese and butter stand at room temperature about 30 minutes to soften. In a medium mixing bowl combine cream cheese, butter, orange peel, and orange juice. Beat with an electric mixer on medium speed about 30 seconds or until combined. Stir in ginger. Cover and chill for 4 to 24 hours.

2 Line work surface with a sheet of waxed paper. On waxed paper toss together coconut and nuts. Shape the cheese mixture into a ball; roll cheese ball in nut mixture to coat. Serve with sweet pepper strips, pea pods, or crackers.

Nutrition Facts per tablespoon: 80 cal., 8 g total fat (5 g sat. fat), 21 mg chol., 72 mg sodium, 1 g carbo., 0 g fiber, 1 g pro.

Thanks to no-sugar-added cranberry-apple juice and sugar substitute, you can adorn your holiday turkey or ham with this classic and festive condiment.

3 g net carb

CRANBERRY RELISH

PREP:

25 minutes

CHILL:

2 hours

MAKES:

about 2 cups

1 12-ounce package (3 cups) cranberries

¾ cup no-sugar added cranberry-apple juice

3 tablespoons no-calorie, heat-stable granular sugar substitute (Splenda)

½ teaspoon ground cinnamon

¼ teaspoon ground nutmeg

Dash ground cloves

½ cup coarsely chopped toasted pecans

1 In a 2-quart saucepan combine cranberries, cranberry-apple juice, sugar substitute, cinnamon, nutmeg, and cloves. Cook and stir over medium-high heat until boiling and cranberries pop; reduce heat. Simmer, uncovered, for 6 to 8 minutes or until mixture thickens, stirring frequently. Transfer to a small bowl. Cover and chill for 2 to 48 hours. Just before serving, stir in pecans. Serve with poultry, pork, or ham.

Nutrition Facts per 2 tablespoons: 37 cal., 2 g total fat (0 g sat. fat), 0 mg chol., 2 mg sodium, 4 g carbo., 1 g fiber, 0 g pro.

This fruit-and-nut condiment is a traditional part of the Jewish Passover celebration. Adjust the ingredients to suit your taste. Try sweet or tart apples, walnuts or almonds, or even pears and finely shredded carrots.

6 g net carb

CHAROSET

6 medium apples (peeled, if desired)

½ cup finely chopped walnuts

1½ teaspoons ground cinnamon

¼ teaspoon ground cardamom

1 cup sweet concord grape wine

1 Using a sharp knife, quarter and core apples. Shred apples into a large bowl. Stir in walnuts, cinnamon, and cardamom. Stir in wine. Cover and chill for at least 1 hour, stirring occasionally. Store in the refrigerator for up to 3 days.

Nutrition Facts per 3 tablespoons: 52 cal., 2 g total fat (0 g sat. fat), 0 mg chol., 1 mg sodium, 7 g carbo., 1 g fiber, 0 g pro.

PREP:
15 minutes
CHILL:
1 hour
MAKES:
24 servings (4½ cups)

Savor the mingling of fall flavors and colors in this easy soup. Serve warm or chilled as weather dictates.

CINNAMON-SPICED PUMPKIN SOUP

PREP:

10 minutes

COOK:

5 minutes

MAKES:

6 servings (about 2¹/₂ cups)

1   15-ounce can pumpkin

1   14-ounce can reduced-sodium chicken broth

1   cup milk

¹/₄   teaspoon ground cinnamon

¹/₈   teaspoon salt

¹/₈   to ¹/₄ teaspoon ground nutmeg

No-calorie, heat-stable granular sugar substitute (Splenda) (optional)

Snipped fresh chives (optional)

1 In a large saucepan stir together pumpkin, broth, and milk. Stir in cinnamon, salt, and nutmeg; heat just to boiling. Reduce heat and simmer, uncovered, for 5 minutes. If desired, sweeten to taste with sugar substitute.

2 To serve, pour warm soup into mugs; if desired, garnish with chives. Or transfer soup to medium bowl; cover and chill for up to 24 hours. Serve soup chilled or reheat in saucepan.

Nutrition Facts per serving: 49 cal., 0 g total fat (0 g sat. fat), 1 mg chol., 254 mg sodium, 10 g carbo., 2 g fiber, 3 g pro.

This tangy red-and-green coleslaw makes a pleasant counterpoint to the holiday turkey or roast beef. The fresh cranberries add a tart, fresh taste and slight pink tint to the dressing.

CRANBERRY COLESLAW

¼ cup mayonnaise or salad dressing

2 tablespoons no-calorie, heat-stable granular sugar substitute (Splenda)

1 tablespoon vinegar

¼ cup chopped fresh cranberries or snipped dried cranberries

5 cups shredded cabbage (1 small head)

1 For dressing, in a small bowl stir together mayonnaise, sugar substitute, and vinegar. Stir in cranberries. Place shredded cabbage in a large serving bowl. Pour dressing over cabbage; toss to coat. Serve at once or, if desired, cover and chill for up to 45 minutes.

Nutrition Facts per serving: 94 cal., 7 g total fat (1 g sat. fat), 5 mg chol., 63 mg sodium, 7 g carbo., 2 g fiber, 1 g pro.

START TO FINISH:

15 minutes

MAKES:

6 side-dish servings

A turkey breast is a great way to enjoy the flavor of roast turkey without days of leftovers.

0 g net carb

SPINACH-STUFFED TURKEY BREAST

PREP:

20 minutes

ROAST:

2¹/₂ hours

STAND:

15 minutes

OVEN:

325°F

MAKES:

8 servings

1	10-ounce package frozen chopped spinach, thawed
¹/₂	of an 8-ounce package cream cheese, softened
3	tablespoons grated Parmesan cheese
2	tablespoons water
1	teaspoon dried basil, crushed
¹/₄	teaspoon ground nutmeg
¹/₄	teaspoon black pepper
1	2¹/₂- to 3-pound turkey breast half with bone

1 Drain spinach thoroughly and squeeze out excess liquid. Place spinach in food processor. Add cream cheese, Parmesan cheese, water, basil, nutmeg, and pepper. Cover and process until well combined.

2 With a small sharp knife loosen breast skin from meat and pull skin back, leaving skin attached along one side. Spread spinach mixture over exposed portion of meat; pull skin back over to cover spinach mixture. Secure skin with wooden toothpicks or skewers along sides of breast. Place turkey skin side up on a rack in a shallow roasting pan. Insert meat thermometer into center of breast, below stuffing. Do not allow thermometer tip to touch bone. Cover turkey loosely with foil.

3 Roast in a 325° oven for 2 hours. Remove foil. Roast ¹/₂ to 1 hour more or until juices runs clear and turkey is no longer pink (170°F). Cover turkey loosely with foil. Let stand for 15 minutes before carving. To carve, start at outside of breast half; slice downward, keeping slices thin. Continue slicing slightly higher up on the breast.

Nutrition Facts per serving: 262 cal., 14 g total fat (6 g sat. fat), 99 mg chol., 183 mg sodium, 1 g carbo., 1 g fiber, 31 g pro.

For a twist on tradition, head outdoors and smoke the holiday bird on your grill. Leftovers make a tasty addition to a cold meat tray.

HICKORY-SMOKED TURKEY BREAST

Hickory wood chips

3 tablespoons Worcestershire sauce

2 tablespoons lemon juice

2 tablespoons butter, melted

1 teaspoon dried oregano, crushed, or dried dillweed

½ teaspoon seasoned salt

¼ teaspoon black pepper

1 2½- to 3-pound turkey breast half with bone

1 Soak wood chips in enough water to cover for at least 1 hour.

2 In a bowl stir together the Worcestershire sauce, lemon juice, butter, oregano, seasoned salt, and pepper; set aside.

3 If desired, remove skin from turkey breast. Place turkey breast bone side down on a rack in a shallow roasting pan. Insert a meat thermometer into the thickest part of turkey breast. Do not allow thermometer tip to touch bone.

4 Drain wood chips. For a charcoal grill, arrange medium-hot coals around the edge of the grill. Sprinkle half of the wood chips over coals. Place roasting pan with turkey breast in the center of the grill (not above the coals). Cover and grill for 45 minutes, brushing turkey breast with butter mixture occasionally. Add more coals to maintain heat; add the remaining wood chips. Cover and grill for 30 to 45 minutes more or until juices run clear and turkey is no longer pink (170°F), brushing occasionally with butter mixture for the first 15 minutes. (For a gas grill, preheat grill. Reduce heat to medium. Adjust for indirect cooking. Add drained wood chips according to manufacturer's directions. Place roasting pan with turkey on the grill rack over the unlit burner. Cover and grill as above.)

5 Remove turkey breast from grill. Cover turkey loosely with foil; let stand for 15 minutes before slicing. Serve warm or refrigerate for up to 24 hours.

Nutrition Facts per serving: 251 cal., 12 g total fat (4 g sat. fat), 100 mg chol., 262 mg sodium, 2 g carbo., 0 g fiber, 31 g pro.

PREP:

1 hour

SOAK:

1 hour

GRILL:

1¼ hours

STAND:

15 minutes

MAKES:

8 servings

Cutting the Cornish hens in half accomplishes two things: It allows them to cook much faster than they would whole, and makes two servings of one bird.

7 g net carb

GAME HENS WITH GRILLED PEPPERS

PREP:

25 minutes

GRILL:

40 minutes

MAKES:

4 servings

2   1½-pound Cornish game hens

¼   cup butter, melted

½   teaspoon salt

½   teaspoon freshly ground black pepper

½   teaspoon ground cumin

3   red, yellow, and/or green sweet peppers, quartered

1   ancho pepper, quartered*

1   medium red onion, cut into ½-inch slices

1 Using kitchen shears or a long heavy knife, cut game hens in half. Twist wing ends under back. For cumin butter, in a small bowl combine melted butter, salt, pepper, and cumin. Divide mixture in half. Use one portion to brush over both sides of hens. Set the other portion aside.

2 For a charcoal grill, arrange medium-hot coals around a drip pan. Test for medium heat above the pan. Place hen halves bone sides down on the grill rack over pan. Cover and grill for 40 to 50 minutes or until hens are tender and no longer pink (180°F). (For a gas grill, preheat grill. Reduce heat to medium. Adjust grill for indirect cooking. Place hen halves, bone sides down, on grill rack over unlit burner. Grill as above.)

3 While the hens are grilling, brush the sweet peppers, ancho pepper, and onion with the remaining butter mixture; add peppers and onion to grill rack over heat. Cover and grill 10 to 15 minutes or until tender and slightly charred, turning once halfway through grilling.

4 Remove hens and vegetables from grill; keep hens warm. Cut peppers into strips; chop onion. Toss together peppers and onion. To serve, divide pepper mixture among 4 dinner plates. Arrange hens on top of pepper mixture.

*NOTE: Hot chile peppers such as ancho peppers contain oils that can burn your eyes, lips, and skin. Wear plastic or rubber gloves while preparing hot peppers and be sure to wash your hands and nails in hot, soapy water afterward.

Nutrition Facts per serving: 493 cal., 35 g total fat (13 g sat. fat), 153 mg chol., 509 mg sodium, 9 g carbo., 2 g fiber, 38 g pro.

Bring simplicity and elegance to a holiday gathering with these rich morsels. To save time, let your fish merchant shuck the oysters, but plan on serving them within a few hours of purchase.

OYSTERS BROILED IN ROQUEFORT BUTTER

¼ cup butter, softened

4 ounces Roquefort or other blue cheese, crumbled

¼ teaspoon black pepper

24 oysters on the half shell*

1 For Roquefort butter, in a small bowl stir together butter, cheese, and pepper until nearly smooth. Cover and chill up to 3 days.

2 Place oyster shells, about half at a time, on rack in broiler pan. Top each oyster with a rounded teaspoon of the Roquefort butter. Broil 4 to 5 inches from the heat for 3 to 5 minutes or until golden and edges of oysters curl. Serve immediately.

*NOTE: For oysters in shells, open each shell. Remove oysters from shells with a knife and drain. Wash shells and place an oyster in the deep half of each shell.

Nutrition Facts per serving: 149 cal., 9 g total fat (5 g sat. fat), 17 mg chol., 238 mg sodium, 5 g carbo., 0 g fiber, 12 g pro.

PREP:
10 minutes

BROIL:
3 minutes per batch

MAKES:
12 appetizer servings

Whip up Citrus Brussels Sprouts (see page 277) to serve with this roast and its savory sauce of mushrooms and green onions. For best results, roast the meat only to medium-rare.

4 g net carb

MUSHROOM-SAUCED ROAST BEEF

PREP:

20 minutes

ROAST:

1½ hours

OVEN:

325°F

STAND:

15 minutes

MAKES:

8 to 10 servings

1	2- to 3-pound beef eye of round roast
2	tablespoons Dijon-style mustard
½	teaspoon coarsely ground black pepper
3	cups quartered fresh mushrooms
4	green onions, bias-sliced into ½-inch pieces
1	clove garlic, minced
2	tablespoons butter
¼	cup unbleached all-purpose flour
½	teaspoon dried thyme or marjoram, crushed
1½	cups beef broth
¼	cup light cream or milk

1 Trim fat from meat. Mix mustard and pepper. Rub onto meat. Place meat on a rack in a shallow roasting pan. Insert a meat thermometer into center of roast. Roast, uncovered, in a 325° oven until thermometer registers 135°F for medium-rare (1½ to 2 hours). Remove roast from oven. Cover with foil; let roast stand for 15 minutes before carving. (Temperature of the meat after standing should be 145°F.)

2 Meanwhile, for sauce, in a medium saucepan cook mushrooms, green onions, and garlic in hot butter until green onions are tender. Stir in flour and thyme. Gradually stir in beef broth. Cook and stir over medium heat until thickened and bubbly. Cook and stir for 1 minute more. Stir in cream. Cook and stir until heated through.

3 Thinly slice meat. Arrange on a serving platter. Pour some sauce over meat. Pass remaining sauce.

Nutrition Facts per serving: 229 cal., 10 g total fat (3 g sat. fat), 75 mg chol., 331 mg sodium, 5 g carbo., 1 g fiber, 29 g pro.

Broccoli and sweet red pepper add crunch and color to this easy Italian egg dish.

3 g net carb

HOLIDAY FRITTATA

1	tablespoon cooking oil
1	cup fresh or frozen broccoli florets
½	of a large red sweet pepper, seeded and thinly sliced
¼	cup chopped onion
½	teaspoon dried Italian seasoning, crushed
¼	teaspoon salt
⅛	teaspoon black pepper
10	slightly beaten eggs
2	tablespoons milk
2	tablespoons finely shredded Parmesan cheese

1 Heat oil in a large skillet over medium heat. Add broccoli, sweet pepper, onion, Italian seasoning, salt, and pepper. Cook and stir until florets are crisp-tender, about 4 minutes for fresh broccoli or about 5 minutes for frozen broccoli.

2 In a medium bowl combine eggs and milk; mix well. Pour over vegetable mixture. As the eggs begin to set, run a spatula around the edge of the skillet, lifting the egg mixture to allow the uncooked portions to flow underneath. Continue cooking and lifting edges until eggs are nearly set. (The surface will be moist.)

3 Remove skillet from heat; sprinkle with cheese. Cover; let stand for 3 to 4 minutes or until set. To serve, cut into wedges.

Nutrition Facts per serving: 166 cal., 11 g total fat (3 g sat. fat), 357 mg chol., 234 mg sodium, 4 g carbo., 1 g fiber, 12 g pro.

PREP:
15 minutes
COOK:
15 minutes
STAND:
3 minutes
MAKES:
6 main-dish servings

With a libation like this, your guests will want to linger. It's a great starter for a dinner, brunch, or a simple evening of appetizers and good cheer.

MULLED CRANBERRY-RASPBERRY JUICE

PREP:

15 minutes

COOK:

5 to 6 hours (low) or
2¹/₂ to 3 hours (high)

MAKES:

10 (6-ounce) servings

1	small orange
8	cups low-calorie cranberry-raspberry juice cocktail
¹/₄	cup no-calorie, heat-stable granular sugar substitute (Splenda)
6	inches stick cinnamon
3	star anise
1	teaspoon whole cloves
	Orange peel strips (optional)

1 Remove the orange portion of the orange peel using a vegetable peeler. Cut peel into strips. Squeeze juice from orange; discard seeds and pulp. In a 3¹/₂- to 5-quart slow cooker combine orange juice, cranberry-raspberry juice, and sugar substitute.

2 For spice bag, cut a 6- or 8-inch square from a double thickness of 100-percent-cotton cheesecloth. Place the orange peel, cinnamon, star anise, and whole cloves in center of cheesecloth square. Bring corners of cheesecloth together and tie with a clean cotton string. Add to slow cooker.

3 Cover and cook on low-heat setting for 5 to 6 hours or on high-heat setting for 2¹/₂ to 3 hours. To serve, discard spice bag. Ladle cider into cups. If desired, garnish with additional orange peel.

Nutrition Facts per serving: 38 cal., 0 g total fat (00 g sat. fat), 0 mg chol., 29 mg sodium, 9 g carbo., 0 g fiber, 0 g pro.

Enjoy every pleasure of holiday dessert with these spiced pumpkin custards. They have all the flavor of pumpkin pie—minus the crust, of course.

6 g net carb

BAKED PUMPKIN CUSTARDS

5	beaten egg yolks
2	cups half-and-half or light cream
⅓	cup no-calorie, heat-stable granular sugar substitute (Splenda)
⅓	cup canned pumpkin
1	teaspoon pumpkin pie spice
1	teaspoon vanilla
⅛	teaspoon salt

1 In a medium bowl stir together egg yolks, half-and-half, sugar substitute, pumpkin, pumpkin pie spice, vanilla, and salt. Beat until combined but not frothy.

2 Place six 6-ounce custard cups in a 13×9×2-inch baking pan. Divide egg mixture among custard cups. Place baking pan on oven rack. Pour boiling water into the baking pan around custard cups to a depth of 1 inch.

3 Bake in a 325° oven about 35 minutes or until a knife inserted near the center of each cup comes out clean. Remove cups from water. Cool slightly. Serve warm.

Nutrition Facts per serving: 166 cal., 14 g total fat (7 g sat. fat), 207 mg chol., 89 mg sodium, 6 g carbo., 0 g fiber, 5 g pro.

PREP:
15 minutes
BAKE:
35 minutes
OVEN:
325°F
MAKES:
6 servings

A short freeze and a whirl in the blender transform homemade eggnog into a creamy, ultra-rich dessert.

ICED EGGNOG CUSTARD

PREP:

15 minutes

COOK:

10 minutes

FREEZE:

2 hours

MAKES:

4 servings

6 beaten egg yolks

$\frac{1}{3}$ cup no-calorie, heat-stable granular sugar substitute (Splenda)

$2\frac{1}{2}$ cups whipping cream

$\frac{1}{2}$ teaspoon vanilla

$\frac{1}{4}$ teaspoon ground nutmeg

1 In a heavy medium saucepan whisk together egg yolks and sugar substitute. Stir in cream. Cook and stir continuously over medium heat until mixture just coats the back of a clean metal spoon. Remove pan from heat. Stir in vanilla. Pour mixture into ice cube trays. Freeze until firm, about 2 hours.

2 Let ice cube trays stand at room temperature for 5 minutes. Break custard mixture into individual ice cubes and place in a large bowl. Using a potato masher, coarsely break up ice cubes. Place in blender or food processor. Cover and blend or process until smooth. Pour into small glasses. Sprinkle with nutmeg. Serve immediately.

Nutrition Facts per serving: 616 cal., 63 g total fat (37 g sat. fat), 524 mg chol., 69 mg sodium, 7 g carbo., 0 g fiber, 7 g pro.

Keep a stash of these chocolate morsels in the fridge year-round. They'll keep for up to 3 days, and with only 2 grams of net carbs per piece, you can enjoy them any time you please.

TOASTED ALMOND-COCONUT BALLS

½ cup toasted slivered almonds

⅓ cup no-calorie, heat-stable granular sugar substitute (Splenda)

⅓ cup unsweetened dried coconut flakes

1 tablespoon unsweetened cocoa powder

2 tablespoons butter, softened

1 tablespoon water

½ teaspoon vanilla

START TO FINISH:
15 minutes
MAKES:
12 balls

1 Place almonds in a food processor. Cover and process until very finely ground. In a medium bowl stir together almonds, sugar substitute, coconut flakes, and cocoa powder. Stir in butter, water, and vanilla.

2 Shape mixture into 12 balls, about 1 inch in diameter. Serve immediately or cover tightly and chill up to 3 days.

Nutrition Facts per ball: 69 cal., 6 g total fat (3 g sat. fat), 5 mg chol., 22 mg sodium, 3 g carbo., 1 g fiber, 1 g pro.

These rich chocolate custards are a handy make-ahead dessert for your holiday meal.
If you like, top them with whipped cream.

CHOCOLATE-MINT POTS DE CRÈME

PREP:

20 minutes

CHILL:

4 hours

MAKES:

8 servings

1½   cups half-and-half or light cream

3   ounces unsweetened chocolate, coarsely chopped

⅔   cup no-calorie, heat-stable granular sugar substitute (Splenda)

4   beaten egg yolks

1   teaspoon vanilla

½   teaspoon peppermint extract

1 In a heavy medium saucepan combine half-and-half, chocolate, and sugar substitute. Cook and stir over medium heat until mixture comes to a boil. (If chocolate flecks remain, use a rotary beater or wire whisk to beat mixture until blended.)

2 Gradually stir half of the hot mixture into egg yolks. Return all of the egg yolk mixture to the saucepan. Cook and stir over medium-low heat just until mixture bubbles (mixture will be very thick). Remove from heat. Stir in vanilla and peppermint extract. Divide mixture evenly into 8 small cups or pot de crème cups. Cover and chill for 4 to 24 hours before serving.

Nutrition Facts per serving: 155 cal., 14 g total fat (7 g sat. fat), 123 mg chol., 25 mg sodium, 7 g carbo., 2 g fiber, 4 g pro.

For a comforting cold-weather dessert, serve these individual baked custards slightly warm.

BAKED CHOCOLATE-CINNAMON CUSTARDS

5 g net carb

½   cup water

1   ounce unsweetened chocolate, chopped

½   teaspoon ground cinnamon

1   cup whipping cream

5   beaten egg yolks

¼   cup no-calorie, heat-stable granular sugar substitute (Splenda)

1   teaspoon vanilla

PREP:
15 minutes

BAKE:
30 minutes

OVEN:
325°F

MAKES:
4 servings

1 In a small saucepan combine water, chocolate, and cinnamon; cook and stir over medium heat until chocolate is melted and mixture is smooth. Gradually stir in whipping cream. Continue to cook and stir until smooth. Remove from heat. Gradually stir chocolate mixture into egg yolks. Add sugar substitute and vanilla; beat with a wire whisk or rotary beater until combined.

2 Place four 6-ounce custard cups in a 2- or 3-quart rectangular baking dish. Divide mixture among custard cups. Place baking dish on oven rack. Pour boiling water into the baking dish around custard cups to a depth of 1 inch.

3 Bake in a 325° oven for 30 to 45 minutes or until a knife inserted near the center of each cup comes out clean. Remove custard cups from water. Cool slightly on a wire rack before serving.

Nutrition Facts per serving: 328 cal., 33 g total fat (18 g sat. fat), 348 mg chol., 35 mg sodium, 6 g carbo., 1 g fiber, 5 g pro.

SAUCES & CONDIMENTS

Adding a touch of seasoning to your favorite foods can make them taste even better. As a low-carb dieter, you still can add flavor and variety to your foods using the carb-friendly choices in this chapter. It's got everything—perfect sandwich spreads, lively salsas, mild sauces, and zesty salad dressings.

Pour this zesty blend over cooked vegetables, such as zucchini, cauliflower, broccoli, or corn.

CAJUN BUTTER

START TO FINISH:

15 minutes

MAKES:

enough for 4 servings

¼ teaspoon chili powder

¼ teaspoon black pepper

⅛ teaspoon garlic powder

⅛ teaspoon cayenne pepper

2 tablespoons butter

2 teaspoons unbleached all-purpose flour

¼ cup chicken broth

1 Stir together chili powder, black pepper, garlic powder, and cayenne pepper. In a small saucepan cook spice mixture in hot butter for 1 minute. Stir in flour. Add chicken broth. Cook and stir over medium heat until thickened and bubbly. Cook and stir for 1 minute more. Serve warm over cooked vegetables.

Nutrition Facts per serving: 56 cal., 6 g total fat (4 g sat. fat), 16 mg chol., 99 mg sodium, 0 g carbo., 0 g fiber, 0 g pro.

Serve this savory spread on vegetables or steaks.

HERB BUTTER

½ cup butter, softened

1 teaspoon dried basil, crushed; or ½ teaspoon dried thyme, crushed, plus ½ teaspoon dried marjoram, crushed

1 In a small bowl stir together the butter and desired herb(s) until combined. Serve immediately or cover and store in refrigerator up to 1 week. Let chilled butter stand 30 minutes at room temperature before serving.

Nutrition Facts per tablespoon: 100 cal., 11 g total fat (7 g sat. fat), 31 mg chol., 116 mg sodium, 0 g carbo., 0 g fiber, 0 g pro.

START TO FINISH:

10 minutes

MAKES:

½ cup

Lemon peel adds a wonderful tang to the mushrooms. Spoon the mixture over grilled steak, chicken, or fish.

MUSHROOM-BUTTER SAUCE

MAKES:

about 1 cup

½   cup butter

2   cups sliced fresh mushrooms

1   clove garlic, minced

1   tablespoon snipped fresh oregano or 1 teaspoon dried oregano, crushed

     Dash black pepper

1   teaspoon finely shredded lemon peel

1 Melt butter in a medium saucepan. Add mushrooms, garlic, oregano, and pepper. Cook about 5 minutes or until mushrooms are tender. Stir in lemon peel. Serve with grilled steak, poultry, or fish.

Nutrition Facts per tablespoon: 53 cal., 6 g total fat (4 g sat. fat), 15 mg chol., 58 mg sodium, 1 g carbo., 0 g fiber, 0 g pro.

Use either sweet or dill pickle relish in this classic seafood sauce.

2 g net carb TARTAR SAUCE

¾ cup mayonnaise or salad dressing

¼ cup drained dill or sweet pickle relish

2 tablespoons finely chopped onion

1 tablespoon snipped fresh parsley

2 teaspoons capers, drained (optional)

PREP:
10 minutes
CHILL:
2 hours
MAKES:
1 cup

 In a small bowl stir together the mayonnaise, pickle relish, onion, parsley, and, if desired, capers. Cover and chill for at least 2 hours before serving. Serve with fish or seafood. (Cover and chill any leftovers for up to 1 week.)

Nutrition Facts per 2 tablespoons: 159 cal., 17 g total fat (2 g sat. fat), 8 mg chol., 168 mg sodium, 2 g carbo., 0 g fiber, 0 g pro.

With the addition of dried tomatoes, this flavored mayonnaise makes a perfect finishing touch for grilled lamb chops.

1 g net carb TOMATO AIOLI

½ cup mayonnaise or salad dressing

2 tablespoons oil-packed dried tomatoes, drained and finely chopped

1 tablespoon snipped fresh basil

1 teaspoon bottled minced garlic (2 cloves)

1 teaspoon snipped fresh thyme

START TO FINISH:
10 minutes
MAKES:
⅔ cup

 In a small bowl combine mayonnaise, tomatoes, basil, garlic, and thyme. Serve immediately or cover and chill for up to 6 hours. Serve with grilled lamb, pork, or chicken.

Nutrition Facts per tablespoon: 75 cal., 8 g total fat (1 g sat. fat), 6 mg chol., 60 mg sodium, 1 g carbo., 0 g fiber, 0 g pro.

Add extra zip to tuna, chicken, or egg salad with this flavorful mayonnaise.

1 g net carb

SCALLION MAYONNAISE

START TO FINISH:

15 minutes

MAKES:

1¹⁄₂ cups

12	green onions, chopped (about 1¹⁄₂ cups)
1	teaspoon cooking oil
1	cup mayonnaise or salad dressing
1¹⁄₂	teaspoons lemon juice
¹⁄₂	teaspoon kosher salt
¹⁄₄	teaspoon cracked black pepper

1 In small saucepan cook half of green onions in hot oil over medium heat for 1 to 2 minutes or until bright green. Remove from heat; cool.

2 In a blender or food processor place cooked green onions, remaining green onions, mayonnaise, lemon juice, salt, and pepper. Cover and blend or process until smooth. Store in a tightly covered container in the refrigerator up to 1 week.

Nutrition Facts per tablespoon: 70 cal., 8 g total fat (1 g sat. fat), 3 mg chol., 91 mg sodium, 1 g carbo., 0 g fiber, 0 g pro.

This velvety, dill-flavored mayonnaise makes a superb accompaniment for roast beef or pork. It also makes a tasty veggie dip.

0 g net carb

HERBED MAYONNAISE

PREP:

10 minutes

CHILL:

1 hour

MAKES:

1¹⁄₄ cups

¹⁄₂	cup mayonnaise or salad dressing
¹⁄₂	cup dairy sour cream
3	tablespoons snipped fresh dill
2	tablespoons snipped fresh parsley
1	clove garlic, minced

1 In a blender or food processor combine mayonnaise, sour cream, dill, parsley, and garlic. Cover and blend or process until almost smooth. Cover and chill at least 1 hour before serving. Store in a tightly covered container in the refrigerator for up to 3 days.

Nutrition Facts per tablespoon: 50 cal., 5 g total fat (1 g sat. fat), 5 mg chol., 34 mg sodium, 0 g carbo., 0 g fiber, 0 g pro.

Dress up roast beef or roast pork with this aromatic spread.

1 g net carb

ROASTED GARLIC MAYONNAISE

1	medium head garlic
2	teaspoons olive oil
½	cup mayonnaise or salad dressing
	Milk (optional)

1 Peel away outer skin from garlic. Cut off the pointed top portion with a knife, leaving the bulb intact but exposing the individual cloves. Place in a small baking dish; drizzle with olive oil. Bake, covered, in a 325° oven for 45 to 60 minutes or until cloves are very soft. Cool slightly. Press to remove garlic "paste" from individual cloves.

2 In a small bowl mash garlic with tines of a fork. Stir in mayonnaise. Thin mixture with a little milk, if necessary. Cover and chill in the refrigerator at least 3 hours. Cover and store in the refrigerator for up to 1 week.

Nutrition Facts per tablespoon: 116 cal., 12 g total fat (2 g sat. fat), 5 mg chol., 76 mg sodium, 1 g carbo., 0 g fiber, 0 g pro.

PREP:
10 minutes
BAKE:
45 minutes
OVEN:
325°F
CHILL:
3 hours
MAKES:
½ cup

Perk up the taste of purchased mayonnaise by adding Dijon-style mustard and fresh lime.

LIME MAYONNAISE

START TO FINISH:

10 minutes

MAKES:

¹/₃ cup

¹/₃ cup mayonnaise or salad dressing

1 teaspoon Dijon-style mustard

¹/₂ teaspoon finely shredded lime peel

1 teaspoon lime juice

1 In a small bowl stir together mayonnaise, mustard, lime peel, and lime juice. Store in the refrigerator up to 24 hours. Serve with beef, pork, lamb, chicken, turkey, or fish.

Nutrition Facts per tablespoon: 106 cal., 12 g total fat (2 g sat. fat), 9 mg chol., 89 mg sodium, 1 g carbo., 0 g fiber, 0 g pro.

This spiced-up mayonnaise is thin enough to drizzle over poultry or fish.
If you want a thicker condiment, leave out the milk.

CURRY MAYONNAISE

START TO FINISH:

5 minutes

MAKES:

¹/₂ cup

¹/₄ cup mayonnaise or salad dressing

¹/₄ cup dairy sour cream

2 tablespoons frozen orange juice concentrate

³/₄–1 teaspoon curry powder

4 to 5 tablespoons milk

1 In a small bowl stir together the mayonnaise, sour cream, juice concentrate, and curry powder. Stir in enough milk to make of drizzling consistency. Serve with chicken, turkey, or fish.

Nutrition Facts per tablespoon: 74 cal., 7 g total fat (2 g sat. fat), 7 mg chol., 46 mg sodium, 3 g carbo., 0 g fiber, 1 g pro.

Use either sour cream or mayonnaise to make this classic meat condiment.

MUSTARD-HORSERADISH SAUCE

1	tablespoon Dijon-style mustard
1/3	cup dairy sour cream, mayonnaise, or salad dressing
1	green onion, finely chopped
1	to 2 teaspoons prepared horseradish

START TO FINISH:

5 minutes

MAKES:

about 1/2 cup

1 In a small bowl stir together mustard, sour cream, onion, and horseradish. Serve with beef, pork, lamb, chicken, or turkey.

Nutrition Facts per tablespoon: 20 cal., 2 g total fat (1 g sat. fat), 4 mg chol., 16 mg sodium, 1 g carbo., 0 g fiber, 0 g pro.

Flecks of parsley freshen this tangy seafood sauce.

LEMON SAUCE

1/4	cup mayonnaise or salad dressing
2	tablespoons dairy sour cream
1	tablespoon snipped fresh Italian flat-leaf parsley
1	teaspoon finely shredded lemon peel
1	teaspoon lemon juice

START TO FINISH:

10 minutes

MAKES:

about 1/3 cup

1 In a small bowl stir together mayonnaise, sour cream, parsley, lemon peel, and lemon juice. Serve with fish or seafood.

Nutrition Facts per tablespoon: 90 cal., 10 g total fat (2 g sat. fat), 9 mg chol., 66 mg sodium, 1 g carbo., 0 g fiber, 0 g pro.

Use this potent pesto in small amounts to season meat, fish, chicken, or vegetables—or even stir a teaspoon of it into eggs for an unbeatable omelet.

CILANTRO PESTO

1   jalapeño pepper, halved (seeded, if desired)*

1   large bunch fresh cilantro leaves, stems removed (about 2 cups)

½   cup loosely packed fresh basil

¼   cup loosely packed fresh mint leaves

2   large cloves garlic

½   cup extra-virgin olive oil

¼   cup water

1   to 2 tablespoons lime juice

½   teaspoon sea salt

1 In a food processor place the jalapeño peppers, cilantro, basil, mint, and garlic. Cover and process with several on-off turns until finely chopped. With processor running, gradually add oil and water. Stir in lime juice and salt. (Or finely chop the jalapeño pepper, herbs, and garlic. Place in a bowl and stir in the oil, water, lime juice, and salt.) Store in a tightly covered container in the refrigerator up to 2 days.

*NOTE: Hot chile peppers contain oils that can burn your eyes, lips, and skin. Wear plastic or rubber gloves while preparing hot peppers and be sure to thoroughly wash your hands and nails in hot, soapy water afterward.

Nutrition Facts per tablespoon: 64 cal., 7 g total fat (1 g sat. fat), 0 mg chol., 78 mg sodium, 1 g carbo., 0 g fiber, 0 g pro.

Brush this fruity condiment on barbecued chicken and pork the last 5 to 10 minutes of grilling.

TANGY APRICOT BARBECUE SAUCE

Nonstick cooking spray

⅓   cup finely chopped onion

1   teaspoon grated fresh ginger

1   cup catsup

⅓   cup reduced-sugar or sugar-free apricot preserves

⅓   cup orange juice

1   tablespoon Worcestershire sauce

Dash black pepper

1 Lightly coat a medium saucepan with cooking spray. Add onion and ginger; cook over medium heat until tender, stirring occasionally. Stir in catsup, apricot preserves, orange juice, Worcestershire sauce, and pepper. Bring to boiling; reduce heat. Simmer, uncovered, about 10 minutes or until sauce is slightly thickened. Remove saucepan from heat; cool.

2 Cover and store any leftover sauce in the refrigerator for up to 3 days.

Nutrition Facts per tablespoon: 18 cal., 0 g total fat (0 g sat. fat), 0 mg chol., 120 mg sodium, 5 g carbo., 0 g fiber, 0 g pro.

PREP:
15 minutes
COOK:
10 minutes
MAKES:
1½ cups

This robust mustard sauce partners well with the distinctive flavors of lamb or beef. The combination of herbs adds a pleasant taste twist.

HERB-DIJON SAUCE

START TO FINISH:

15 minutes

MAKES:

1¹/₃ cups

1   8-ounce jar Dijon-style mustard

¹/₃   cup dry white wine

¹/₄   cup cooking oil

2   cloves garlic, minced

1   teaspoon dried rosemary, crushed

1   teaspoon dried basil, crushed

¹/₂   teaspoon dried oregano, crushed

¹/₂   teaspoon dried thyme, crushed

¹/₄   teaspoon black pepper

1 In a small bowl stir together the mustard, wine, oil, garlic, rosemary, basil, oregano, thyme, and pepper. To use, brush chicken, shrimp, fish, or pork with some of the sauce during the last few minutes of grilling or broiling. Cover and refrigerate remaining sauce up to 2 weeks.

Nutrition Facts per 2 tablespoons: 71 cal., 6 g total fat (1 g sat. fat), 0 mg chol., 108 mg sodium, 2 g carbo., 0 g fiber, 1 g pro.

Add the almonds just before serving this fruity condiment so they keep their crunch.

PEAR-CHUTNEY SALSA

½   cup bottled chunky salsa

3   tablespoons chutney, large pieces cut up

1   medium pear, peeled, cored, and chopped (1 cup)

½   cup chopped, seeded, peeled cucumber

2   tablespoons toasted slivered almonds

1 In a medium bowl stir together the salsa, chutney, pear, and cucumber. Serve immediately or cover and chill up to 4 hours. Before serving, stir in almonds. Serve with pork, ham, or chicken.

Nutrition Facts per tablespoon: 12 cal., 0 g total fat (0 g sat. fat), 0 mg chol., 10 mg sodium, 2 g carbo., 0 g fiber, 0 g pro.

START TO FINISH:

10 minutes

MAKES:

2 cups

To peel the fresh ginger, cut off one of the root ends and use a vegetable peeler to remove the brown outer layer. Store any remaining ginger in the refrigerator for up to 2 weeks or freeze for up to 6 months.

FRESH GINGER RELISH

⅓   cup peeled and minced fresh ginger

2   tablespoons finely chopped red sweet pepper

2   tablespoons cider vinegar

2   tablespoons orange juice

    No-calorie, heat-stable granular sugar substitute (Splenda)
    or other sugar substitute (optional)

1 In a small bowl stir together ginger, sweet pepper, vinegar, and orange juice. If desired, sweeten to taste with sugar substitute. Cover and chill in the refrigerator at least 4 hours. Store in the refrigerator up to 1 week. Serve with beef, pork, lamb, chicken, turkey, or fish.

Nutrition Facts per 2 tablespoons: 14 cal., 0 g total fat (0 g sat. fat), 0 mg chol., 2 mg sodium, 3 g carbo., 0 g fiber, 0 g pro.

PREP:

5 minutes

CHILL:

4 hours

MAKES:

½ cup

Grilling out tonight? Serve this fruity topper with grilled or broiled chicken breasts, slices of pork tenderloin, or lamb chops.

MINTED PINEAPPLE RELISH

START TO FINISH:

10 minutes

CHILL:

1 hour

MAKES:

6 to 8 servings

1   cup canned pineapple chunks (juice-pack), drained

½   cup lightly packed fresh mint leaves

1   tablespoon coarse-grain brown mustard

1 In a blender or food processor combine the pineapple, mint, and mustard. Cover and blend or process just until combined. Cover and chill in the refrigerator for 1 to 24 hours. Serve with chicken, pork, or lamb.

Nutrition Facts per serving: 29 cal., 0 g total fat (0 g sat. fat), 0 mg chol., 35 mg sodium, 7 g carbo., 0 g fiber, 0 g pro.

This sweet and spicy salsa is great on chicken or fish.

FRESH PEACH SALSA

2　cups chopped, peeled fresh peaches

¼　cup chopped sweet onion

3　tablespoons lime juice

2　to 3 tablespoons finely chopped, seeded fresh jalapeño peppers*

1　clove garlic, minced

1　tablespoon snipped fresh cilantro

PREP:

10 minutes

CHILL:

1 hour

MAKES:

2 cups

1 In a medium bowl stir together peaches, onion, lime juice, jalapeño peppers, garlic, and cilantro. Cover and chill for 1 to 2 hours.

*****NOTE:** Hot chile peppers such as jalapeños contain oils that can burn your eyes, lips, and skin. Wear plastic or rubber gloves while preparing hot peppers and be sure to thoroughly wash your hands and nails in hot, soapy water afterward.

Nutrition Facts per tablespoon: 12 cal., 0 g total fat (0 g sat. fat), 0 mg chol., 0 mg sodium, 3 g carbo., 1 g fiber, 0 g pro.

Fresh salsa, made from your own garden vegetables, surpasses any store-bought version.

FRESH TOMATILLO SALSA

10g net carb

PREP:

40 minutes

STAND:

30 minutes

CHILL:

1 hour

MAKES:

about 3 cups

¼ cup finely chopped red onion

¼ cup ice water

2 tablespoons white wine vinegar

4 tomatillos, husked, rinsed, and finely chopped

¾ cup finely chopped yellow cherry tomatoes

⅔ cup finely chopped Roma tomatoes

1½ teaspoons snipped fresh cilantro

1 medium fresh serrano chile pepper, seeded and finely chopped*

1 teaspoon lime juice

Salt

Black pepper

1 In a large bowl combine onion, ice water, and vinegar; let stand for 30 minutes. Drain onion mixture; stir in tomatillos, cherry tomatoes, Roma tomatoes, cilantro, serrano pepper, and lime juice. Season to taste with salt and black pepper. Cover and chill for 1 to 24 hours.

*NOTE: Hot chile peppers such as serranos contain oils that can burn your eyes, lips, and skin. Wear plastic or rubber gloves while preparing hot peppers and be sure to thoroughly wash your hands and nails in hot, soapy water afterward.

Nutrition Facts per ¼ cup: 79 cal., 4 g total fat (1 g sat. fat), 0 mg chol., 78 mg sodium, 11 g carbo., 1 g fiber, 1 g pro.

The peppers you choose will vary the spiciness of this salsa. Anaheime and jalapeños will give you a fairly mild salsa. Turn up the heat with poblanos or serranos.

CHUNKY HOMEMADE SALSA

7	pounds tomatoes (about 20)
10	Anaheim chile peppers or poblano chile peppers*
3	jalapeño peppers or serrano chile peppers*
2	cups chopped onion
½	cup snipped fresh cilantro or parsley
5	cloves garlic, minced
1	cup vinegar
½	of a 6-ounce can (⅓ cup) tomato paste
1	teaspoon salt
1	teaspoon black pepper

PREP:
1 hour
STAND:
30 minutes
COOK:
1 hour 10 minutes
MAKES:
5 pints
(140 one-tablespoon servings)

1 Wash tomatoes. Remove peels, stem ends, cores, and seeds. Coarsely chop tomatoes. Measure 14 cups. Place in a large colander. Let drain 30 minutes. Place drained tomatoes in an 8-quart stainless steel Dutch oven. Bring to boiling; reduce heat. Simmer, uncovered, for 1 to 1¼ hours or until thickened, stirring frequently.

2 Meanwhile, seed and chop Anaheim or poblano chile peppers; measure 3 cups. Seed and chop jalapeño or serrano chile peppers; measure ⅓ cup. Add chile peppers, onion, cilantro, garlic, vinegar, tomato paste, salt, and pepper to tomatoes. Return mixture to boiling; reduce heat. Simmer, uncovered, for 10 minutes. Remove from heat.

3 Ladle salsa into hot, clean pint canning jars, leaving ½-inch headspace. Wipe jar rims and adjust lids. Process jars in a boiling-water canner for 15 minutes (start timing when water returns to boil). Remove jars from canner; cool on racks.

*NOTE: Hot chile peppers contain oils that can burn your eyes, lips, and skin. Wear plastic or rubber gloves while preparing hot peppers and be sure to thoroughly wash your hands and nails in hot, soapy water afterward.

Nutrition Facts per tablespoon: 10 cal., 0 g total fat (0 g sat. fat), 0 mg chol., 25 mg sodium, 2 g carbo., 1 g fiber, 1 g pro.

This creamy dressing is delicious over lettuce, but for a change of pace, try it over steamed vegetables such as cauliflower or summer squash.

5 g net carb

CHUTNEY SALAD DRESSING

START TO FINISH:

10 minutes

MAKES:

1³/₄ cups

¼ cup mango chutney

1 cup mayonnaise or salad dressing

½ cup dairy sour cream

1 Using kitchen scissors, cut up any large pieces in chutney. In a small bowl stir together chutney, mayonnaise, and sour cream. Cover and store in the refrigerator for up to 1 week.

Nutrition Facts per 2 tablespoons: 143 cal., 14 g total fat (3 g sat. fat), 12 mg chol., 98 mg sodium, 5 g carbo., 0 g fiber, 0 g pro.

This classic dressing is named for the Thousand Islands of New York because all the little chunks of relish, hard-cooked egg, and onion are said to resemble the many islands.

1 g net carb

THOUSAND ISLAND DRESSING

START TO FINISH:

20 minutes

MAKES:

2 cups

1½ cups mayonnaise or salad dressing

¼ cup chili sauce

1 hard-cooked egg, chopped

1 tablespoon finely chopped onion

1 tablespoon pickle relish

1 In a small bowl stir together mayonnaise, chili sauce, egg, onion, and relish. Use at once or cover and chill in the refrigerator for up to 3 days.

Nutrition Facts per tablespoon: 80 cal., 8 g total fat (1 g sat. fat), 10 mg chol., 87 mg sodium, 1 g carbo., 0 g fiber, 0 g pro.

This mild oil-and-vinegar Roquefort dressing is delicious over torn spinach or any combination of mixed salad greens.

ROQUEFORT SALAD DRESSING

1 cup olive oil

2 ounces Roquefort cheese, crumbled

⅓ cup white wine vinegar

⅓ cup lemon juice

2 tablespoons capers, drained

¼ teaspoon salt

¼ teaspoon garlic salt

¼ teaspoon black pepper

PREP:
15 minutes

CHILL:
1 hour

MAKES:
about 2 cups

1 In a small bowl gradually stir about half of the olive oil into the cheese until combined. Transfer to a screw-top jar. Add remaining oil, vinegar, lemon juice, capers, salt, garlic salt, and pepper. Cover tightly and shake well. Chill in the refrigerator for at least 1 hour, or up to 24 hours, to blend flavors. Shake again before serving.

BLUE CHEESE SALAD DRESSING: Prepare salad dressing as directed except substitute 2 ounces blue cheese, crumbled, for the Roquefort cheese.

Nutrition Facts per 2 tablespoons: 134 cal., 15 g total fat (2 g sat. fat), 3 mg chol., 133 mg sodium, 1 g carbo., 0 g fiber, 1 g pro.

Use this sugar-free version in any recipe that calls for ranch salad dressing.

BUTTERMILK DRESSING

PREP:

10 minutes

CHILL:

30 minutes

MAKES:

1¼ cups

¾ cup buttermilk

½ cup mayonnaise or salad dressing

1 tablespoon snipped fresh parsley or 1 teaspoon dried parsley, crushed

¼ teaspoon black pepper

¼ teaspoon onion powder

¼ teaspoon dry mustard

1 clove garlic, minced

1 In a small bowl stir together buttermilk, mayonnaise, parsley, pepper, onion powder, mustard, and garlic. If necessary, stir in additional buttermilk to make dressing of desired consistency.

2 Cover and chill dressing for 30 minutes before serving. Cover and store in the refrigerator for up to 1 week.

Nutrition Facts per tablespoon: 44 cal., 5 g total fat (1 g sat. fat), 2 mg chol., 38 mg sodium, 1 g carbo., 0 g fiber, 0 g pro.

Toss this tangy dressing with greens or in any recipe calling for bottled poppy seed dressing.

POPPY SEED DRESSING

⅓ cup orange juice

3 tablespoons salad oil

1 tablespoon Dijon-style mustard

1 teaspoon poppy seeds

2 to 3 dashes bottled hot pepper sauce

1 In a small bowl whisk together orange juice, oil, mustard, poppy seeds, and hot pepper sauce. Use at once or cover and store in the refrigerator for up to 3 days. Stir before using.

Nutrition Facts per tablespoon: 54 cal., 5 g total fat (1 g sat. fat), 0 mg chol., 11 mg sodium, 1 g carbo., 0 g fiber, 0 g pro.

START TO FINISH:

5 minutes

MAKES:

½ cup

Powdered fruit pectin adds body to this fat-free, sugar-free dressing. With only 8 calories and 2 grams of carbs per serving, it fits into any diet plan.

OIL-FREE HERB DRESSING

PREP:

15 minutes

CHILL:

30 minutes

MAKES:

about ¹/₂ cup

1 tablespoon powdered fruit pectin

³/₄ teaspoon snipped fresh oregano, basil, thyme, tarragon, savory, or dill, or ¹/₄ teaspoon dried herb, crushed

¹/₂ teaspoon no-calorie, heat-stable granular sugar substitute (Splenda)

¹/₈ teaspoon dry mustard

¹/₈ teaspoon black pepper

¹/₄ cup water

1 tablespoon vinegar

1 small clove garlic, minced

1 In a small bowl stir together pectin, desired herb, sugar substitute, dry mustard, and pepper. Stir in water, vinegar, and garlic. Cover and chill for 30 minutes before serving. Cover and store remaining dressing in the refrigerator for up to 3 days.

Nutrition Facts per tablespoon: 8 cal., 0 g total fat (0 g sat. fat), 0 mg chol., 3 mg sodium, 2 g carbo., 0 g fiber, 0 g pro.

Add a little heat to your salads with this spicy dressing. If you like, double the recipe and serve it as a dip.

JALAPEÑO DRESSING

¼   cup dairy sour cream

1   tablespoon lime juice

1   to 2 fresh jalapeño peppers, seeded and finely chopped*

¼   teaspoon paprika

¼   cup dairy sour cream

     No-calorie, heat-stable granular sugar substitute (Splenda) or other sugar substitute (optional)

PREP:

10 minutes

MAKES:

about ²/₃ cup

1 In a blender combine ¼ cup sour cream, the lime juice, jalapeño peppers, and paprika. Cover and blend until nearly smooth. Transfer to a small bowl. Stir in ¼ cup sour cream until combined. If desired, sweeten dressing with sugar substitute to taste. Use immediately or cover and chill up to 24 hours.

*NOTE: Hot chile peppers such as jalapeños contain oils that can burn your eyes, lips, and skin. Wear plastic or rubber gloves while preparing hot peppers and be sure to thoroughly wash your hands and nails in hot, soapy water afterward.

Nutrition Facts per tablespoon: 28 cal., 2 g total fat (1 g sat. fat), 4 mg chol., 5 mg sodium, 2 g carbo., 0 g fiber, 0 g pro.

Garlic, basil, and oregano season this classic dressing. If fresh herbs are unavailable, dried Italian seasoning makes a pleasing substitute.

ITALIAN DRESSING

PREP:

10 minutes

MAKES:

1 cup

½ cup salad oil

⅓ cup cider vinegar

3 cloves garlic, crushed

1 tablespoon snipped fresh basil and 1 tablespoon snipped fresh oregano or 2 teaspoons dried Italian seasoning, crushed

½ teaspoon salt

¼ teaspoon black pepper

1 In a screw-top jar combine oil, vinegar, garlic, herbs, salt, and pepper. Cover and shake until smooth. Use immediately or cover and store in the refrigerator for up to 3 days.

Nutrition Facts per 2 tablespoons: 125 cal., 14 g total fat (2 g sat. fat), 0 mg chol., 147 mg sodium, 1 g carbo., 0 g fiber, 0 g pro.

Either coarse-grain brown mustard or Dijon mustard will give a robust flavor to this tangy salad dressing.

LEMONY MUSTARD DRESSING

_{1 g net carb}

⅓ cup salad oil

2 tablespoons lemon juice

2 tablespoons coarse-grain brown mustard or Dijon-style mustard

1 clove garlic, minced

No-calorie, heat-stable granular sugar substitute (Splenda)

1 In a small bowl whisk together oil, lemon juice, mustard, and garlic. Sweeten to taste with sugar substitute. Use at once or cover and store in the refrigerator up to 3 days. Whisk before using.

Nutrition Facts per 2 tablespoons: 113 cal., 12 g total fat (2 g sat. fat), 0 mg chol., 77 mg sodium, 1 g carbo., 0 g fiber, 0 g pro.

START TO FINISH:

10 minutes

MAKES:

¾ cup

Walnut oil gives this citrusy dressing a rich nutty flavor. It goes well with mild greens such as leaf lettuce, but try drizzling it over grilled chicken, too.

2 g net carb

LEMON-NUT VINAIGRETTE

START TO FINISH:

10 minutes

MAKES:

²/₃ cup

- ¼ cup walnut, salad, or olive oil
- 1 teaspoon finely shredded lemon peel or lime peel (optional)
- ¼ cup lemon juice or lime juice
- 2 tablespoons ground walnuts, almonds, or pecans

  No-calorie, heat-stable granular sugar substitute (Splenda) or other sugar substitute (optional)

1 In a small bowl stir together oil; lemon peel, if desired; lemon juice; and nuts. If desired, sweeten to taste with sugar substitute. Use at once or cover and store in the refrigerator for up to 3 days. Stir before using.

Nutrition Facts per tablespoon: 66 cal., 6 g total fat (1 g sat. fat), 0 mg chol., 0 mg sodium, 2 g carbo., 0 g fiber, 0 g pro.

Toss this tangy ginger-scented salad dressing with mixed greens or drizzle it over grilled fish or chicken.

1 g net carb

LIME VINAIGRETTE

START TO FINISH:

10 minutes

MAKES:

¹/₃ cup

- ¼ cup salad oil
- ¼ teaspoon finely shredded lime peel
- 2 tablespoons lime juice
- ¼ teaspoon grated fresh ginger or dash ground ginger

1 In a screw-top jar combine oil, lime peel, lime juice, and ginger. Cover and shake well. Use at once or store in the refrigerator for up to 3 days. Shake well before using.

Nutrition Facts per tablespoon: 98 cal., 11 g total fat (2 g sat. fat), 0 mg chol., 0 mg sodium, 1 g carbo., 0 g fiber, 0 g pro.

Drizzle this yogurt dressing over mixed greens and sliced cooked turkey breast for a savory main-dish salad.

APRICOT NECTAR DRESSING

½   cup plain yogurt

⅛   teaspoon ground cinnamon

    Dash nutmeg

¼   to ½ cup apricot nectar

    No-calorie, heat stable granular sugar substitute (Splenda) or other sugar substitute

START TO FINISH:
5 minutes
MAKES:
¾ to 1 cup

1 In a small bowl stir together yogurt, cinnamon, and nutmeg. Add apricot nectar to make the dressing of drizzling consistency. Stir until smooth. Sweeten to taste with sugar substitute. Use at once or cover and store in the refrigerator for 3 to 5 days.

Nutrition Facts per tablespoon: 12 cal., 0 g total fat (0 g sat. fat), 1 mg chol., 8 mg sodium, 2 g carbo., 0 g fiber, 1 g pro.

Prepare this dressing in the summertime when fresh watermelon and strawberries are at their best. The pureed fruit gives the dressing body.

BERRY MELON VINAIGRETTE

1   cup seeded watermelon chunks

1   cup hulled, halved strawberries

2   tablespoons white balsamic vinegar

1   teaspoon finely shredded orange peel

    No-calorie, heat-stable granular sugar-free substitute (Splenda) (optional)

START TO FINISH:
15 minutes
MAKES:
about 2 cups

1 In a blender or food processor combine watermelon, strawberries, vinegar, and orange peel. Cover and blend or process until smooth. If desired, sweeten vinaigrette with sugar substitute. Use at once or cover and store in the refrigerator for up to 3 days. Shake well before using.

Nutrition Facts per 2 tablespoons: 11 cal., 0 g total fat (0 g sat. fat), 0 mg chol., 1 mg sodium, 3 g carbo., 0 g fiber, 0 g pro.

INDEX

Recipes Listed by Grams of Net Carbohydrates

METRIC INFORMATION

The charts on this page provide a guide for converting measurements from the U.S. customary system, which is used throughout this book, to the metric system.

Product Differences

Most of the ingredients called for in the recipes in this book are available in most countries. However, some are known by different names. Here are some common American ingredients and their possible counterparts:

- **All-purpose flour** is enriched, bleached or unbleached white household flour. When self-rising flour is used in place of all-purpose flour in a recipe that calls for leavening, omit the leavening agent (baking soda or baking powder) and salt.
- **Baking soda** is bicarbonate of soda.
- **Cornstarch** is cornflour.
- **Golden raisins** are sultanas.
- **Green, red, or yellow sweet peppers** are capsicums or bell peppers.
- **Light-colored corn syrup** is golden syrup.
- **Powdered sugar** is icing sugar.
- **Sugar** (white) is granulated, fine granulated, or castor sugar.
- **Vanilla** or vanilla extract is vanilla essence.

Volume and Weight

The United States traditionally uses cup measures for liquid and solid ingredients. The chart below shows the approximate imperial and metric equivalents. If you are accustomed to weighing solid ingredients, the following approximate equivalents will be helpful.

- 1 cup butter, castor sugar, or rice = 8 ounces = 1/2 pound = 250 grams
- 1 cup flour = 4 ounces = 1/4 pound = 125 grams
- 1 cup icing sugar = 5 ounces = 150 grams

Canadian and U.S. volume for a cup measure is 8 fluid ounces (237 ml), but the standard metric equivalent is 250 ml.

1 British imperial cup is 10 fluid ounces.

In Australia, 1 tablespoon equals 20 ml, and there are 4 teaspoons in the Australian tablespoon.

Spoon measures are used for smaller amounts of ingredients. Although the size of the tablespoon varies slightly in different countries, for practical purposes and for recipes in this book, a straight substitution is all that's necessary. Measurements made using cups or spoons always should be level unless stated otherwise.

Common Weight Range Replacements

Imperial / U.S.	Metric
1/2 ounce	15 g
1 ounce	25 g or 30 g
4 ounces (1/4 pound)	115 g or 125 g
8 ounces (1/2 pound)	225 g or 250 g
16 ounces (1 pound)	450 g or 500 g
1 1/4 pounds	625 g
1 1/2 pounds	750 g
2 pounds or 2 1/4 pounds	1,000 g or 1 Kg

Oven Temperature Equivalents

Fahrenheit Setting	Celsius Setting*	Gas Setting
300°F	150°C	Gas Mark 2 (very low)
325°F	160°C	Gas Mark 3 (low)
350°F	180°C	Gas Mark 4 (moderate)
375°F	190°C	Gas Mark 5 (moderate)
400°F	200°C	Gas Mark 6 (hot)
425°F	220°C	Gas Mark 7 (hot)
450°F	230°C	Gas Mark 8 (very hot)
475°F	240°C	Gas Mark 9 (very hot)
500°F	260°C	Gas Mark 10 (extremely hot)
Broil	Broil	Grill

*Electric and gas ovens may be calibrated using celsius. However, for an electric oven, increase celsius setting 10 to 20 degrees when cooking above 160°C. For convection or forced air ovens (gas or electric), lower the temperature setting 25°F/10°C when cooking at all heat levels.

Baking Pan Sizes

Imperial / U.S.	Metric
9×1 1/2-inch round cake pan	22- or 23×4-cm (1.5 L)
9×1 1/2-inch pie plate	22- or 23×4-cm (1 L)
8×8×2-inch square cake pan	20×5-cm (2 L)
9×9×2-inch square cake pan	22- or 23×4.5-cm (2.5 L)
11×7×1 1/2-inch baking pan	28×17×4-cm (2 L)
2-quart rectangular baking pan	30×19×4.5-cm (3 L)
13×9×2-inch baking pan	34×22×4.5-cm (3.5 L)
15×10×1-inch jelly roll pan	40×25×2-cm
9×5×3-inch loaf pan	23×13×8-cm (2 L)
2-quart casserole	2 L

U.S. / Standard Metric Equivalents

1/8 teaspoon	= 0.5 ml
1/4 teaspoon	= 1 ml
1/2 teaspoon	= 2 ml
1 teaspoon	= 5 ml
1 tablespoon	= 15 ml
2 tablespoons	= 25 ml
1/4 cup = 2 fluid ounces	= 50 ml
1/3 cup = 3 fluid ounces	= 75 ml
1/2 cup = 4 fluid ounces	= 125 ml
2/3 cup = 5 fluid ounces	= 150 ml
3/4 cup = 6 fluid ounces	= 175 ml
1 cup = 8 fluid ounces	= 250 ml
2 cups = 1 pint	= 500 ml
1 quart	= 1 litre